Women
Counseling
Women

ELYSE
FITZPATRICK
GENERAL EDITOR

HARVEST HOUSE PUBLISHERS

EUGENE, OREGON

Cover by Koechel Peterson & Associates, Inc., Minneapolis, Minnesota

Cover photo © Blend Images Photography / Veer

WOMEN COUNSELING WOMEN
Copyright © 2010 by Elyse Fitzpatrick
Published by Harvest House Publishers
Eugene, Oregon 97402
www.harvesthousepublishers.com

Library of Congress Cataloging-in-Publication Data
   Women counseling women / Elyse Fitzpatrick, general editor.
      p. cm.
   Includes bibliographical references.
   ISBN 978-0-7369-2998-1 (pbk.)
   1. Christian women—Religious life. 2. Peer counseling in the church. 3. Women—Pastoral counseling of. I. Fitzpatrick, Elyse, 1950-
   BV4527.W5935 2010
   253.5082—dc22
                                                             2009052334

12 13 14 15 16 17 18 / BP-SK / 10 9 8 7 6 5 4 3

*To the thousands of women who share their biblical
wisdom with other women in ways private and
unheralded—the Lord sees and loves it.*

Contents

Part 4:
A Woman and Specific Problems

Appendices

Women Who Teach
What Is Good

What you're holding in your hands right now is a gold mine. I know that's quite a claim. A gold mine…really? While it might not have the physical appearance or financial worth of real gold, it's a gold mine nevertheless. What makes this book so valuable that we would call it a gold mine? Simply this: The thoughts and words you'll find here are the culmination of thousands upon thousands of hours of training and experience by nearly two dozen women who have had just one goal in mind: knowing and teaching other women what is good, according to God's Word.

As you'll soon learn, every woman who contributed to this book has done so because she has a love for the Lord and for you. At great personal expense of both finances and time, every one of these women have given their lives to be trained in the truth of the Bible and especially in how that truth applies to the daily lives of women just like you. But that doesn't mean these women are supersaints who have all the answers and no longer struggle with sin and sorrows. No, these are women who face the same kind of day that you do.

Many of them have families and all the demanding responsibilities that correspond to them. They change diapers and make dinner and try to figure out how to buy shoes for feet that never seem to stop growing. Some of them are single and have to balance the demands of taking care of themselves, working, serving other women, and hoping their car makes it another 1000 miles. Some of them are young, wondering what the Lord has for their lives. Others have lived a life of faith, walked through the fire, have been tempered by the disappointments and heartaches of living in a broken world, have held on when it seemed as though all was lost. They've found their God faithful. They're just like you. They understand.

In addition to sharing your experience, they've also given themselves to studying and learning how to apply the truth of the Bible to the struggles that are common to us all. They're like your best friend in the sense they can relate, but they're also like your pastor in the sense they can offer guidance. What a treasure!

Women Teaching Other Women

This book is not only a gold mine because loving, wise, mature women have contributed to it; it's also a gold mine because it is the result of godly obedience. Every one of these women has willingly responded to the command of Paul to Titus (and us) over 2000 years ago: "Older women...are to teach what is good, and so train the young women" (Titus 2:3-4). Every one of these women believe that God has called mature women to counsel, mentor, teach, and disciple other women. And to that they have dedicated their lives.

In commanding Titus to train mature women and to, in turn, have them train other women, Paul made a very significant point: *No one is better equipped to train a woman than another godly woman.* In saying this, we're not suggesting that male teachers and pastors cannot or should not train women. We recognize and are thankful for the roles that godly men have played in our lives by teaching us God's Word and modeling for us how it is to be lived out. Every one of these women have male pastors they love and respect. What we're saying is simply this: When it comes to one-on-one discipleship, *no one* does this better in the life of a woman than another godly woman.[1] Every one of the women who have contributed to this book have done so because they believe God has commanded them to teach other women what is "good," and they have joyfully embraced this calling.

You should also know that none of these women, including this editor, will gain any personal remuneration for their contribution to this book. All the royalties that accrue from the sales of it will go directly into a scholarship fund to train other women in biblical counseling. The women you'll hear from in this book are committed to fulfilling God's call on our lives and to helping other women do so also. So when you purchase this book and encourage other women to do so, know that your dollars are multiplying training and help for thousands of other women. Thank you!

Jesus Is the Source of All Wisdom and Knowledge

Finally, and most significantly, this book is a gold mine because it will faithfully point you to the only source of lasting help, Jesus Christ. In writing to the church at Colossae, the apostle Paul made an astonishing assertion. He claimed that in Jesus Christ were "hidden *all* the treasures of wisdom and knowledge" (Colossians 2:3). Just think of that: *All* the treasures of wisdom and knowledge are hidden in Christ, in the gospel, in the story of His life, death, resurrection, and ascension. That statement should astound you. It should make you shake your head in wonder. *All? Really? All?*

But what about all those other voices: the Dr. Phils, Oprahs, Deepak Choprahs, and Eckhart Tolles of modern media? What about the favorite pop psychologists? What about all those seemingly innocuous maxims like "God helps those who help themselves," or "You'll be happy when you learn to really love yourself"? What about books that claim to be spiritual but neglect the gospel and insinuate that there are other more spiritual wisdoms that will help us? "Ignore them all," Paul said in essence. You don't need special visitations from angels or old women who make you feel cozy, like God is your grandmother. You don't need special, more friendly words from special, more spiritual sages. All you need is Jesus Christ and Him crucified.

This is a hard truth; it isn't tidy. It doesn't caress our egos or feed our self-esteem. Christ's crucifixion for our sin is not a fluffy concept. But it's the only medicine that will cure the human heart. We don't need fluff. We need life-transforming truth. He is the truth we need because *all* the treasures of wisdom and knowledge are hidden *in Him*. He's the gold mine. He's the treasure. His life, death, and resurrection are *all* you need.

Wisdom You Can Rely On

Does that sound too simple? It is simple, but it's not shallow or simplistic. In fact, the gold in this mine is so plentiful that the vein of His wisdom will run on for eternity. You could spend thousands and thousands of years digging out these treasures and you would barely have even scratched the surface. So, when all the voices of our modern age have been silenced, when the human wisdom of this age has finally been played out and found empty, the wisdom and knowledge of Jesus Christ will still stand like a rock. You can build your house on this foundation and be assured that it will stand forever (Luke 6:46-49).

In every way that this book is faithful to the truth about Jesus, to the story of His life and love for us, it presents His wisdom and knowledge. And it will transform your heart if you believe it. When Paul commanded women to teach what is good, he wasn't hoping we'd figure it out on our own or develop some homemade recipe for goodness. He was telling us to teach the gospel and all the ways that the gospel applies to life.

So whether you're a pastor's wife, a biblical counselor, a woman who has friends who need help, or just someone wondering if the Bible really does have all the answers, this book is for you. And whether you choose to read straight through it or pull it off your bookshelf only at the times that someone calls and asks for help, we're here for you. We invite you to dig in, to mine these riches, to discover gold for yourself and share the riches with everyone you know.

You'll see that we've divided the book into five parts. The first, "A Woman and the Word," will help you see the importance of thinking biblically about your problems and your daily life. It will help you understand what we mean when we talk about biblical counseling and how to think about God's promises. It will also train you how to read your Bible and discern truth from error.

In Part Two, "A Woman and Her Emotions," you'll learn what the Bible teaches about the emotions that most of us face: fear, depression, and anger. You'll also find help for discerning biblical answers to questions about the use of psychiatric medicines.

In Part Three, "A Woman and Her Relationships," nine women will walk with you through the different stages of life a woman may face. From singleness to caring for the elderly, you'll find godly advice and real hope for change from women who are walking through these stages themselves.

In Part Four, "A Woman and Specific Problems," four women will help you walk through the difficulties of addictions—whether to food, pornography, homosexuality, or the maze of what is sometimes referred to as "generational sins." In limiting our chapters about addictions to these four, we're not proposing that those are the only addictive behaviors a woman might struggle with. What we're hoping is that you'll find the general principles in these chapters applicable to other types of addictions and weaknesses.

And finally, in one of the three appendices at the back of the book you'll find a list of recommended resources for further study, as well as training centers where you can learn more about becoming a biblical counselor.

Our encouragement to you is this: This wisdom is for you whether you're just beginning the Christian walk or have been a believer for decades. You don't need to have completed a college course or even know where the book of John is in your Bible. We're here to help you, but we're not all the help there is. You can take courage. You don't have to try to uncover these treasures on your own. No, if you're Christ's, the Holy Spirit has been given to you to enable you to understand and believe truth. You can trust in Him and, by faith, dig in.

Part 1

A Woman
and the Word

Chapter 1

BIBLICAL COUNSELING: REAL HELP FOR REAL WOMEN

∮ Elyse Fitzpatrick ∮

Like you, I frequent grocery stores. And like you, I scan the headlines of the magazines and newspapers while I wait my turn to slide the debit card and be on my way. Although there are times when the headlines of some "newspapers" are laugh-out-loud funny—"Monkey Boy Actually Nostradamus!"—most of the headlines are heartbreaking: "Famous Starlet Arrested Again!" "Beautiful Couple's Marriage on the Rocks!" "Celebrated Director in Drug and Alcohol Rehab!" And these are reports of the lives of people we're tempted to envy. They're the ones who are able to take long and luxurious vacations, who have achieved the American dream, who have access to all the "best" help. And yet something is desperately wrong. Not money, fame, nor beauty can shelter any of us from it. We're not shocked by the troubles of the rich and famous because, at heart, we know they're just like us. We know that *we're all in trouble and we all need help.* How would the headlines of our lives read? Aside from the paparazzi, are we all that different?

Yes, we've got significant problems and we're all looking for answers. No one will argue with you about that. Now, they may argue with you about the *source* of our troubles or whether our troubles are as bad as we think they are. But everyone acknowledges that things just aren't as they should be. We look around at the state of affairs in our country, in our family, in our hearts, and we know, without anyone telling us, something is desperately wrong.

And so we search and search for a solution to this innate "wrongness" that we feel, that we see. We read articles, we surf the Web, we watch programs featuring the latest self-help guru who assures us that he's finally found the answer we've been looking for. But nothing satisfies. Nothing really solves the problem. Yes, perhaps for a day or two, or even a month or two, we seem to find some relief, but then we find ourselves back at our starting point again: We're still in trouble, we still need help.

So we start over again and eventually discover much to our dismay, that every one of these "helpful" voices offers a different solution to our problem. We're not only in trouble and in need of help, but everyone seems to have a different (and usually conflicting) answer! Some of the answers we're given assure us that we can solve our problems ourselves—that we've got everything we need inside us already. We just need to believe in ourselves and access our own power, they say.

Others tout their special secret formula for success—and at $19.99, they tell us it's quite a bargain. If we would just follow their advice carefully, we would find our problems disappearing. And then still others tell us that there aren't any true-for-all-time answers, life just is as it is, and we should give up trying to change and learn to live with it.

So our days go by and troubles multiply as we try one futile strategy after another. We try hard for a season, but then either the strategy or our willpower fails. So we pick up another strategy and after a bit it fails, too. And on and on it goes until we just give up for a season and go watch TV or take a nap…that is, until we hear about another exciting new fail-safe solution, and we feel hopeful and start all over again.

The One Light Shining in the Dark

Standing in stark contrast to this dismal, futile cycle of trouble-hope-despair-trouble-hope-despair, the Bible shines as a beacon of ageless wisdom and eternal hope. Without mincing words, it clearly identifies the source of all our troubles while it also powerfully displays the only way to true life transformation. But don't be confused. The Bible is not a self-help book. Written on every page is this truth: We *can't* help ourselves.

The Bible teaches us to be properly hopeless about our ability to change. No, it isn't very flattering to us. It tells us that our problems are so bad, so deeply rooted, so intrinsic to our very nature that we're utterly unable to change, or as the Old Testament prophet Jeremiah put it, "Can…the leopard [change] his spots? Then also you can do good who are accustomed to do evil" (Jeremiah 13:23). Can you transform the bent of your own heart? No, of course you can't. You know that's true because you've tried…and failed. Yes we can move the furniture of our lives around or tidy things up a bit. But we can't truly change who we are at heart—especially when we're alone or when we think no one is watching. The Bible says we're powerless to change ourselves.

Although the Bible's perspective on our abilities seems discouraging at first, the truth is that it's really very freeing. While it's counterintuitive, there's actually great freedom and hope in knowing and accepting our limitations. It's like this: If I had contracted a crippling disease but was unaware of it, I would undoubtedly be frustrated and discouraged when I tried to walk. I would keep raging against my stupid legs and trying to insist that my muscles work as I think they should. I would continually try to get myself going, only to end up in failure and despair once again. But, once I get an accurate diagnosis, even if that diagnosis is heartbreaking, I'll begin to embrace my inability and know that if I want to get around I'll need to find a new way, and learn to live life within my weakness. That's just what the Bible does for us. It tells us that we're too far gone to expect any help from ourselves. It teaches us to rely on help from outside. It's a hard truth but it's a good and necessary one.

We're the Source of Our Troubles

The Bible is very clear about the source of our troubles, too. This is one of those places where the truth of God's Word and the "wisdom" of the world collide dramatically. The world assures us that our problems stem from any of a number of places: our upbringing, our education, the economy, the environment, the government, "those" people, our brain chemicals, and on and on.

But the Bible paints a different picture. It teaches us quite clearly about the source of our troubles. As the well-known British scholar, G.K. Chesterton, once quipped in response to a newspaper reporter's query, "What's wrong with the world today?" His answer? "Dear Sir, I am." The Bible clearly teaches that *we* are the source of our problems. And specifically, our sin is the fountainhead from which all sorrow, suffering, difficulty, and death in the world flows. Of course, that's not to say that there is always an exact one-for-one correlation between a specific sin we commit and some difficulty that we face—although, of course that may be true. It's just that sin is the cause of all the trouble everyone in the world faces.

Let me try to illustrate this for you. Just think for a moment what the world would be like if there were no sin. No one would cut you off on the freeway; no child would go to bed hungry; no one would waste away in prison or waste themselves in drug-induced oblivion. And imagine what you would be like. You would always love and it wouldn't ever be a question or a struggle to do so. You would love others because you loved to do so. You would never be cranky or selfish or worried or self-indulgent because you would know that you are loved and you love. When we view sin from the perspective of living a life of love in a loving world, it's easy to see how we're the problem. Chesterton was right. What's wrong with the world today? We are.

The Bible says that what's wrong with our lives and everyone else's life is that we sin—this poverty of love is called sin. Sin is a refusal to love God or our neighbor, ignoring the two great commands of God's law (Matthew 22:36-40). And why don't we love God or others like we should? We don't love because we don't believe that we've been loved (1 John 4:19). We refuse to believe that God is as loving as He says He is. And because we don't believe that "God is love" (1 John 4:8,16), we fall short of God's loving intention for our lives and we create other lesser gods to take His place—gods that make us feel loved, gods like acceptance, power, safety and comfort.

This is called idolatry. All of our sin flows out of unbelief and idolatry: *unbelief* that God is as loving and good as He says He is; *idolatry* that we have to live for and worship no one but ourselves in order to be happy. And even though some of us have been Christians for decades, we all struggle to believe in God's goodness and worship Him alone. We're all sinners—unbelieving, idolatrous sinners. Here's one way that the Bible describes our condition: "for my people have committed two evils: they have forsaken me, the fountain of living waters, and hewed out cisterns for themselves, broken cisterns that can hold no water" (Jeremiah 2:13). We forsake the loving God and we make other gods to take His place.

The Solution to the Sinner's Problem

The sin that we *all* commit when we fail to love God above all else or to love others the way we already love ourselves is the source of *all* the world's problems. And it is, in some measure, the source of all the problems we're facing today. Perhaps you are trying to love but someone else is being hateful to you. Or, perhaps you've been consistently unloving and now you're facing the consequences of a broken marriage or habitually angry children. In any case, our unbelief and idolatry, our lovelessness are the reasons for the troubles we face today, whether we're sinning against someone or they're sinning against us, and it's why we're constantly looking for help.

We're assuming that up to this point, you've probably agreed with most of what we've said. Yes, sin—everyone's sin—is the problem. Yes, we've all failed to love. But if sin is the problem, what is the solution? Is there a solution that really helps? Really transforms? Yes, of course there is. But the answer doesn't originate in anything we can do. This answer bypasses all our "self" help. And this is another place where the Bible's answers collide violently with the answers from the world...and even from some people in the church.

Here's an illustration of the many different kinds of answers we can encounter: Let's say that Jane is married and the mom of three. Let's also say that her husband, Joe, is disengaged and spends his leisure time golfing and watching television. Jane is tired, angry, distant, sullen, and demanding. She vengefully spends more money than she should.

Joe is oblivious, self-centered, and immature. He can't understand what Jane's problem is: He goes to work and provides for her. So why shouldn't he reap some of the rewards for his labors on the golf course? Besides, he goes to church with her on Sunday and he wishes Jane were more submissive to him. Both Jane and Joe would say that they're Christians and that they believe that Jesus died for their sin. But they're in need of real help and that old gospel story seems insufficient, weak, and hackneyed.

Now, how would you help Jane and Joe? If you believe that Jane is an empty love-cup who needs to be filled by Joe's attentions, you might tell her to demand more of his time or learn how to communicate her needs in a way that satisfies her desires. If you believe that Joe requires more respect and needs to let his wild masculinity run free, you'll encourage him to tell Jane more about his needs and not be a slave to her demands. After all, both Jane and Joe need to love themselves more and take care of meeting their own needs before they can meet the needs of the other, right?

If, on the other hand, you believe that Jane and Joe are both victims of dysfunctional homes, you might have Jane write a letter to her parents, telling them how their continual fighting has ruined her ability to communicate lovingly with Joe. You might tell her to sign up for assertiveness training or classes on communicating in her own special love language. Or you might have Joe confront his dad how his alcoholism and distance has wrecked his relationship with Jane so that he is cold and unloving. Perhaps Joe should join a recovery group for children of alcoholics so he can be with other people who understand him.

Or, you might simply say that both Jane and Joe's problems stem from some sort of chemical imbalance in their brains and advise them to see a physician and get on medication.

Obviously, the problem with such solutions is that they don't solve our unbelief-idolatry-love problem. In fact, they make it worse. Instead of teaching Jane and Joe that the goal of their life is to bring glory to God by loving God and neighbor, these solutions end up showing them ways to get more of what they selfishly crave. They teach them strategies to serve their idols, to love themselves, to dismiss God's great love for them. So perhaps they'll be a little happier for a season, but their hearts won't be transformed, and that deadly, poisonous root will remain just as entrenched as it ever was. And, sadly, in the end, every one of these methods is doomed to failure.

Rather than turning to the empty philosophies of the world that bend us in on ourselves, Jane and Joe (and the rest of us) need to look outward, away from ourselves and our "wisdom" to a wisdom that is from above (James 3:17). We need God's wisdom, and His wisdom is found in Scripture, and particularly in Scripture's testimony to the good news about Jesus Christ.

Jesus…Again?

You'll remember that we said that the Bible is not a self-help book. That's because, as we've seen, God knows we're unable to help ourselves. We don't need self-help; we can't use it. We need Other-help. We need a Savior. We need Someone outside of ourselves who can rescue us from ourselves, our sin, our unbelief, and our idolatry. Those of us who are already Christians believe this truth: Jesus Christ came into the world to save sinners (1 Timothy 1:15). I'm sure that about now you're nodding and saying, *Yes, I believe that. But I need something more right now. I believe the gospel, but I don't see how it applies in my situation.* Though we may know that the gospel story is true, we can easily assume or think that its significance pretty much ends after we get saved. Jesus again…really?

The Bible teaches that it is the gospel of Jesus Christ—the good news about what He's *already* done for us—that transforms our lives. This good news is the true story about the life, death, resurrection, and ascension of the Son of God and it really is astonishing! It tells us that although we are unbelieving, idolatrous, unloving sinners, we've been loved and adopted by God! At great cost to Himself, at great cost to His Son, our heavenly Father has made a way for us to return to Him and to be transformed into people who resemble Him. Every true Christian believes these wonderful truths, and yet there seems to be a disconnect for people like Joe and Jane when it comes to their personal problems. How exactly is the gospel relevant when our lives aren't progressing like we thought they would?

Let's revisit the story of Joe and Jane again to see how the Bible and specifically the gospel would help them. Because the Bible clearly teaches the husband is the head of his household (Ephesians 5:23), we'll start with Joe. Although he is a good provider, Joe has missed the point entirely. The Bible tells him to love his wife as Christ loved the church and "gave himself up" for her (Ephesians 5:25). Joe is giving his wife money but he's withholding himself. He isn't giving up his time or his heart to her. No, he's holding onto his own life. So, although he says he loves Jane, he doesn't live like that is the case. He serves his idols of fun and relaxation and a veg-out zone. He loves himself more than his nearest neighbor. And he's forgotten how he's been loved by God.

You see, if he really remembered God's great love for him, he would know that he didn't need to hang onto his life. He could freely lose it in order to gain it.

Jesus wouldn't advise Joe to learn how to procure respect from Jane. He'd tell him,

> Whoever would save his life will lose it, but whoever loses his life for my sake will find it. For what will it profit a man if he gains the whole world and forfeits his soul? Or what shall a man give in return for his soul? (Matthew 16:25-27).

But that's not all Joe needs to remember. He also needs to remember he has a Savior, a loving Bridegroom who has done what Joe has neglected to do. Jesus gave up His life so that Joe would live. Christ perfectly loved His bride so that Joe would have a record of perfect love before his Father, the Holy Judge. Joe has forgotten the gospel he says he believes.

In light of the love Jesus has bestowed on Joe, he can learn to love Jane. That means that on the commute home from work he should pray that the Lord would grant him the energy and interest to take an active part in his home. Although he'll be tempted to plop down in front of the television, Joe should sit down with his kids and listen to what they have to say. He could help out in the kitchen or offer to take the kids out for ice cream while Jane relaxes in a warm bath. All the while he will have to remember he isn't doing these things because he's trying to get something from Jane, earn an early tee-time on Saturday, or gain brownie points from God.

As long as Joe's motivation remains self-centered, then he is doing good only for himself, out of self-love, rather than out of love for God or Jane. Instead, Joe should remember that he is to love Jane because he's been loved by God, as the apostle John pointed out: "Beloved, if God so loved us, we also ought to love one another" (1 John 4:11). So when Joe does what is right, whether Jane responds in kind or not, Joe can take satisfaction in knowing that he's living in grateful obedience to God.

Jane needs the gospel, too. Jane began her marriage hoping that Joe would be the answer to all her dreams. She's longed to have a deep relationship with him, but as the kids came along and Joe pulled away, she's found satisfaction in her children and friends and especially in shopping. Vengefully she thinks, *If he thinks that money is all I want, then fine. I'll just spend it faster than he can make it.*

Although Jane's attitude may be understandable, she is guilty of unbelief, idolatry, and selfishness, too. To begin with, Jane craved something from her husband that he was never meant to give her. She wrongly believed that he would be the "love of her life" who would satisfy her deep desire to know and be known. She looked to him to save her from a life of loneliness, insecurity, and boredom. But Joe was never meant to be her savior; no, that position is already filled.

In addition, Jane has forgotten the servant-love of Jesus Christ, the One who washed the feet of those who were about to desert Him in His most desperate hour. The disciples slept as He wept in the garden. They ran away into the night and denied that they even knew Him. One even betrayed the King of Love. Yes, Joe has also been guilty of deserting Jane, but she's done worse to her Savior. She's erected idols in her heart and she's worshipped them by acting in unkind, self-indulgent ways. She's let hopelessness infect her soul and obliterate her faith.

But Jesus hasn't forgotten Jane. Even now He's bearing her flesh, interceding for her before the throne of her Father, praying for her, guiding and protecting her. She's withheld her love from Him, but He hasn't returned her evil. He's overcome her evil with good.

And so, in light of what Jesus has done for Jane, she can love Joe. She can begin by repenting of idolizing him and expecting him to do something for her he was unable to do. He can't satisfy the longings of her heart; he can't make her truly blessed.

Jane can then walk in the footsteps of her Savior and learn what it means to love the disengaged and selfish. She can tell Joe that she loves him and that she wants to have a relationship with him but if he refuses, she can continue to love because she's been loved. And then, in all the ways that Jane will continue to fall back into her old sullen patterns of sinful self-pity and self-indulgence, she can rest in the glorious truth that she's been the recipient of the perfect record of Jesus Christ. She's not just forgiven, she's righteous! His loving record is hers before God—when He looks at her, He says, "This is My beloved daughter. She makes Me happy."

Real Women and Their Real Savior

We're all very well aware of the fact we've got problems. We sin. Others sin against us. We live in a sin-cursed world. We also know that there are as many different answers to our problems as there are problems themselves. But there is only one answer strong enough to transform us into loving, humble servants. Every other answer only takes us more toward sin, unbelief, idolatry, and lovelessness. The answer we need is found in the Bible and because every part of the Bible testifies about Jesus (Luke 24:44), the answer is found in Jesus Himself.

The Bible isn't a self-help book. It isn't a book of heroes (aside from One!), nor is it a book of rules. The Bible is the story of God's love for us and His determination to have a people for His own pleasure and our unending joy. The Bible is the only book that can correctly diagnose our sin problem. It reveals our deepest hearts, even down to our inmost thoughts and motives (Hebrews 4:12). No other system of help can do that.

The Bible is also the only book that can give us real hope, power, and motivation for change. Because of God's love demonstrated in the gospel and most powerfully at Calvary, we can have hope. As Paul put it so beautifully thousands of years ago, "He who did not spare his own Son but gave him up for us all, how will he not also with him graciously give us all things?" (Romans 8:32). In typical ancient near-Eastern fashion, Paul argued for our hope from the greater to the lesser. "Look," he said, "if God is willing to give up His beloved Son for you, why would you doubt His love? If He is willing to give you the greatest gift ever given, why would He withhold any blessing from you?" You can have hope today simply because God loved you so dearly that He gave his Son for you and then powerfully raised Him from death so that you could live with Him eternally. Now *that's* something to hope in.

There is also power for you to experience change because of the resurrection. The Bible tells us that the enslaving power of sin in our lives was broken when Christ overcame the punishment for sin—that is, death—through His resurrection.

> We were buried therefore with him by baptism into death, in
> order that, *just as Christ was raised from the dead by the glory of*

the Father, we too might walk in newness of life...We know that
our old self was crucified with him in order that the body of
sin might be brought to nothing, *so that we would no longer be
enslaved to sin* (Romans 6:4,6, emphasis added).

The only hope we have to overcome our sin, idolatry, unbelief, and
lovelessness is the resurrection of Jesus Christ. But what a lively hope
that is! He died once and will never die again so that right now He's
providentially protecting and providing everything we need to persevere through this difficult life and join Him in eternal happiness.

And finally, there's only one motive that will stand the test of time,
that will enable us to keep serving, keep obeying, keep believing, even
when the trials we face seem interminable. The motive: love. But how
can we love? What will make us love? This *and only* this: God's prior
love for us. If we start our day thinking about our obligation to love,
serve, and believe, we'll very shortly find ourselves falling into either
pride (because we're doing so well) or despair (because we're not). But
if we start (and stay) with this thought: Jesus Christ loves me and gave
Himself up for me, ensuring my Father's smile on me no matter how
the day wears on, we'll know the joys of obedience and repentance.
We'll understand the promise in our Savior's words: "If you love me,
you will keep my commandments" (John 14:16).

The Bible is the only book that has sufficient, deeply profound and
yet amazingly simple answers to life's problems. Yes, we have a problem: We're sinners. But that's not all. We've been given real help: We've
been loved. And this love is powerful enough and long-lasting enough
to change everything about us and about our world. This love is genuinely and eternally life-transforming. It makes us new.

Now, this love isn't some impersonal force. This love is embodied
in human form in our Savior, in the One who has gone through every
temptation we face and so is able "to sympathize with our weaknesses"
(Hebrews 4:15). He knows that we have real problems and He's given
us a real answer: Himself. He was willing to leave the bliss of heaven
and become a real man with thoughts and feelings and desires just like
ours. He embraced us when He embraced our mortal flesh. He was
stripped of His glories so we could be clothed in His goodness. And

He forfeited the pleasure of uninterrupted fellowship with His beloved Father so we could share in that relationship forever.

Yes, we have real problems, but Christ has given us His life. Yes, we're real women who need real answers, but He's a real Savior who has supplied all we need. And so we look to Him, solely to Him, and we find that our hearts are satisfied. Our lives are transformed and our deepest problems are solved in the shadow of the cross.

Recommended Resources

Fitzpatrick, Elyse and Dennis Johnson. *Counsel from the Cross.* Wheaton, IL: Crossway, 2009.

Chapter 2

Do God's Promises Apply to You?

Janet Rickett

I have observed—and maybe you have, too—that we often use the word *promise* too freely and frequently with little regard for what it truly means. For instance, most likely you've had times when you've run into a friend whom you haven't seen recently and, because neither of you had time to visit, you promised to call and talk in a few days, but after six months neither of you have made that phone call. Unfortunately, even though we all know what a promise is, many times we fail to keep them.

Though we are inconsistent when it comes to keeping our promises, there is someone we can always trust to keep His—someone who always means what He says and says what He means. The only person in all of creation who is perfectly consistent when it comes to giving and fulfilling His promises is God. King Solomon expressed the faithfulness of God when he said, "Blessed be the LORD who has given rest to his people Israel, according to all that he promised. *Not one word has failed of all his good promise,* which he spoke by Moses his servant" (1 Kings 8:56, emphasis added). That amazing benediction demonstrates the confidence Moses had in God's absolute faithfulness. God's promises are completely trustworthy.

Second Peter 3:9 says, "The Lord is not slow to fulfill his promise." Not only is the Lord faithful about fulfilling His promises, but He does so in His perfect timing. The Lord is never late in fulfilling His promises. No, He's always right on time and always does exactly what He says He will. He's the only faithful Promise-Keeper.

Yes, God's promises are wonderful. But we must not overlook one key fact about the promises of God: Not only do His promises include blessings for those who have a personal relationship with Jesus, they also include judgment for those who do not.

Considering God's Promises

Every one of the authors of this book are ultimately writing about *God's promises of blessings.* His blessings overflow with magnificent benefits to His children. God's promises grant those who have embraced the gospel to have joy and perseverance even in times of trial (James 1). What's more, they allow believers to live triumphantly in the midst of their difficulties and sufferings. God's blessings include the assurance of eternal life in heaven and a confident hope for the future—a wonderful gift when we're facing trouble and heartache.

In addition, those who have faith in Jesus Christ can go to God in prayer just as a child goes to her father. We can ask Him for help, pour out our concerns to Him, and pray for strength and grace to live faithfully every day. When we struggle with our sins, we have the promise of the ability to put off sinful habits and enslaving addictions and replace them with righteous deeds (Ephesians 4, Colossians 3). God's blessing of salvation motivates us to put off selfishness and instead focus on loving others who are suffering.

And because God is our Father, He lovingly disciplines His dear children. Of course, discipline doesn't sound like such a great blessing, but we learn in Hebrews 12:10 that discipline is ultimately for our good so that we may share in God's holiness. Because of God's blessings, we can overcome temptations and learn to walk by the power of God's Holy Spirit (Galatians 5:16).

Finally, those who have a personal relationship with Jesus are no longer under God's wrath and judgment, but receive His grace and mercy forever and ever! These are wonderful blessings indeed. Here's what one well-known Christian writer says: "Indeed there are ten thousand gifts that flow from the love of God. The gospel of Christ proclaims the news that he has purchased by his death ten thousand blessings for his bride [the church]."[1]

You may be thinking, *That sounds great! I have heard all about these blessings and they are wonderful. I want to receive every one of them!* I appreciate your enthusiasm but before we move on, we must finish the quote from the Christian writer above. He goes on to say, *"...but none of these gifts will lead to final joy if they have not first led to God.* And not one gospel blessing will be enjoyed by anyone for whom the gospel's greatest gift was not the Lord himself."[2]

Is Jesus Christ your greatest gift? Have you embraced Him as your Savior and Lord? Is He everything to you? These are important questions because the blessings promised in the Bible, those we are discussing in this book, are only for those who love Jesus Christ, repent of their sins, and embrace the gospel.[3] Which leads me to ask: Are you one of His children? Can you say for certain that God's promises of *blessing* apply to you?[4]

Remember, God has made promises to everyone (blessings for those who have a relationship with Him and judgment for those who reject His Son, Jesus). The question is, which promises are for you? Do you know for certain you are a recipient of God's blessings? Helping you answer this question is the main focus of this chapter. God's Word tells us that we must all be *"diligent* to make [our] calling and election sure" (2 Peter 1:10). That is, those of us who claim to be believers must confirm we really are, that we really do have a personal relationship with Jesus Christ.

Has Jesus Christ granted you salvation from God's wrath? Remember, no one can save us from the wrath of God but Jesus Christ (Romans 5:9). Our rebellion against God's laws keeps us bound to our sin. The Bible explains that is why each of us will eventually die; death is the consequence of our sin. Because God is perfectly holy and righteous, He cannot look upon sin. So He lovingly sent His perfect Son, Jesus, to pay the ultimate price for our sins. Jesus gave His life so that we might live. In order to have spiritual life,[5] we must turn from the sin (repent) that separates us from God, and trust in Jesus Christ. "Whoever believes in the Son has eternal life; whoever does not obey the Son shall not see life, but the wrath of God remains on him" (John 3:36). Author Burk Parsons, in his book *Assured by God,* gently counsels:

> Although many have unwisely presumed otherwise, assurance of salvation does not flow from a proud heart that boasts of

one's ability to maintain a bold profession of faith. On the
contrary, God assures us of our salvation in Christ precisely
because our hearts have been broken and humbled by God
himself…He assures us not by giving us confidence in ourselves but by bringing us to the end of ourselves so that we
might know and love him.[6]

This chapter was written because many have never heard the gospel, many others have heard a false gospel, and still many others have
believed only the historical facts about the Christ of the gospel without ever having met the One whose life *is* the gospel. And there is one
other reason: Many have forgotten the sweet joy of receiving the gospel and the greatness of that good news! My prayer is that God will use
this chapter to help ensure that you know Him, love Him, and worship Him.

Identity Theft

Identity theft is a very frightening phenomenon that has become
more prevalent in recent years. Part of what makes it so alarming is the
randomness with which it occurs. Reports of identity theft can show
up in the most unlikely places and happen to the most unlikely victims. Recently I learned of an instance of identity theft that surprised
many people. They were shocked when it was reported that Ben Bernanke, chairman of the Federal Reserve, had his identity stolen after his
wife's purse was nabbed at a Washington, D.C. coffee shop. Seemingly
someone in chairman Bernanke's position and of his influence would
be one of the last people you would expect to have his identity stolen.
This occurrence serves as a vivid reminder that everyone, regardless of
station in life, is subject to this devastating problem.

But imagine for a moment that you could be involved in identity
theft as an unwitting culprit. Worse than having someone steal your
identity to gain access to your financial information is *falsely believing
you are the recipient of God's blessings* when in fact you are not.

Just like the man who wanted to claim the identity of Mr. Bernanke
in order to gain access to his resources, some people identify themselves as children of God because they so desire His blessings. In other
words, many people falsely identify themselves as a Christian when

there is no real basis for this assurance. They are self-deceived, believing their identity is in Christ and they are going to heaven when in fact they are not.

Pastor and author Steven Lawson addressed this very problem in his book *Absolutely Sure*. While on an out-of-town couples retreat, he heard the disturbing testimonies of many who had previously been self-deceived regarding their relationship to God. He wrote,

> Again and again, they shared that years earlier they had gone to church, walked an aisle, talked with a counselor, prayed a prayer, been baptized and presented to the church as a new Christian. But by their own sad admission, their life never changed. Despite this initial step toward Christ, they continued to live indifferently toward God, to run with the world, and to pursue sin with increasing pleasure.[7]

What Is Your True Identity?

Unfortunately, such self-deception is present throughout churches all across the world. Many people claim to know Jesus and identify themselves as Christians but continue to walk in darkness. In *The Gospel According to Jesus*, pastor and author John MacArthur writes about many such churchgoers when he states, "When put to the test, they consistently deny the Lord either by their silence, by their actions, or by their words." He goes on to say that a person

> may claim to believe, but everything about his way of living exudes denial. Churches are filled with such people masquerading as disciples, but denying the Lord in some very disturbing ways. Christ will deny them before God.[8]

These two pastors have written about the very issue that Jesus warned about in several parables. In the parable of the sheep and the goats, the Lord described the separation of the sheep (believers) from the goats (unbelievers) at the end time during the judgment of the nations (Matthew 25:32-46). Christ said that when He appears as judge at the final day, He "will separate people one from another, as a shepherd separates the sheep from the goats" (verse 32). He will do this by gathering the sheep (believers) on His right hand and the goats (unbelievers) on His left hand. He will usher the sheep into eternal life in heaven, and He will send the goats away into eternal punishment. The most shocking aspect of this parable is that those who were goats were seemingly surprised to be characterized as such.

Look with me at another section of Scripture where Jesus again addresses this same issue in the parable of the wheat and the tares (or weeds), which is found in Matthew 13:24-43. He compares our world to a wheat field with Himself as the sower of the wheat. The wheat represents Christians, and the tares, or false Christians, are sown by the devil. Both the wheat and the tares grow in the field together virtually indistinguishable from one another until they mature and are harvested, at which time they are separated. The text identifies the reapers as angels (verse 39) who carry out the work of separating the wheat and the tares for judgment at the end of the age. At that time, explains Jesus, the reapers will "throw them into the fiery furnace. In that place there will be weeping and gnashing of teeth" (Matthew 13:42).

Note that both the wheat and tares grow together and appear to be the same on the outside until they produce fruit. God's Word tells us the same will be true about people. Many claim to know Jesus and may even attempt to look like Christians, but Jesus does not necessarily know them. In fact, Jesus states this outright in Matthew 7:21: "Not everyone who says to me, 'Lord, Lord,' will enter the kingdom of heaven, but the one who does the will of my Father who is in heaven."

This may sound alarming to you and it should. This problem is not new. It was such a widespread issue during the New Testament days that the apostle John wrote the book of 1 John to help readers know whether they were indeed a Christian. We will look at this more in depth later.

Pathways to False Identities

There are many people who teach a false Christianity under the guise of tolerance and diversity. In fact, in the present postmodern climate, tolerance is increasingly the one standard under which many liberal and mainline churches join together. This standard tells us to tolerate or allow teachings or beliefs that are not found in the Bible.

Yet God strongly warns us against adding anything to His Word: "You shall not add to the word that I command you, nor take from it, that you may keep the commandments of the LORD your God that I command you" (Deuteronomy 4:2). Teaching anything other than what the Bible teaches is sin, and a tolerance that brushes aside biblical truth actually covers up sin. By contrast, the gospel of Jesus Christ *exposes* our sin. Author Carolyn McCulley explains:

> Until I heard the gospel, I didn't see sin very clearly in myself. If I saw weaknesses, shortcomings, or failures in myself, I was good at blaming other people for them or minimizing them in me. I was blind to the sins of envy, anger, self-righteousness, judgment, greed, and pride...I was all about myself and maximizing my own comfort, opportunity, and pleasure.[9]

For some of you, such warnings come as a reminder of the importance of being certain about where you stand with God. Others, however, may have never heard any of this before. Consider, for example, what the apostle Paul said about false teaching in Galatians 1:8: "Even if we or an angel from heaven should preach to you a gospel contrary to the one we preached to you, let him be accursed." Paul warned us to not accept false teachings. "Be careful here," writes pastor Joshua Harris. "At first glance, most churches will appear to teach God's Word. You'll see it printed in the bulletin, written on the walls, or sprinkled through the services. But these references to Scripture don't necessarily mean a church is submitted to God's Word,"[10] or to the gospel of Jesus Christ.

Many churchgoers are greatly confused about the gospel because they listen to false teachers. God has warned us about believing in a false gospel. A false gospel is any teaching that does not stress we repent of our sin by grace through faith in Christ alone. Any other "gospel" is empty and has no saving value. All other conceptions of the so-called gospel lead only to God's promises of judgment and ultimately God's wrath.

Why all these warnings? Because of the reality that there are many false Christians who believe a false gospel taught by false teachers. These people claim to belong to Christ but don't. We don't want that to be true about you. So many people are walking down this road today. In

Matthew 7:13 Jesus said, "The gate is wide and the way is easy that leads to destruction, and those who enter by it are many." Jesus doesn't say a few are on this destructive path, but *many*! Many people think they are the beneficiaries of God's blessings because they have achieved material comforts when in reality they are headed straight for the wrath of God. Satan has deceived them into believing they are receiving God's blessings when they are not. First John 2:16 boldly declares, "For all that is in the world—the desires of the flesh and the desires of the eyes and pride in possessions[11]—is not from the Father but is from the world."

Now you can see why Scripture tells us to "examine yourselves, to see whether you are in the faith. Test yourselves" (2 Corinthians 13:5).

Inspecting Your Fruit

The Bible uses metaphors (a word or phrase describing one object or idea to describe something else) to illustrate believers and unbelievers.[12] Each metaphor is selected to help us understand a certain point being made. I want to share with you one metaphor in particular in which Jesus describes the difference between a true believer and a false one. In John 15:5-6 He says,

> I am the vine; you are the branches. Whoever abides in me and I in him, he it is that bears much fruit, for apart from me you can do nothing. If anyone does not abide in me he is thrown away like a branch and withers; and the branches are gathered, thrown into the fire, and burned.

In those verses, Jesus says the true believer is like a vine that bears fruit. Thus fruit is an identifying characteristic of someone who is truly saved. This is a great reminder that there are, in fact, visible signs that validate the genuineness of a person's spiritual condition.

As mentioned earlier, the book of 1 John presents a number of identifying characteristics that will reveal a person's true spiritual identity. Each of these indicators will be present in some form in a believer's life, although they may be more prominent in some people than in others. Let's take some time to walk through several spiritual indicators and discover some crucial questions about whether or not your identity truly is in Christ.

Spiritual Identity Indicators

Identity Indicator #1—Fellowship with the Father

The true believer has fellowship with the Father. This means fellowship with God is synonymous with salvation. Communion with God and fellowship with His Son Jesus Christ is a fact of the reality of a person's true conversion. Fellowship with the Father means that you want to be near Him, hear what He says, and seek to live a life that reflects how wonderful your relationship with Him is. Fellowship with God produces joy within the believer and a longing to be with the Father (1 John 1:3-4).

Identity Indicator #2—Confession of Sin

A genuine believer has a biblical view of sin. Every believer realizes he is a sinner and knows that even though he is saved, he continues to struggle with sin. When we confess our sin to God, He is faithful to forgive us and cleanse us of our sin. The true Christian desires to *put off* sin because he loves God and wants to obey Him (1 John 1:8-10; see also Ephesians 4:31-32; Colossians 2:13).

Identity Indicator #3—Keeping God's Word

True believers love God's Word and greatly desire to keep it, even though they might not understand everything about it. Their love for God produces obedience to His Word and a desire to live a life that may be called biblical (1 John 2:3-6; see also 1 Peter 1:14). This doesn't mean that a true believer always knows what she should do or that she always does what she knows to do. It simply means that she'll have a hunger for God's Word and a lifelong desire to obey it.

Identity Indicator #4—Love for Other Believers

True believers have a genuine love for others, especially fellow believers in Christ. This love is a sign that they've come to know God's love for themselves. Once a person becomes a believer, he is born into the family of God. All believers are then part of a new family and become brothers and sisters in Christ (1 John 2:9-11; 3:14-17; see also 1 Peter 1:22). The realization that we belong to one another because we all belong to Christ grows within the heart of every true believer.

Identity Indicator #5—No Longer Love the World

The true believer no longer loves the things that the world has to offer. This doesn't mean that she doesn't enjoy the earthly blessings in the world. It simply means that she no longer lives for them or believes that they will ultimately satisfy her. Compared to her love for the Lord, every other love is like a hatred. She knows the sinful enticements of the world will lead to death and although she may fall prey to them from time to time, she longs to live a holy life. She has been given new desires that consist of the things of God (1 John 2:15-17; see also Ephesians 2:1-3; Colossians 2:8).

Identity Indicator #6—Love for the Truth

Genuine believers desire to hear and be taught the truths in God's Word. They are able to understand God's Word because the Holy Spirit enlightens them, giving them the ability to comprehend spiritual truths that unbelievers cannot grasp. This doesn't mean that genuine believers understand *everything* in the Bible; it means that they're growing in the truth and their love for it. The Holy Spirit also helps the Christian to discern between truth and error (1 John 4:6; see also 2 Corinthians 4:2).

Identity Indicator #7—Becoming More Christlike

True believers are characterized by a life of love and righteousness; they seek to put off sin daily and delight in following in their Savior's footsteps. A woman who really belongs to the Lord is one who is growing in her character—she's becoming more loving, more gentle, more patient every day. The anticipation of Christ's eventual return causes every Christian to examine her life through the lens of Scripture so she is not ashamed when He comes (1 John 2:28-29; see also 1 Corinthians 4:1-5).

Identity Indicator # 8—Conflict with the World

Genuine believers are hated by the world because of their godly lifestyle and righteous deeds. The righteous conduct of God's children serves as a rebuke to the wicked lives of unbelievers, so often believers will find themselves at odds with unbelievers and the objects of undeserved hostility. Jesus was hated by the world; therefore, all those who follow Him will be hated by the world (1 John 3:11-13; see also John 15:19).

Identity Indicator #9—Confidence in Prayer

A genuine believer has the confidence that God hears her when she prays. And not only that—she knows that whatever she asks according to His will, it will be answered in God's perfect timing (1 John 5:14-15). Again, this doesn't mean she never has any doubts or that she always walks in perfect confidence. Many godly men and women have experienced difficult times when their faith and their faithfulness to prayer were tried. But as the years go by, a true believer will live out a lifestyle of faithful, humble prayer and trust in God's good answers.

Being Certain of Your Identity

Now, my dear friend, I have to ask you a very pointed but loving question: Will you *promise* to test yourself to make sure you have a personal relationship with God? Perhaps to you, this chapter seems too hard, too narrow. But the truth is that God's promises are only for God's children, and we love you enough to encourage you to ask yourself whether you are, in fact, His child. If you are, even if you're nowhere near perfect, you can rest in the great comfort of knowing that *all* of God's gracious promised blessings are for you.

> *Submit yourselves therefore to God. Resist the*
> *devil, and he will flee from you. Draw near*
> *to God, and he will draw near to you*
>
> (JAMES 4:7-8).

Recommended Resources

Lawson, Steven. *Absolutely Sure.* Sisters, OR: Multnomah Publishers, 1999.

MacArthur, John. *The Gospel According to Jesus.* Grand Rapids: Zondervan, 1988.

Parsons, Burk. *Assured by God.* Phillipsburg, NJ: Presbyterian & Reformed, 2007.

Peace, Martha. *Attitudes of a Transformed Heart.* Bemidji, MN: Focus Publishing, Inc., 2002.

Piper, John. *Finally Alive.* Fern, Scotland: Christian Focus, 2009.

———. *God Is the Gospel.* Wheaton, IL: Crossway, 2005.

Chapter 3

INTERPRETING GOD'S
WORD ACCURATELY

Barbara Enter

S o many opinions, so many voices...to whom should we listen? Where should we go to find clear answers to the problems we face? What should we do about the many voices who speak totally different opinions while supporting their views with the Bible? Could it be that the Bible is being misinterpreted to support these various opinions?

To get answers, we need to turn to hermeneutics. "What is hermeneutics?" you ask. Webster's dictionary defines *hermeneutics* (hər-mə-nü-tiks) as the "science of interpreting, especially the Scriptures..."[1] Bible scholar Roy Zuck defines hermeneutics simply as the science and art of interpreting the Bible.[2] It is a science because it involves principles and rules for Bible interpretation. And it is called an art because it takes skill to apply those rules. The problem is that many people who read and teach the Bible do not understand and follow these interpretive rules; therefore, they have weak skills when it comes to applying them.

The Problem of Incorrectly Interpreting the Bible

This lack of understanding has caused confusion and even harm. When we read the Bible for guidance yet do not interpret it accurately, we end up arriving at wrong applications or conclusions. In addition, when we lack the skills for interpreting Scripture, we will not know whether other people are teaching the Bible correctly. The result is confusion—especially when we hear teachings that are supposedly from the Bible but are contradictory with one another.

For instance, some Christian financial advisors would tell us that it is not wise to buy a new car. They go on to say that we are to be good stewards of God's money; therefore, it is better to buy a used car. On the other hand, I have heard of a television preacher who said that God does not want His people to buy used cars; instead, they should purchase brand-new cars. These two views claim to be based on the Bible; yet, these views are totally opposite of one another and confusing to the listener.

I happen to agree with the Christian financial advisors who say it's better to buy a used car because they support their opinions with wisdom from the book of Proverbs. While the television preacher supported his teaching with a Bible verse, he plucked that verse out of context. He pointed to the time when Jesus rode into Jerusalem on a young donkey that had never been ridden (Mark 11:1-8). This preacher misused this verse to support his view that God's people should buy new cars because Jesus rode on a colt that had never been ridden or "used." If the people listening to that preacher understood the rules for good Bible interpretation, they would realize this story about Jesus doesn't apply to buying new cars.

The television preacher broke a very important interpretive rule: Each portion of Scripture must be understood in its context. Understanding a verse in its context means it must be understood in relationship with the surrounding verses. When a verse is taken out of context, it can be misused to support any false notion.

Taking verses out of context can cause a lot of unnecessary harm. For example, when my son Travis was born, the umbilical cord was tied around his neck. He started having seizures when he was six weeks old. After seeking much medical advice, he was diagnosed with epilepsy. As a young mother, it was very difficult for me to watch my son suffer with this neurological condition. However, my pain was intensified when I was told by a Christian friend that if I just had enough faith, Travis would be healed because Christ came to heal us of all of our diseases. She quoted Isaiah 53:5 from the Bible, which says, "He [Christ] was wounded for our transgressions; he was crushed for our iniquities; upon him was the chastisement that brought us peace, and with his stripes we are healed" (Isaiah 53:5). My friend was setting me up for disappointment. She was saying that if my son wasn't healed, it meant we lacked faith. However, Isaiah 53:5 does not talk about physical healing. If we read Isaiah 53:5 in the context of the surrounding verses, we learn that it is speaking of the *spiritual* healing that the cross of Christ will bring to those who turn from their sin and turn toward Christ in dependence and faith.

The counsel I received from my Christian friend was unbiblical, confusing, and harmful because it added to my grief. Her counsel made me feel responsible and guilty that I did not have enough faith for my son's healing. Later, when I learned about proper Bible interpretation, I came to realize my friend had pulled the verse out of context. I realized that my son's condition didn't mean I lacked faith.

This leads me to an important question: Who controls the meaning of the Bible?

Who Controls the Meaning of the Bible— the Author or the Reader?

This question is a good one when reading any literature, but it is especially important in relation to the Bible. Often you will hear people say, "This portion of Scripture means this to me...," or "I think this verse means such and such..." These types of statements often come from people who think a verse can mean different things to different people. That is, the reader controls and determines the meaning of the Bible. But such a perspective is not correct, nor is it logical.

Consider the following example: Say you are driving a car and you come to a stop sign. You say to your friend who is riding with you, "To me, this sign means that I should just slow down." (Imagine saying that to a police officer!) Now suppose you come to a four-way intersection, and there are cars waiting from every direction. What if each driver decided to interpret their stop sign in a different way? Obviously, much confusion and possibly even harm would occur if the drivers failed to interpret the signs properly and caused collisions.

The same type of confusion and harm occurs when we as readers think that we can determine for ourselves the meaning of what God has written. *God is the One who determines the meaning of the Scriptures because He is the Author of the Bible.* Second Timothy 3:16-17 says, "All Scripture is breathed out by God and profitable for teaching, for reproof, for correction, and for training in righteousness, that the man of God may be competent, equipped for every good work."

This verse tells us the Scriptures were spoken by God. The apostle Peter then added to our understanding when he wrote, "No prophecy of Scripture comes from someone's own interpretation. For no prophecy was ever produced by the will of man, but men spoke from God as they were carried along by the Holy Spirit" (2 Peter 1:20-21).

In other words, God breathed out the Scriptures and used men who were borne along by the Holy Spirit, just as a sailboat is carried by the wind that fills its sails. The Bible means what *God* intended it to mean. Each verse means only what *He* intended for it to mean.

As the author of the sacred Scriptures, God is in control over them. This means He controls the intended meaning of the words. Interpreting the Scriptures was never meant to be a guessing game with interpretations that vary from reader to reader. The Bible is clear and is written in such a way that with the exception of some of the more difficult passages, its teachings are understandable by all who will read it with a teachable, humble attitude. There is only one meaning for every verse in the Bible; otherwise, it could have no clear meaning at all. Our task as readers of the Bible is to draw out the single meaning intended by God—not to determine it by our own subjective opinion.

Learning how to draw out the single meaning of each verse is what helps protect us from contradictory or harmful teachings. This is where hermeneutics comes in. As stated before, there are principles and rules to follow when we interpret the Bible. Learning hermeneutics is crucial for many reasons, but the chief reason is to discover what *"God has said in Sacred Scripture…*There is no profit to us if God has spoken and we do not know what He has said…The result of an erratic hermeneutic is that the Bible has been made the source of confusion rather than light."[3]

So let's consider some general rules for Bible interpretation so we can understand the Scriptures better and avoid the confusion and harm caused by poor interpretation.

The General Rules for Correctly Interpreting the Bible

Many books have been written to teach the rules for proper Bible interpretation. My goal in these few pages is to teach you some basic, general rules that will get you off to an excellent start. I hope to whet your appetite for further study on this topic. Without the help of sound hermeneutical principles, we will not be able to find God's solutions to life's problems. In addition, we will miss the message of the Bible and we'll fail to understand God Himself.

Principle #1: Context Determines the Meaning

A good place to start in understanding God's Word is this: *Context determines the meaning of any biblical text.* A good motto to follow is a "text without a context is a pretext for a proof text."[4] This slogan is not intended to be a tongue twister! Rather, it is teaching that the Bible out of context is not the Bible.

There are three contexts to consider when you read a portion of Scripture, and all three are important if you want to understand what God has spoken. The Bible must be understood in its historical-cultural context, the literary genre context, and the literary Bible book context.

THE HISTORICAL-CULTURAL CONTEXT

What do I mean when I say the historical-cultural context? This refers to the varied historical and cultural contexts at the time the different books of the Bible were written. We need to remember that the Bible was written in three different languages—Hebrew, Aramaic, and Greek—over a period of approximately 1500 years. Therefore, the context of the Bible was written in the context of different cultures (and it's wonderful that the Bible's timeless truths apply to all cultures!).

One passage in which cultural context is key is Romans 16:16, which says we should "greet one another with a holy kiss." This manner of greeting people was a common cultural practice among the Jews in Bible times. However, we do not greet one another in this manner in twenty-first-century America. Instead, we greet one another with a "holy handshake"! The timeless *principle* of Romans 16:16 is still true today in that we should extend a warm greeting to one another as an expression of care.

When it comes to understanding historical-cultural background, study Bibles are often helpful. Also, much of the historical-cultural context of Scripture can be discovered by careful observation of the Bible book that we are reading. It helps to pay attention to details about the author and those who received the book. We can also find cultural clues through political, religious, economic, legal, agricultural, domestic, and geographical information. Roy Zuck writes, "When we go to the Scriptures, it is as if we are entering a foreign land…If we fail to give attention to these matters of culture" then we may be guilty of putting our Western twenty-first-century ideas into the meaning of the Bible.[5] It is extremely important to note the historical-cultural context when interpreting Bible passages so we can understand God's intended meaning of those passages.

THE LITERARY GENRE CONTEXT

Genre (zhän-rǝ) is a French word that simply means a "kind…a type of category, especially of works of art and literature."[6] The term *literary genre* refers to the different kinds of literature found in the Bible. We should read and understand all literature, secular and biblical, according to the type of literature it is. I certainly read a cookbook differently than I would read a love letter from my husband—or at least I had better! I also read a restaurant menu quite differently than I read directions to a friend's house. Various genres have special qualities we must consider when we interpret the Bible. We should read and interpret the poetry in the Psalms differently than we would read a letter from the apostle Paul. We should also read and interpret the historical narratives in Genesis differently than we would read prophecy that is found in the book of Revelation.

Much confusion has resulted from people interpreting the various genres of literature without noting their varied characteristics. For example, many parents have been told to cling to the "promise" of Proverbs 22:6, which states, "Train up a child in the way he should go; even when he is old he will not depart from it." There are some who teach that if parents train their child in the ways of the Lord, their child will continue on a godly path when he grows up.

However, this ignores the fact that the book of Proverbs is wisdom literature. Proverbs contains insights and general principles that are more often true than not.[7] But the proverbs are not specifically promises. In fact, Proverbs 22:6 is actually a warning, not a promise. Solomon, who wrote most of Proverbs, was warning parents that if they withheld discipline and instruction from their child, the child was likely to proceed in his own foolish way unhindered, even when he grew older. That's simply a general truth Solomon was stating, and we know that because that's the nature of wisdom literature.

Most Bible scholars divide the literary genres of the Old Testament into the following categories: narrative, law, poetry, wisdom, and prophecy. And the New Testament's literary genres are gospel, history, letters, and apocalyptic writings. Both Testaments include subgenres within their larger genres, such as parables, riddles, sermons, and prayers.

Many good books have been written about how to properly interpret the various types of Bible literature. One such book is *Living by the Book* by Howard Hendricks and his son, William Hendricks. There are special rules for correctly interpreting the different literary forms, and learning these rules will help you to understand your Bible more accurately.

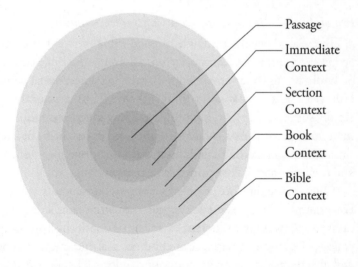

THE LITERARY BIBLE BOOK CONTEXT

The last context we will consider is the literary Bible book context. This refers to understanding a portion of Scripture within its (1) immediate context; (2) then within the larger section surrounding

the passage, such as a chapter; (3) then in light of the entire book of
the Bible in which the passage is found; and (4) within the context of
the entire Bible. The diagram above illustrates how we should seek to
interpret a passage of Scripture within the successively larger contexts
around it.

When we isolate verses out of their context, we risk misinterpreting
them. For example, Philippians 4:13 says, "I can do all things through
[Christ] who strengthens me." Some people take the first half of that
verse too literally to promote self-confidence. I don't know about you,
but I cannot do *all* things. In fact, at my age there are more and more
things I can no longer do! For example, I can say, "I can do all things
through Christ who strengthens me" all day but I cannot jump over
a six-foot-high wall or stay up half the night and still function the
next day. This verse was not meant to be isolated and used in that way.
Rather, the apostle Paul was referring to contentment that can be found
in any and every circumstance. He was talking about Christ being our
strength for that.

Principle #2: Scripture Can Never Contradict Scripture

The second general principle of good Bible interpretation is this:
Scripture can never contradict Scripture. Although the Bible consists of
66 books written by approximately 40 human authors over a period of
1500 years, it is a book with a unified theme. The theme of the Bible,
simply stated, is that God has provided a way to redeem sinful, fallen
man through the person and work of the Lord Jesus Christ. Because of
this unified theme, the Bible cannot teach one principle in one book
and teach a contradictory principle in another book.

Often in the Bible we will read *seemingly* contradictory statements.
For example, the apostle Paul appeared to write conflicting instructions to widows in two different letters. In 1 Timothy he instructed the
younger widows to "marry, bear children, manage their households,
and give the adversary no occasion for slander" (1 Timothy 5:14). But
in another place Paul told some widows "that it is good for them if
they remain single" like him (1 Corinthians 7:8). Those two passages
appear to contradict one another, yet we know the Bible cannot contradict itself. If it did, then it's not consistently truthful and therefore

it's not trustworthy. So how do we reconcile the seemingly opposing statements? Well, Paul's instructions to widows must be interpreted in the context in which it appears. A close look shows he was addressing two different situations.

In the letter to Timothy, Paul was writing so Timothy, who was a young pastor, "may know how one ought to behave in the household of God, which is the church of the living God, a pillar and buttress of the truth" (1 Timothy 3:15). Paul was explaining how the church was to view older widows who have no family, and was to instruct young widows who might be tempted to become idle gossips and give in to sensual desires (1 Timothy 5:11-16).

By contrast, in 1 Corinthians 7, Paul told the widows it would be better if they remain unmarried because of a "present distress" (verse 26). At that time and place in church history, there was great persecution. Paul wrote that a person who was single would have fewer "worldly troubles" or concerns. He was trying to spare these widows from the added burden of having to care for a family while enduring severe persecution (1 Corinthians 7:28).

Again, Scripture is its own best interpreter, especially when it appears two statements are in conflict. When you are uncertain about seemingly conflicting statements, look more carefully at the context because Scripture cannot contradict Scripture.

Principle #3: Vague Passages Must Not Determine Our Doctrine

The third general principle for good biblical interpretation is this: *Vague passages must not determine our doctrine.* An unclear verse should never be interpreted in such a way that we end up making it contradict a plain biblical text. For example, Paul wrote that women will be "saved through childbearing—if they continue in faith, love and holiness with propriety" (1 Timothy 2:15 NIV). This verse *appears* to state that women will receive salvation through the work of giving childbirth.

Yet any careful student of the Bible knows 1 Timothy 2:15 could not possibly be teaching that a woman is brought to salvation through childbearing! That would contradict the straightforward biblical teaching that salvation is by grace alone, through faith alone, in Christ alone. Ephesians 2:8-9 teaches that very plainly: "By grace you have been saved through faith. And this is not your own doing; it is the gift of God, not a result of works [such as childbirth], so that no one may boast."

So, when interpreting the Bible, we cannot build any doctrines on vague passages. When we are uncertain, we should look to clearer passages for help.

The three general hermeneutical principles stated above should govern how you interpret Scripture. They are applicable to every book of the Bible, no matter what type of literature you are reading. And when you use these principles, you help to ensure that you will arrive at biblical answers to your life problems.

Walking in the Light

God's Word declares that it is a lamp to our feet and a light to our paths (Psalm 119:105). However, much of the light of God's Word is often hidden through faulty interpretation. Our paths are cloudy and we stumble because we do not take the time to apply the principles of hermeneutics that will enable us to discover God's guidelines on how we are to live. It is easy for people to make a human opinion *sound* biblical by wrapping a Bible verse around it. But mere human opinions will lead us astray—only God's Word has the guidance we need. I could write a book on the bad teaching that I and others have embraced because we were following opinions and not truth. Biblical counselor Jay Adams once said, "Opinions are like noses. Everyone has one!"[8] We do not need yet another human opinion; we need God's authoritative guidance about the solutions to our problems.

J.I. Packer writes that if you "disregard the study of God [in His Word]...you sentence yourself to stumble and blunder through life blindfolded, as it were, with no sense of direction and no understanding of what surrounds you. This way you can waste your life and lose your soul."[9]

If we desire to learn how to live a wise, righteous life, we need to understand Scripture properly and take it to heart. Near the end of his life, Moses spoke to the Israelites and said, "Take to your heart all the words with which I am warning you today, which you shall command your sons to observe carefully, even all the words of this law. For it is not an idle word for you; *indeed it is your life*" (Deuteronomy 32:46-47 NASB; emphasis added).

The Bible contains God's life-giving words, and we are in desperate need to hear what God has spoken. His words are not futile words we can ignore. If we do not know how to correctly interpret the Bible with the help of sound hermeneutics, then we will not truly have God's valuable words, nor will we find God Himself, even if we are reading the Bible.

Every Christian woman has been given both the privilege and responsibility to learn about God and His ways through the Bible. And even if we've never taken a formal course on Bible interpretation, we can have hope that we can learn how to understand His Word properly because we've been given the Holy Spirit, who will open our eyes to truth and teach us. So, don't be afraid! Why not write those three interpretive principles on an index card and place it in your Bible right now so you are always ready to have a clear understanding of God's Word?

Recommended Resources

ESV Study Bible. Wheaton, IL: Crossway, 2008.

Pearch, Dora Leigh. *Back to the Source: 10 Steps for Personal Bible Study.* Mesa, AZ: Pearch Publishing, 2007.

Zuck, Roy B. *Basic Bible Interpretation.* Colorado Springs: Victor, 1991.

Chapter 4

SPIRITUAL DISCERNMENT:
HOW CAN I KNOW WHAT IS TRUE?

§ *Karen Avinelis* §

Joy was anxious to discover the cause for her friend's excitement over the latest book everyone was talking about. She bought a copy of the book herself and was captivated by each word she read. It was as if the author had written this story with Joy in mind. Her heart was racing with excitement! She now understood the reason this book had hit the bestseller list so quickly: It helped her feel important and in control of her destiny.

Can you identify with Joy? She is attracted to ideas that feel and sound good. However, that which seems appealing from our perspective doesn't always agree with the Bible. That which looks good may not be good at all! We find ourselves drawn to promises of help and success only to discover later that the promises are empty.

What is it that leads us to succumb to the fads and trends that offer a lot of promises that later turn out empty? Have you found yourself looking for answers in the wrong places?

You are not alone. I have struggled with this as well. Counterfeit promises saturate our world. World-born lies steal our time, confuse our minds, and complicate our lives. Many of these lies contain enough truth to appear "for real" at first. How do we deal with that?

This shows our need to recognize wrong from right. We need the ability to see error wherever it is, no matter what it hides behind. Our need for spiritual discernment is critical—especially when we consider the number of messages thrown our direction every day. The only way to get this kind of discernment is by being a child of God who desires it, prays for it, and seeks for it in the only place it can be found—God's Word.

The Bible is the only source of accurate and absolute truth that directly pertains to our daily life situations. Second Timothy 3:16 tells us that God has given us His words to live by. God's truths are relevant and will never lead us down a wrong path. God's Word teaches us how to live, warns us of danger, corrects our thinking, and trains us to distinguish right from wrong. Things that sound too good to be true, outside of God's Word, usually are.

The purpose of this chapter is to give you the tools that will enable you to grow into a more mature, spiritually discerning woman of God (Hebrews 5:14). We are bombarded with information every day; we need to test or measure all of it for accuracy. Not just any measuring stick will do, however—God's standard for truth is perfect, and it alone is adequate for the task of helping us to separate right from wrong. We learn to discern truth from error by constant and close study of the real thing, God's Word. Developing a warning system much like that of the U.S. Department of Homeland Security[1] will help us to lift up a flag of caution when we come across information that at first glance sounds good but doesn't seem quite right. The world's wisdom cannot be trusted, and the Bible is our instruction manual for life (Psalm 119:129-130). We must learn it and live by it.

The Gospel and Spiritual Discernment

Growing in the ability to *discern* truth from error without becoming legalistic and pronouncing unloving judgments on those who speak or write in error is hard work. This is the reason that God's Holy Spirit is our essential Helper and Wise Counselor in this process. If you are in any way unsure whether you are a child of God, please take the time, right now, to go to Appendix Two on page 321. Without the Holy Spirit's presence in your heart, biblical spiritual discernment will never be yours.

Spiritual discernment is all too rare in the Christian community today. Many believers have become lazy in the pursuit of gaining wisdom from the Bible. Every believer is called to develop and grow into the constant use of spiritual discernment (1 Corinthians 2:12-16). This involves thinking biblically about every aspect of daily life and every event in the world around us (Romans 12:2). Thinking biblically means thinking on the reality of the gospel, the power of God, every waking moment. The gospel truth has endured the test of history and constant attack by the world that surrounds us. Therefore, God's Word is the only tool strong enough to help us take a stand against the constant stream of wrong and destructive information that tempts our minds and seduces our hearts away from God. As women who have been given new and changed hearts by the gospel message, God's plan for us now is to stand firm against these attacks and rest in the power and protection of Jesus our Lord.

Spiritual Discernment Defined

Spiritual discernment is the learned ability to understand and apply the truths found in God's Word so that we are able to separate truth from error and right from wrong.[2] Let's take this definition apart and see what it is exactly that God is calling every believer to do when it comes to spiritually discerning truth from error, half-truths, and partial truths.

The Skill of Understanding

We are not born with an innate ability to separate wrong from right. Watch any infant for a while and it will become glaringly apparent that this little bundle of joy will need help in learning the appropriate manners and habits that accompany living in harmony within a family structure. In fact, the skill of discernment is one that we continue to develop all through life.

So how do we develop this skill? There are four basic steps, as outlined by the acrostic S-T-O-P:

1. **S**tudy of God's Word

2. **T**ime to succeed and fail

3. **O**bservation of others who are spiritually discerning

4. **P**ractice of the truths already learned every day

This acrostic, STOP, will help you to apply the principles of discernment to daily life. The more we know what truth looks and sounds like through the *study* of God's Word, the more easily we will recognize wrong information. Taking the *time* to apply God's truth will help us grow more successful at separating right from wrong. *Observing* other Christians who are more mature and set a good example is helpful and encouraging. And *practicing* the truths you learn through the previous three steps will lead to maturity in spiritual discernment.

Study God's Truth

Discernment involves the study of that which is right and true day after day. First Thessalonians 5:20 speaks about taking in God's Word rather than rejecting it. When we accept God's truths and think about them, the Holy Spirit is then able to use these principles to teach us how to respond to different situations in daily life.

Imagine sewing together a garment for the first time. The first step is to purchase a pattern that shows you how to cut and size the fabric. You must then carefully follow all the directions and measure your fabric just so. Otherwise, the end-product will turn out quite interesting, to say the least. By following the pattern carefully, you will be able to fit the garment to the person it was meant for.

God's truths require attention and adherence to its specific instructions. When you apply the Bible's truth to a situation, when you understand and follow the intended meaning of a passage, then God is pleased. His Word has been accepted not rejected (Hebrews 11:6).

Time to Succeed and Fail

When we carefully examine and weigh thoughts, ideas, or information and compare it to the guidelines in the Bible, we are practicing *discernment*. We are measuring all things against God's truths like a yardstick. As women, we must carefully divide truth from error and choose to respond in ways that are good and right.

Look at the magazines at the checkout line in the grocery store, and the need for discernment meets you immediately. You may find things that look appealing or enticing, and find yourself itching for more. In 2 Timothy 4:4 the apostle Paul talks about "itching ears" that want to follow those who say what makes them feel good. Paul goes on to say that people who succumb to this itch will "turn away from listening

to the truth and wander off into myths." All of us today are in a battle
for our minds, a battle in which we must separate truth from error. It
takes time and close examination to recognize what causes our ears to
itch for more and whether that "more" is good or evil.

Spiritual Discernment in Action

The most exciting and rewarding step in the process of spiritual
growth is when you put your discernment into practice. It helps when
you spend time with another believer who has successfully recognized the difference between good and evil. Perhaps you know of a fellow believer who has survived a difficult trial or tragedy by choosing
to do what was right rather than doing what the world says or does.
The Christian who has walked through life's struggles and has found
strength within the pages of God's Word usually has a track record for
spiritual discernment. She can be a wonderful resource for you and a
rich source of godly wisdom and understanding (James 1:2-4), and she
can serve as an example you aspire to follow.

Practice God's Truths You Have Learned

Let's look at how we can put discernment into practice. You are at
the grocery store and a magazine catches your eye. There is an article
on power, and you are feeling exceptionally weak and vulnerable today.
You pick up the magazine and begin reading what it takes to assert
power and control over your life so that those around you do not control you. Well, that sounds good, doesn't it? What's wrong with wanting to be in control? That's a really good question. Is what the magazine
teaches you antithetical to Scripture? In other words, is it the opposite
of what God wants for you? What you are reading may sound pretty
good, but is it?

Warning level blue—guarded: Does this teaching line up with Scripture? Is the message you are reading drawing you closer to God? Does
what the author suggests line up with biblical truth? Suppose the writer
mentions God's blessing on those who take time to prepare themselves through meditation and aligning their spirit on their inner power.
Warning level orange—high: If what the author says sounds too good to
be true, then it is probably false teaching. Remember the alert system?

It sounds as though Satan (the accuser, Revelation 12:10) is using some juicy tidbit of half-truth to knock you off course.

It's now 3:00 p.m.; time for your favorite afternoon talk show. Guess what? The featured guest this afternoon, a respected woman in her field, is sharing with the audience how to develop their inner power in daily life and guard themselves from the control of others around them. Wow! This is no accident. This woman even mentions God. So immediately you know this afternoon was meant for you. Both the magazine and TV show are about the same thing! Warning level red—severe: Are you allowing your feelings to determine what truth is? Have you sought God and asked for wisdom and discernment? James 1:5 invites us to ask Him for wisdom whenever we need it.

Practicing spiritual discernment requires right thinking and doing. You have a decision to make: God's way or the world's way? Which will you choose?

As you read the words in the magazine, you must examine them in the light of the gospel of Jesus Christ. Is Christ center-stage as the source of power? If the magazine article does not align with God's truths, then what keeps you reading further? If the talk show guest is not sharing encouragement that points you back to Christ and God's Word, then what keeps you tuned in? God's Word clearly states that man's wisdom is not profitable: "Has not God made foolish the wisdom of the world?" (1 Corinthians 1:20). We have to learn to say no to what the world offers us as wisdom. Let God alone be the source of truth and instruction for you and your family.

God's Word Is Truth

In a prayer to His heavenly Father, Jesus said in John 17:17, "Sanctify them in the truth; your word is truth." He wants His followers to be sanctified. The word *sanctify* means "to be set apart" for holy service to God. Followers of God are to be different, set apart from the world, not doing what the world does. When we do what the world does, people around us are unable to see what makes a Christian different. As followers of God, we are to (1) study God's Word, (2) hear God's Word preached regularly, (3) memorize God's Word, and (4) be a member of a church that practices what God's Word teaches by serving one another in biblical love.

The result of diligent study of the Scriptures is a changed heart and mind. Genuine heart change is only possible when we follow God's instructions for life each day. Jesus said in John 14:15, "If you love me, you will keep my commandments." As you believe and do what Jesus teaches in His Word, life will change. That doesn't mean your life will be free of struggles; God never promises that in His Word. But as you let God's instruction guide you in the choices you make each day, you will develop a biblical worldview (1 John 2:15-17). That is, you will see this world more and more the way God views it.

Separate Truth from Error, Right from Wrong

The Bible is like a magnifying glass. When you look at something that seems fuzzy and put it under the magnifying glass of God's Word, the details become clear. The Bible is an important "magnifying glass" that helps provide clarity for you as you sift through all the messages the world throws at you. Christian women are challenged every day, for example, by the world's lies about outward beauty and the shape of their bodies. We're told that's what really counts. But God's Word tells us, in 1 Peter 3:4, that you should "let your adorning be…the imperishable beauty of a gentle and quiet spirit, which in God's sight is very precious." How does that compare to what a magazine or talk show will tell us? As you can see, it is important to measure everything against the yardstick of God's Word.

Believers in Christ are to "test everything; hold fast what is good. Abstain from every form of evil" (1 Thessalonians 5:21-22). Believers are to examine what they think, hear, see, and do, and measure it all against what God's Word says. What you think of and understand about God (that is, your theology) will always drive your responses to everything in life. When a woman lives out the world's expectations for her, you can know that she desires the world's acceptance of her and not God's direction for her.

You need to practice discernment in what you believe and in what you do with what you believe because you are a daughter of the King. This is "walking your talk." Tim Challies, author of the book *The Discipline of Spiritual Discernment,* oversees a Web site dedicated to book reviews of newly published works for the Christian community.[3] His ministry is dedicated to helping the naïve or undiscerning become wise in God's ways. He exhorts Christians to test everything, because if we accept a wrong idea or concept as truth, then we will *assume* it is reliable truth—even when it isn't.

God Is the Source of All Spiritual Discernment

When God offered to give King Solomon whatever he wanted, Solomon asked for the gift of wisdom and discernment (1 Kings 3:9-12). With God's help, he became the wisest man who ever lived. Solomon desired God's wisdom for the purpose of *discerning* good from evil as he governed God's people, Israel. Solomon's request was in alignment with God's good purposes, and God freely granted his request. Solomon is the author of many proverbs and Scriptures in the Bible that still give us encouragement, instruction, and hope today (see Romans 15:4). As in the case of Solomon, our request for spiritual discernment must also line up with God's will for us (James 1:5-8; 3:13–4:3).

The Spirit's Power to Discern

The Holy Spirit of God is our Helper (John 16:7). He is the power behind every believer's spiritual life; He is always active in our learning, growing, and changing process. His work is to transform every believer into the image of Jesus Christ (John 16:7-15).

Does the Holy Spirit live in your heart? Is He your Helper? If you are a Christian, then the answer is yes. But not until you submit to His guidance will you succeed in living a life that pleases God, bringing you peace and contentment even in the worst of situations. Pastor and author John MacArthur says, "The Holy Spirit is the only one who can prove God's Word is true; and He does this as He works in the heart and mind of the Christian in whom He dwells."[4]

The Process of Growth

The process of growing in spiritual discernment is just that: a process. It begins when you become a daughter of God through saving faith in the person and work of Jesus Christ (Ephesians 2:8-10). Then, like King Solomon, you must desire this ability by admitting to God your need (Proverbs 2:2-5) and praying for it as the Word of God instructs you to (James 1:5). You will further your progress in this process when you learn from the examples of other godly women through involvement in a Bible-teaching church (Hebrews 10:23-25). Then, in dependence upon the Holy Spirit, as the true Discerner who guides us through God's written Word, you will be lead into a clear understanding of how to please God and live in His ways of truth (John 16:13). You will accomplish all this as you commit yourself to the faithful study of God's Word (2 Timothy 2:14-16).

Above all else, you need to love God—above yourself, your family, your material possessions, and everything else you treasure more than God. This sounds difficult because it is. But only when we love God above all else does everything in our lives come together as it should. This is the only way you will know true joy and contentment.

What Is Your Ultimate Purpose?

As a child of God, your chief purpose on the earth is "to glorify God and enjoy Him forever."[5] Practically speaking, this means that whatever you think, say, and do, is to bring glory to God. As you live this way, you will get greater pleasure in your relationship with your heavenly Father through the person of Jesus Christ (Ephesians 1:3-13). Imagine: You are a child of the King! When you are enticed by the things that "itch your ears," you must remember your ultimate purpose: It isn't to be entertained. It is to bring glory to God.

Learning to separate truth from error, to recognize partial truth sprinkled in with wrong thinking is one way to bring God honor. When we bring honor to God, we actually will please Him and gain enjoyment from doing so. We will enjoy being His people, being in His family, being associated with Him and His purposes, and receiving His mercies and graces in daily life. Instead of living life so it's all about us, we'll live it so it's all about Him and His glory.

Consider all that the Lord has done for us. Jesus prayed for us on the way to the cross (John 17). He prayed for us to be changed and set aside for God's own purposes and plans. We are "a people for his own possession, that you may proclaim the excellencies of him who called you" (1 Peter 2:9). What this means is that we belong to God. Through Jesus' perfect payment of our sin and His redemption of us, we become the property of God (1 Corinthians 6:19-20). This should encourage us to study and hide God's Word in our hearts so that we may live in a way that pleases and glorifies Him. When we struggle with making right choices in our lives, it helps to remember why God sent His Son and His call to salvation. To become a Christian, we had to acknowledge our sin and repent, and agree with God that we are unable to keep His law perfectly. When we asked God for His mercy and grace and to save us from our sin, He transferred us from the kingdom of darkness to the kingdom of light (Colossians 1:13-14). Go back and ponder these truths again, and offer a prayer of praise and thanksgiving to your heavenly Father for all He has done for you! Though as sinners we deserved condemnation, He gave us forgiveness and makes it possible for us to bring Him honor and enjoy our relationship with Him through Christ Jesus (Ephesians 2:2-10).

Spiritual Discernment in Action

At the beginning of this chapter we met Joy, who had been enticed by the promises offered in a bestselling book. How did Joy come to discern truth from error in the pages of the book that captivated her imagination that day?

First, she spent time in prayer, asking God to help her understand the truth. Joy realized she could not rely on her emotions, feelings, or imagination to let her know what was right. She saw her need for spiritual discernment. The Holy Spirit would need to help her discern the truth.

Next, she turned to God's Word to discover God's guidance for her. She then determined to spend more time at her local church learning and growing in spiritual discernment. As a result of reading the Word and studying biblically solid books, she has learned to avoid those grocery-store tabloids and bestselling books that try to entice us with the latest promises and fads that come from human wisdom. Because Joy had never really studied about discernment before, she asked her elders to help her find a spiritually mature and discerning woman at church who could disciple her.

Ultimately, Joy learned what we all need to learn: *that God's Word is the only source of eternal, unchanging truth we can rely on.* She began to rely on and find her hope and security in the Bible alone. This put her on the path to spiritual discernment. That doesn't mean life suddenly became easy. We will always struggle as we attempt to discern truth from error and right from wrong. But God is always faithful to help us even when we are not faithful to Him (2 Timothy 2:13).

Do You Desire Spiritual Discernment?

Are you willing to pursue God and earnestly desire the discipline of spiritual discernment? When you become a daughter of God, you are commanded to grow in your ability to separate God's truth from man's error-laden wisdom. You can remember to STOP before you believe anything you read or hear because...

- God's has given you the Helper, the Holy Spirit.

- God has given you His Word.

- God has given you the privilege of coming to Him in prayer.

- God has given you His church, your family, to offer support.

- God has created you for His glory.

Guard the deposit of God's truth that has been given to you for safe-keeping (1 Timothy 6:20). Avoid error and partial truths—even if the world calls them knowledge or wisdom. This means holding on tightly to the ancient Word of God that will never pass away or return empty (Isaiah 55:11). And God, in His perfect plan, will help change you and bring the work He began in you to completion (Philippians 1:6).

Recommended Resources

Adams, Jay E. *A Call to Discernment.* Woodruff, SC: Timeless Texts, 1998.

Bridges, Jerry. *The Gospel for Real Life.* Colorado Springs: NavPress, 2002.

Challies, Tim. *The Discipline of Discernment.* Wheaton, IL: Crossway, 2007.

Lutzer, Erwin W. *Who Are You to Judge?* Chicago: Moody, 2002.

MacArthur, John. *Fool's Gold.* Wheaton, IL: Crossway, 2005.

Chapter 5

Establishing a Biblical Ministry to Women

⧛ *Maureen Bonner* ⧛

In times of crisis, women frequently turn to and pour out their hearts to one another. Female friends make themselves available to one another for support, advice, and practical guidance. Younger women especially look to their older, more mature "sisters" as role models. This "sisterhood" didn't just happen by chance. No, the amazing fact is that God has created women in such a way that we love to nurture and help one another. In fact, helping is part of what it means to be a woman (Genesis 2:18).

As you learned in the introduction to this book, God has ordained women to help and to disciple other women (Titus 2:3-5). It is plain from this passage that this woman-to-woman ministry is to be carried out primarily in the context of the local church. In the book of Titus, the apostle Paul gave Titus guidelines for establishing and overseeing young congregations on the island of Crete. Paul wrote that members of the church were to teach and disciple one another.

Jesus, the builder of God's house, the church (Hebrews 3:6), is intently focused on both the teaching and discipling of His people. When He lived here on earth, He taught both by word and deed. He excelled at it. Then, at the end of His earthly ministry, He commanded the church to carry out His mission of teaching and discipleship (Matthew 28:19-20). Christian discipleship is simply the process of one person passing on to another person the application of truth from God's Word. The goal of this discipleship is that ultimately every believer would become so firmly grounded in God's Word that she would know how to apply God's truth to the troubling situations and difficult circumstances she faces. In addition, as she matures in her faith, she is then able to come alongside other women, equipping, teaching, and discipling them.

Because biblical counseling has to do with instructing and building up others in the Word, it is also a part of the discipleship ministry in every local church. Like all teaching and discipleship, biblical counseling is primarily concerned with helping people apply God's Word to all of life; what sets it apart is that it's more focused on applying Scripture to specific problems faced by specific people. It is teaching and discipleship done one-on-one. The Bible teaches that all Christians ought to be involved in a discipleship/counseling ministry to one another. Here's how the writer to the Hebrews put it: "Exhort one another every day, as long as it is called 'today,' that none of you may be hardened by the deceitfulness of sin" (Hebrews 3:13; see also Romans 15:1,14; Galatians 6:1-2; 1 Thessalonians 4:18; 5:11).

Christ ordained the local church as the instrument to help believers grow into His likeness. One of the ways that the church helps believers mature is through discipleship and counseling. Because Christ's goal for all believers is that they become more and more like Him (Romans 8:28-29), every church needs to intentionally focus on the progressive sanctification—or growth—of every member of the body. Then and only then will you have a God-centered model for biblical change and Christian growth.[1] So then, because it is the mission of the church to make disciples, a biblical ministry to women must have as its foundation a robust ministry of both discipleship and counseling.

Discerning the Foundation of Your Ministry to Women

Although Christ's command to the church is obvious, many churches do not emphasize the mission of the church "to go...and make disciples." There are churches that, even though they are Bible-believing, Bible-teaching churches, do not teach the *whole* Scripture with the intention of helping their congregations apply it to the different circumstances and trials of life. Because of this neglect, Christians are not taught that the Scriptures are sufficient for all of life's struggles, problems, and circumstances (2 Timothy 3:15-17; 2 Peter 1:3). Instead they are taught ideas borrowed from popular psychology—ideas that are promoted as though they were as valid as Scripture. People are wrongly taught that they need to love and forgive themselves and to build up their self-esteem. They're taught that the goal of life is to feel good about oneself, and that life is all about pursuing one's own happiness. Such ideas are often integrated with the truths of God's Word, creating a mixture that at first glance seems harmless yet is dangerous because it's tainted with human wisdom.

Making Disciples or Teaching Psychology

There are only two approaches to life, and these two approaches affect how we do ministry within the local church, especially as we disciple others. One is man-centered and the other is God-centered. One focuses on me, my wants, and my desires, and the other focuses on God and His desires for me. One develops a worldview that at its core is humanistic; the other is a worldview that places God and His Word at the center of all of life.

Today's church has not been exempt from the subtle influence of modern-day philosophies and psychologies. Many churches use study materials for discipleship purposes that are infected by modern psychological principles. Even in seemingly solid churches many women are encouraged to read and study materials that are based more upon a secular or humanistic[2] foundation rather than upon the principles of God's Word. Again, much of this material is man-centered rather than God-centered. In this way, the goal of women's ministries changes from discipleship and becoming more like Christ to attaining temporal happiness and feeling fulfilled in life. These are not biblical goals for any ministry in the local church, including ministry to women.

It is vital that every woman who desires to disciple and counsel other women take the time to become familiar with secular philosophies so that she can discern and identify the presence of error when an idea or concept poses as truth. We must wisely scrutinize all that we hear and teach to ensure it is biblical. As defenders of God's Word, the leadership of a church must examine what is being taught in every discipleship ministry of the church. And women's ministry leaders must also do the same. We must question the books and materials presented to the women for study, always asking if they are fully based on the truths of God's Word or if they are tainted by secular, humanistic ideas. In short, are they God-centered or are they man-centered? Women, like men, should desire the same commendation given to the Bereans, a group of believers in the early church who "received the word with all eagerness, examining the Scriptures daily to see if these things were so" (Acts 17:11).

Our churches and our ministry to women should be tethered to the truth that "all Scripture is inspired by God and profitable for teaching, for reproof, for correction, for training in righteousness; so that the man [or woman] of God may be adequate, equipped for every good work" (2 Timothy 3:16-17 NASB). That passage assures us that God's Word changes lives. It is the only word in all the universe that has the power to deeply transform us. What is this Word? Yes, it is codified for us in the Bible, but this Word is also embodied in Jesus Christ (John 14:6). He is the Living Word, the truth of God (John 17:17). Second Peter 1:3 reveals that we can experience grace and peace in our lives only when we know God through our Lord Jesus. To "know" God implies an intimate knowledge—a genuine, personal sharing of life with Christ, based on repentance from sin and personal faith in the work He's already done on our behalf.[3]

A Biblical Mission in Women's Ministry

If you have decided to launch a women's ministry within your church or would like to revamp the existing one, one of the first steps you'll need to take is to establish a biblical discipleship ministry that will include the public teaching of the Word and the private application of the Word (in counseling). You'll want the women to understand God's Word and live out its principles. You'll want to provide more than just a little devotional thought every now and then. You'll want to help women develop a biblical worldview that preserves and protects them from the secular teachings so prevalent today. You'll want to encourage them to understand doctrine, or the Bible's teachings on specific topics. Simply defined, *doctrine* is what the Bible teaches about a particular subject.

Change in our own lives and in the lives of the women entrusted to us will occur when we understand our place in God's world, the nature of God, and the work of His Son. Many of the difficulties women face today flow out of faulty ideas about Bible doctrines. They're confused about God's disposition to them; they don't understand what His plans for them are. That's why it's not enough to simply help women acquire knowledge of the Bible. We need to help them live out the Bible's teachings so that lives are changed. *That* is the goal of any ministry to women in the church (1 Timothy 6:3-4; see also Psalm 1:2-3; 119:5,9-16).

Key Doctrines to Teach

Every doctrine in the Bible has significant implications in how we are to live out our lives as godly women. There isn't enough space to discuss all of them here, so we'll focus on a few key ones for now. In the meantime, there are several good theology and research books you can use to become more informed about the doctrines in Scripture. (Some such books are mentioned at the end of this chapter.)

The Doctrine of the Word of God

The major teachings about the Bible itself can be classified as follows: (1) the authority of the Scripture, (2) the clarity of Scripture, (3) the necessity of Scripture, and (4) the sufficiency of Scripture.[4] These are the basic truths that women need to know about the Bible so that they better understand its essential place in their lives.

The Authority of Scripture

That Scripture possesses authority means that the Bible claims for itself that all its words are God's words. This goes hand in hand with the fact Scripture is inerrant—the Bible is without error. It is wholly reliable and truthful. It was inspired by God through the agency of the Holy Spirit as He directed the different authors to write. Therefore, as you disciple other women, you can speak the directives of God's Word with authority. You can speak with assurance that God's words are truthful. You can know that God's Word will produce lasting change when believers respond in faith to it. You can have full confidence in His Word as you disciple and counsel your sisters in Christ.

THE CLARITY OF SCRIPTURE

The Word of God is clear—you can understand what the Bible says when you read it, meditate on it, and seek God's help (Psalm 1:1-2; 19:7). For that reason, as you disciple women, you can have the assurance that its truths can be clearly communicated to them. Often God's people will have a difference of opinion regarding a particular issue, doctrine, or topic, but for the most part, God's Word is clear. And when it comes to understanding Scripture, we are not alone. We have the help of the Holy Spirit, and we've been blessed with biblical scholars who have provided guidelines for properly interpreting Scripture. *Hermeneutics* is the study of the methods of interpreting Scripture (see chapter 3). The more involved you become in women's ministry, the more you'll need to learn the skill of accurately interpreting God's Word. Otherwise, lofty, good-sounding, unbiblical theology will lead women astray, leaving them in confusion and deceived.

As you learn the rules for interpreting Scripture accurately, you will develop a greater love and devotion to the Bible and the Lord. You cannot be a student of God's Word without coming to know the Author better. He will reveal Himself to you in the most wonderful and surprising ways. When women complain that they feel far from God, it's probably because they are not spending time in His Word. His nearness can be experienced as they take time to read, study, and meditate upon Scripture.

THE NECESSITY OF SCRIPTURE

The Bible is necessary "for knowing the gospel, growing in spiritual maturity, and knowing God's will, but it is not necessary for knowing that He exists or to know His moral law or character."[5] In Deuteronomy 29:29 we read, "The secret things belong to the LORD our God, but the things revealed belong to us and to our children forever, that we may do all the words of this law." In other words, God does not reveal everything to us through His Word, but He reveals enough for us to be obedient in what He asks of us. In this way, Scripture is necessary. It helps us grow and know how to live. It helps us discern truth from error so we know what to believe.

THE SUFFICIENCY OF SCRIPTURE

As women immerse themselves in the Word of God, they will see the depth and relevance of Scripture. They will know that it is sufficient for their everyday lives. *Sufficiency* simply means that the Bible is adequate, it is all that we really need. The apostle Paul described sufficiency when he wrote to Timothy: "From childhood you have been acquainted with the sacred writings, which are able to make you wise for salvation through faith in Christ Jesus" (2 Timothy 3:15). The Word of God is always sufficient to accomplish its intended purpose: "So shall my word be that goes out from my mouth; it shall not return to me empty, but it shall accomplish which I purpose, and shall succeed in the thing for which I sent it" (Isaiah 55:11).

Second Corinthians 3:5 demonstrates another facet of this sufficiency by saying that the truths we learn in Scripture actually make *us* sufficient: "Not that we are adequate in ourselves to consider anything as coming from ourselves, but our adequacy is from God" (NASB). The ESV says simply, "Our sufficiency is from God." Faith in the truths presented in God's Word makes us sufficient to answer every problem that we or other women face. The gospel of Jesus Christ is the answer to our most basic needs and problems (See John 15:3; Acts 20:32; Romans 10:17; 15:4; Ephesians 5:26; Hebrews 4:12). May we be women who are radically sold out to God and His truth!

The Doctrine of God

If we want to understand the relationship between God and His creation, it is necessary to know His nature. Thankfully, God has revealed Himself to us through creation and His Word (Psalm 19:1-2; Romans 1:19-20). Scripture reveals that He is love, that He is light, that He is just and righteous, and that we come to know Him personally through this revelation of Himself. God is magnificent and can answer every need we have at any moment. He is our peace, our comforter, and our refuge in times of trouble. This has clear and beneficial implications for the women you disciple and counsel.

Sadly, many women would rather make God into a different sort of person. They want to "experience" Him in their own way, rather than in the way He has revealed Himself through the Bible. They conjure a distorted image of God that suits their own desires. But we need to understand God as revealed in His Word, not according to our own flawed perspective.[6] When we embrace God as He has revealed Himself in the Bible, we can have great hope as we disciple and counsel women whose problems seem horrific. We can always assure them that God is a present help in time of trouble (Psalm 3; 18:1-5; 27:1-2). This reality of who God is and what He does for us brings comfort and hope!

The Doctrine of Man

Modern-day "enlightenment" and humanistic influences have skewed our understanding of the nature of man and his problems, thus also skewing our understanding of the solutions to these problems. Before we can apply the Word of God rightly to our lives, we first must understand ourselves from God's perspective. It's hard for us to see ourselves as fallen people, marred by sin, and in need of a Savior. But it is only as we understand who we truly are that we can be healed by the prescription God offers for our sin-sick souls.

It doesn't help that the world constantly tells us that we are here on earth only to enjoy ourselves and find self-centered fulfillment. But Scripture teaches that we have been created by God and redeemed by His grace for His own glory (Isaiah 43:7; Ephesians 1:11-12). Therefore, rather than living for ourselves, we are to "do all to the glory of God" (1 Corinthians 10:31). The fact that we as weak, sinful, confused creatures can bring glory to God has wonderful implications for us. Even in the most mundane of our days we have a purpose in life, and that is to glorify Him. What a delight and privilege is ours! This reality of created purpose should bring hope and joy to every woman who finds herself frustrated by the struggles of life. We can find joy and purpose, no matter what the situation because God calls us to make His name known and admired wherever we go.

There are many more doctrines within Scripture that help us to disciple other women biblically—such as the doctrine of sin, the doctrine of salvation, and the doctrine of the church. You'll want to get a good basic resource on Bible doctrine, because all these doctrines have vast implications for women as they seek answers for the predicaments they face in life.

Implementing a Discipleship/Counseling Ministry

There is no greater joy than sacrificing one's self for others and serving them. If God lays upon your heart the desire to help begin a women's ministry in your church so that you can teach or mentor other women, or if He calls you to help with an existing women's ministry, know that He will supply the resources you need (Philippians 4:13; 1 Timothy 1:12; see also Deuteronomy 31:7-8). And remember, as you move forward, this is Jesus' ministry, not yours. This perspective will spare you much grief as you walk with women through the trials of their lives.

Developing the Vision

As you share your vision with the leaders at your church, especially women's leaders, you may meet with some resistance. In fact, Satan may try to discourage you and put roadblocks in your path. Do not yield to his temptations nor fall for his lies. Resist the impulse to claim this ministry as your own. Instead, humble yourself before the leaders of the church and before God (James 4:1-8) and ask for the Holy Spirit's help.

In Ephesians 6:10-19, the apostle Paul describes what you must do when you come up against resistance. You are to find your strength in God and in the soul-comforting truths of the gospel. The armor of God, rooted in the gospel, is to serve as your hope and courage. Pray for yourself and have others pray for you. Then persevere as you share the ways women can benefit from a biblical discipleship and counseling ministry.

When it comes to ministry service, God, in His kindness, may bring other women alongside you who will stand with you. Ask Him to show you one or two others who have a heart for this kind of ministry and who have the same perspective on discipleship as you do. Pray together for God's wisdom and discernment as you endeavor to move forward. You might consider inviting your pastor's wife to be a part of your team. Then using the Titus 2 passage as a ministry model, ask your pastor to teach the older women biblical principles that they, in turn, can then teach to the younger women. As always, do all of this in a spirit of humility.

If there is already a women's ministry in place at your church and you believe change needs to occur, identify the problems and be prepared to humbly explain what they are. Is biblical discipleship/counseling the foundation of all ministry? Or is there some other focus? Survey the curriculum to see if it is biblical. Is the Word of God integrated with psychology, or are women being fed the "pure spiritual milk" of God's Word (1 Peter 2:2)? If the answers to these questions point to a foundation other than the truths of God's Word, ask the pastor and leaders of your church if they would be willing to hear your concerns as well as your suggestions for a change in ministry focus. Then, after much prayer, present your ideas to them. Be prepared, organized, and factual.

If the leadership of the church is not enthused about your vision, then wait and continue to trust the Lord for His timing. You can keep working to prepare yourself and to encourage and counsel women in the Word of God. You can write a vision and purpose statement in which you define what you believe the purpose and goals of a women's ministry should be. You can come up with ideas for program options. And as you wait, God may, in time, change the hearts of the church's leadership to be more responsive on these issues.

Studying the Biblical Principles

Spend time studying the biblical principles for woman-to-woman ministry found in Titus 2:3-5. Here you'll find an excellent outline for implementing ministry to women in the church. Earlier Paul told Titus to "teach what accords with sound doctrine" (Titus 2:1). Paul wanted the people in the church to know doctrine first so that their hearts and lives would know change. As we have already seen, sound doctrine is the remedy for false teaching.

Remember, the passage in Titus 2 is not a suggestion; it is a mandate. It is part of the strategy for the Christian education of the church. Titus 2:3-5 lays out the biblical foundation and framework for a discipleship and counseling ministry to all women—both older and younger. Paul clearly gives us the *what* of ministry and the *how* of ministry to women. These are the two basic building blocks: what to do, and how to do it. As we follow these commands, joyfully serving the Lord in obedience, the young women will grow in godliness, the older women will be enriched personally, the church will reap the benefits of these godly relationships, and the community will be blessed—all because God's Word has been honored. As women, we can celebrate the truth that God has given us a mandate for women's ministry that will fulfill what God intended for women to accomplish in the church.

Certainly, Titus 2:3-5 is not all God has to say to women, but it is an excellent place to start. From there you can take women to other passages of Scripture that will address other parts of their life and teach them how to grow in godliness (2 Peter 1:3). And He might use you to help them apply His commands and principles with greater diligence.

God has called women to disciple and counsel one another with His Word. And it is amazing what an effective ministry *to* women *by* women will do. It can touch their lives in ways that nothing else can. And as Titus 2:3-5 affirms, it is God's plan for women to minister to each other.

The Fruit of Biblical Women's Ministry

Because women-to-women ministry is God's idea, it will bring Him much glory when we follow His lead. As women teach women the truths of the Bible, hearts and minds will be transformed by the power of God and will reflect God's glory. All that, of course, will show how great He is. "For what we proclaim is not ourselves, but Jesus Christ as Lord...For God, who said, 'Let light shine out of darkness,' has shone in our hearts to give the light of the knowledge of the glory of God in the face of Jesus Christ" (2 Corinthians 4:5-6).

To God be the glory!

Recommended Resources

Buckley, Ed. *Why Christians Can't Trust Psychology.* Eugene, OR: Harvest House, 1993.

Duncan, J. Ligon and Susan Hunt. *Women's Ministry in the Local Church.* Wheaton, IL: Crossway 2006.

ESV Study Bible. Wheaton, IL: Crossway, 2008.

Grudem, Wayne. *Systematic Theology.* Grand Rapids: Zondervan House, 1994.

House, Wayne. *Charts of Christian Theology & Doctrine*. Grand Rapids: Zondervan, 1992.

Ryken, Leland. *The Word of God in English*. Wheaton, IL: Crossway, 2002.

Tripp, Paul. *Instruments in the Redeemer's Hands*. Phillipsburg, NJ: Presbyterian & Reformed, 2002.

Part 2

A Woman
and Her Emotions

Chapter 6

Dealing with Your Emotions God's Way

§ Mary Wilkin §

Susan is a 30-year-old single career woman. Last week her boss met with her to tell her she was not doing her job as well as he had hoped. He attempted to give her some guidelines that would help improve her job performance. Rather than listening respectfully, Susan flew into a rage. She screamed at her boss, smashed her coffee mug on his desk, and slammed his office door hard. Not surprisingly, after this outburst, Susan was fired.

Although most of us haven't broken coffee mugs on our boss's desk, we all have felt overwhelming anger before. We have all experienced the wide range of emotions that come naturally to us as humans: anger, fear, sorrow, love, jealousy, happiness. In fact, when a person is unable to experience emotions, we know that something is desperately wrong.

Though we all know what it's like to feel emotions, we rarely take time to consider where they come from or what they might mean about us. We seldom stop to consider what our emotions might be telling us about our values, beliefs, and desires. And we almost never think about what they tell us about our relationship with God.

For most of us, our experience of emotions usually follows a three-step progression. First, a situation presents itself, such as when Susan's boss evaluated her work. Second, the situation or circumstance seems to trigger an inner emotional response. In Susan's case, her boss's negative evaluation made her afraid, so she became angry. The final step in this progression is that we respond—we act out what we're feeling. Susan smashed her coffee cup and stormed out of the office. Susan could have responded in a different, more godly way, but she didn't. She sinned against her boss and, more importantly, against the Lord. Susan was in such a rage that she didn't stop to consider what she had done until she was in her car, crying. Amid her tears, she asked herself, *Why do I get so angry? How can I be a Christian and still act this way?* She dearly longed to stop exploding in people's faces, but didn't have any idea how to go about it.

What do we say to the Susans in our lives? What do we ourselves do when we are overrun by our emotional responses? What do our responses tell us about ourselves? What can we learn from our emotions, and how can we bring them under control?

There are many voices trying to answer these kinds of questions. A Google search revealed over 59 million hits to the word *emotion*. And in the field of psychology, there have been more than 90 definitions of *emotion* proposed over the past 100 years. One psychologist who studies emotions has said that with so many theories, it is no wonder there is still confusion about how to help people understand and deal with their emotions.[1]

God's Word Is Our Standard

Does it have to be this hard to discover the truth about our emotions? Is there any hope for change? With so many choices, how do we choose the best way to help ourselves and others deal with emotions? And most important of all, where does God fit into this?

God provides hope for mastering our emotions as well as instruction on the best way to deal with them. His answers have survived the test of time and have never needed changing because He alone, as our Creator, knows what will work. God provides instruction to us in the Bible that is based on His perfect knowledge so that we do not need to turn to the confusing and contradictory suggestions of fallen mankind. He teaches us that we can understand and respond properly to our emotions (Genesis 4:1-16; Ephesians 4:22-24; 2 Timothy 3:16-17). Not only does God provide guidance; He also provides us with the power to change. Christ's work on our behalf has made that possible.

God's Word can give Susan hope by helping her see the world, her life, and the source of her problems from God's point of view. It can help her bring the gospel to bear on every area of her life and free her from her pattern of self-destructive and God-dishonoring anger.

Created in God's Image, Fallen, Restored in Christ

The Bible teaches that our emotions come from within us, from our inner person or heart. Contrary to our Western perspective on the heart, the Bible teaches that the heart is much more than what or how we feel. When the Bible uses the word *heart*, it refers to the soul or spirit, the immaterial you. The heart is everything about us that is not our physical body. It is the inner you that no one sees directly, but is revealed by your actions. Susan's inner anger was revealed to everyone in her office when she had her tantrum.

All people, believers and unbelievers alike, are made in the image of God. Because God does not have a physical body, His image in us is seen in our inner person, our soul or heart. The heart includes our conscience as well as our ability to think and reason, to make choices, to feel emotions, to imagine, to desire, and to plan. When Adam and Eve sinned in the Garden of Eden, their action caused death not only to their physical body, but also to their inner person, the spiritual heart. The Bible teaches that this death passed from Adam on to all people who were born after him (Romans 5:12).

Now, spiritual death does not mean we have completely lost our ability to think, feel, desire, or choose. It's obvious that even unbelievers still do all those things. Rather, it means that our hearts are dead to the things of God and all our inner faculties are skewed by sin's deceptions. We have sinful emotions for the same reason we have sinful thoughts and behavior. Sin has infected every part of our being: our inner person, the heart, and our outer person, the body. The image of God in us is shattered by sin; our ability to emote without sinning has been shattered as well.

The good news of the gospel is that by His sinless life, death, resurrection, and ascension, Christ has restored our relationship with God and made our dead, stony hearts alive (Ezekiel 36:26). While this new life is immediate and pervasive, no part of us, including our inner person, becomes sinless—that won't happen until we reach heaven. Even as Christians we all continue to struggle with the sin and death that has twisted our thoughts and emotions. Susan's anger made her question her faith; she wondered why she hadn't completely changed. Susan needs to know that even though she is truly saved, she won't be completely free from sin during this life.

God has a plan not only for restoring our relationship with Him, but also for restoring His image in us. His goal is that we become holy, or pure, like He is, in our inner person, the heart. This gradual restoration of His image within us is called *sanctification*. The Holy Spirit works in us to eliminate sin in our hearts and to make us more like Him. Since emotions are a part of our fallen hearts, the process of sanctification includes restoring our emotions so that they more closely mirror Christ's. It is God's plan for us to look like His Son, even in our emotions. And because God always accomplishes what He purposes to do, Susan can have hope that her emotions can change and God will complete the work He has begun in her (Philippians 1:6).

The solution for Susan and us is not merely a program to learn how to change our outward behavior. The problem with our emotions is much deeper than that.

In Matthew 15:17-20 Jesus teaches that our sinful behavior flows out of our hearts, so the only solution to sinful emotions is sanctification, or heart-change. Of course, it may be possible to change our outward behavior and do the right thing with the wrong motives. If Susan's motivation for changing is simply to get her job back, she might be successful for a time. But she won't be able to sustain that change for long because what is in our hearts *always* comes out eventually. God wants us to bring change in our hearts. When our hearts change, then our behavior will follow. Godly actions will naturally flow from a pure heart.

The power for a changed life does not come from within, but from Christ. In fact, Jesus Himself said that we cannot bear any lasting fruit in our own power. We will bear fruit only when we are dependent on Him (John 15:4).

The Biblical Understanding of Emotional Responses

When people view their emotional responses in terms of the process described earlier (situation, emotion triggered, emotion acted out), they often do not realize that they are leaving God out of the picture. Because God is in the process of restoring us—as Christians—to the image of His Son, we must learn to look at all of life, including our emotions, through His eyes.

God's Word gives us a different way to view our emotions. Typically we blame our circumstances for evoking certain emotions. However, the situations we face are *not* the cause of our emotional reactions. Our hearts are always active, thinking, desiring, and planning. It is here, in our hearts, that our emotions begin. Our emotions are already present even before situations confront us and before we sense the emotion. Situations simply serve to *expose* the things we are thinking about, desiring, and planning. They simply give rise to an emotion already present in us. God wants to use our emotions like a mirror to show us what is going on in our heart. We are then to choose to respond to various situations based on what *God* desires of us, not what we want and desire.

Let's look at each of these steps in more detail. As we do, we will compare the roots and response of Susan's anger with the roots and response of Jesus' anger. Because Jesus is sinless, His life defines what is normal for us, what we would have been like if sin had not entered the world. He models how we are to interact with our Creator. He sets the standard for every human behavior, attitude, or use of emotion. If we want to see what God's perfect image in us should look like, we can look to Jesus. "He is the radiance of the glory of God and the exact imprint of his nature" (Hebrews 1:3).

The Root of the Problem—Our Hearts

Again, the situations we face expose what is already going on in our hearts. There was something going on in Susan's heart before her boss confronted her. Biblical counselor Wayne Mack uses this illustration to make this point: If a sponge is full of clean water, clean water will come out when you squeeze it. If a sponge is full of black ink, black ink will come out. When life's circumstances squeeze our hearts, what comes out is what was already in our hearts.

Jesus said in Mark 7:21-23, "From within, out of the heart of man, come evil thoughts, sexual immorality, theft, murder, adultery, coveting, wickedness, deceit, sensuality, envy, slander, pride, foolishness. All these evil things come from within, and they defile a person." The heart is where all of our thoughts, desires, and choices have their beginning. The roots of our emotions start here. Susan became angry because her boss's words squeezed her heart. What was going on in Susan's heart before this interaction with her boss?

Susan's emotions have roots in her life experience, in her desires, and in her perception of right and wrong. Susan's single mother juggled two jobs to support five children. Although she loved her children, she did not discipline them. She thought that her children should make all of their own decisions so they could be self-sufficient. So Susan learned to be her own authority figure and to take charge of her world. She took pride in having overcome a difficult childhood. She saw herself as the primary authority in her life. She was in charge of her decisions, her goals, and her dreams. It was up to her to get where she wanted to go in life.

Unfortunately, Susan's thoughts and desires left God out of the picture. She understood her need for a Savior and God's role in her salvation, but she did not understand God's desire to love her, provide for her, and to make her more like Him—sometimes through suffering. Her heart focused on herself, not on God.

In contrast, Jesus' heart was completely submitted to His Father. The goal of His every thought, desire, and choice was to please and glorify God (John 8:28-29). He responded to all of the circumstances of His life without sin because the content of His heart was pure and without sin.

The Sovereignty of God and Our Emotions

Many people see life as they do through their emotions—they see their circumstances as random events that just happen. They do not understand that every situation in life comes from God's hand. God determines what happens to us and when. He is sovereign; nothing can happen to us outside of God's control. There are numerous passages in Scripture that teach this. For example, Lamentations 3:37-38 says, "Who has spoken and it came to pass, unless the Lord has commanded it? Is it not from the mouth of the Most High that good and bad come?"

God did not create the world then leave it to run on its own. He is actively involved in everything that happens in the world today—including every detail of our lives. This should be a comfort to us. But often we forget God is involved, or we think we could run the world better than He does. We fail to see the circumstances of our life as selected specifically for us, by His loving hand, and intended for our good and for His glory (Romans 8:28-29).

Trusting in God's sovereign control over the world and our lives is one of the ways we change in our inner person and thereby change our emotional responses. We must believe that God loves us and is watching over us even if our life circumstances seem to say something different.

And yes, there were circumstances that angered Jesus. But how could He be angry and still not sin? Anger, like all of our emotions, is not necessarily sinful. It is an emotion that is aroused when someone or something opposes our desires. Because Jesus' desires were always the same as His Father's, His anger was toward anyone who opposed God. We see this when He overturned the money changers' tables in the temple and when He was angered by the Pharisees' view of doing good to another person on the Sabbath (Mark 3:5; John 2:14-17).

Though Jesus became angry at sins against His Father, He still trusted God's sovereign control over His life. He endured difficult circumstances that continually tested His heart. People hated Him and sought to kill Him from the time He was born. He was mocked and mistreated. His friends betrayed and abandoned Him. He was tortured, then murdered despite having lived a perfect and innocent life. And in the face of all that, He never let His anger out of control.

Unlike Jesus, Susan did not acknowledge or trust God's activity and control in her job struggles. When people at one job did not respect her work, she simply changed jobs. She saw people and circumstances as the problem, as random events that made her life miserable.

Susan needs to understand that God is intimately involved in every situation in her life. He allowed her to experience each difficult situation so He could to expose a heart that was determined to be in control. God wanted to teach Susan that *He* is in control. God did not do this out of anger toward Susan; His desire was to show her He loved her and she could trust Him with every aspect of her life. Her jobs and her bosses did not cause her anger. They were what God's sovereign hand used to squeeze the sponge of her heart so that she could see what filled her heart.

The Need for a Heart Examination

Emotions are part of what it means to be a human made in the image of God. God does not ask us to suppress our emotions, but He does not intend for emotions to guide our life either. Our emotions flow from fallen hearts that are deceitful and impossible for us to completely understand; only God can know what is in the heart and mind of a person (Jeremiah 17:9-10). So when it comes to determining what is true of God and of our hearts, we need to turn to Scripture (Psalm 19:7-9; Hebrews 4:12).

In order to be more like Christ, we need to examine our hearts in light of Scripture. We need to let God's Word inform our mind and let His Spirit convict our conscience. Sometimes, we also need other believers to help us see ourselves as we really are. These three things—God's Word, His Spirit, and His church—are the means He uses to help us to become more like Him and learn how to control our emotions.

We Must Choose to Think Right

Because our emotions are always the result of our thoughts,[2] we cannot change our emotional responses until we change the way we think. This includes our expectations, desires, beliefs, and motives. And the Bible teaches us how we should think. It tells us to "take every thought captive to obey Christ" (2 Corinthians 10:5) and to renew our minds by considering God's mercy (Romans 12:2; Ephesians 4:23). This renewal is not something we can do on our own; it is something God does for us through His Word and His Spirit. *God makes our emotions new and different by changing the way we think.*

When the Word of God reveals that our thinking does not line up with God's, we need to confess our sin and repent. To confess our sin means we say the same thing about our sin that God does. We admit that we are wrong. Repentance is the process of turning from our wrong thoughts, emotions, desires, and attitudes and choosing to follow God's design for us.

When Susan became angry, she was reacting to what she believed. She was not consciously thinking about whether her innate beliefs were true. She needed to learn the truth about her expectations, desires, and attitudes, and she needed to realize the lies she had believed her whole life—lies about how she needed to be self-sufficient and in control. Susan believed that she was her own boss, that she needed to look out for her own interests even at the expense of others. She had forgotten that Jesus had submitted His desires to the Father and counted others as more significant than Himself (Philippians 2:1-10). She needed to see that God had created her to be dependent on Him and that she could trust Him to take care of her.

Susan also believed that she deserved respect, admiration, and success. She had placed these desires ahead of her desire to please God. Because her allegiance was focused on herself, when she felt threatened, her anger controlled her. She was willing to sin to get what she wanted and avoid the loss of what she valued most: success and respect.

The Word of God brought conviction to Susan. She was humbled when she realized how she had mistreated others to further her quest for respect. Susan began to see that her sinful anger was the result of wrong thinking and desires. Her thoughts about herself and what she wanted were too high and her thoughts about God were too low. Her desire for respect had become so powerful that she tried to use God to achieve it. *She saw that her anger had resulted from her desire to achieve her own goals.*

We Must Choose to Act Right

Right thinking is important when it comes to our emotions, but right thinking alone will not ensure we make right choices. Knowledge alone does not make us holy. It's possible for us to believe everything that God says about Himself and still want to live our own way. The demons believe the Bible, but do not obey it (James 2:19). In order to change from sinful to godly emotions, we need to *choose* to do right. True repentance includes a willingness to do the right thing.

We make choices based on what we desire most. We do what we do because we want what we want. We must ask ourselves, "What is ruling my heart? What or who am I worshipping?" We can *know* that what God says is right yet still want what is wrong!

Even in the midst of strong emotions, Jesus always did what was pleasing to God (John 8:29). His greatest desire was to glorify or elevate God. His love for and understanding of God provided this motivation.

Eventually, Susan responded with repentance to God's Word and with gratitude for His love. She confessed her sinful anger to God. She sought His forgiveness and was joyful when she understood that Jesus' death paid for all of her anger. Her desire to make amends with her boss was further evidence of her repentance. She committed to seeking his forgiveness even if she did not get her job back.

When Susan asked for her boss's forgiveness, he offered it freely. He was amazed at the change in Susan, especially her humility in admitting she was wrong. He decided to give her another chance. He also asked her what caused this change in her. Susan was able to share her faith in Christ and the hope she possessed for growing more like Him. She was able to see that even despite her sinful outburst, God had used the situation for His glory.

God Created Us with Robust Emotions

In a world that often seems controlled by the sinful emotions of people all around us, God is sovereign. He is in control. He determines the situations of our lives and commands us to put our emotions in their proper place. This can happen only by His grace, only as we choose to live in submission to God rather than as slaves to our emotions. This does not mean we are to completely suppress or subdue our emotions. Rather, we are to respond to God with our emotions just as we respond to Him with our thinking and our choices.

Jesus Christ was not wimpy or subdued in His emotions. His emotions were deep, strong, and robust. Every emotion of Christ reflects His love. Robert Law describes Jesus' anger as the anger of love: "His love to God and zeal for God's worship makes Him indignant at whatever dishonours God."[3]

Jesus' hatred of sin, His jealousy for God's honor and glory, His joy in doing God's will, and His love and compassion for sinners led to the bravest and most sacrificial act in the history of the world. He willingly died in the place of sinful humans and absorbed God's anger at our sin.

Jesus' love and compassion toward us continues. He teaches and empowers us to hate sin; to be jealous for God's glory; to be angry when God is dishonored; to have joy in doing God's will; to have compassion on others; to love God with all of our heart, soul, mind, and strength; and to love our neighbor as ourselves. And when we commit ourselves to dealing with our emotions God's way, the world will see the good deeds that result from pure hearts…and God will get the glory.

> Let your light shine before others, so that they may see your good works and give glory to your Father who is in heaven (Matthew 5:16).

Recommended Resources

Borgman, Brian. *Feelings and Faith.* Wheaton, IL: Crossway, 2009.

Bridges, Jerry. *Trusting God: Even When Life Hurts.* Colorado Springs: NavPress, 1988.

Fitzpatrick, Elyse. *Idols of the Heart.* Phillipsburgh, NJ: Presbyterian & Reformed, 2001.

Lane, Timothy S. and Paul David Tripp. *How People Change.* Winston-Salem, NC: Punch Press, 2006.

Williams, Sam. "Toward a Theology of Emotion." *Southern Baptist Journal of Theology,* volume 7 (Southern Baptist Theological Seminary, 2003; 2006), p. 58.

Chapter 7

CHRIST, GOD'S ANSWER TO YOUR FEAR

§ *Janie Street* §

W ho…me? I'm not a 'fraidy cat!"
How many times have we heard this from children at play—often pretending not to be afraid? Perhaps you think that you are not a fearful person. Or maybe you know that you are, but hate to admit it. We adults are as masterful as children are when it comes to putting on a brave front while concealing fear. It seems as though we're afraid to let others know how fearful we really are.

The truth is that no one is completely free of fear. Even the most seemingly self-confident, accomplished people have fears. For example, they might fear someone who is better-looking, richer, or more skilled than them. They might fear losing the high regard of their peers or business associates. Perhaps they are afraid that someone younger, better trained, or more savvy will catch the boss's eye. Yet to the casual observer, they appear to fear nothing. All that to say, fear is common to everyone, even those who don't show it. As one author has stated so well, "There are as many forms of fear as there are situations in life."[1]

When Fear Paralyzes

Even though we all struggle with fear at various times in our lives, there is fear…and then there is *fear*. Some of us experience truly paralyzing fear. Some of us are shut down by fears about the future, about our finances. We fear the loss of a job or home or car during unpredictable economic times. We fear others' mistreatment of us. Then there are irrational fears, like the fear that our heart may stop beating at any moment even though we don't have heart disease. Irrational fear can produce terrifying panic and paralysis.

It is these kinds of fear that can end up controlling our daily life. They become our uninvited yet constant companion. Even though we want to shake them off, we find that they are not so easily dismissed. Oftentimes they produce a habitual response to life's situations. We feel trapped by such fears, and it doesn't matter how many times we tell ourselves that we're being irrational.

Fear Not?

Many times in Scripture, God has commanded us not to fear. He simply says, "Fear not." For instance, when the shepherds were startled by the angels who announced Jesus' birth, He told them not to be afraid. In Matthew 10:28, Jesus said to His disciples, "Do not fear those who kill the body." In Proverbs 3:25, the Lord counsels us, "Do not be afraid of sudden terror nor of the ruin of the wicked, when it comes" (Proverbs 3:25). How can God expect us not to be fearful when we find ourselves in very frightening circumstances? And how are we to overcome our irrational fears when we seem enslaved to them?

Then, to complicate things even more, there are Scripture passages that tell us a certain kind of fear is good and even commanded. For example, at the end of Matthew 10:28 Jesus said, "Rather fear him [God] who can destroy both soul and body in hell." Psalm 33:8 says, "Let all the earth fear the Lord." In fact, there are great benefits promised to those who fear God, as Psalm 31:19 says: "How abundant is your goodness, which you have stored up for those who fear you." It's apparent, then, that not all fear is bad or sinful. In fact, we are to pursue and nurture the fear of God.

There is also another category of fear that can be called natural fear. In his book *Fear Factor*, Dr. Wayne Mack uses the term *prudence* to describe this kind of fear. He writes, "In one sense, fear is an acknowledgement that you are just a human being, that you are not in control of everything, that there are things greater than you."[2] Proverbs 22:3

declares, "The prudent [man] sees danger and hides himself, but the simple go on and suffer for it."

It is prudent or wise for us to run away from harm or evil. Prudence teaches us to avoid walking in front of moving cars, to protect ourselves and our loved ones from danger. Again, Dr. Mack says, "It's not good to be completely fearless. God gave us the emotion of fear for a specific reason."[3]

There is a point, however, when fear, even prudence, can become sinful. Consider the parents who never let their children leave home, *for any reason*, because they fear something bad might happen to them. That is an extreme example, but it serves to point out how even natural fear—that good, wise, prudent fear given to us by God—can overwhelm and enslave us to the point of withholding good things from our loved ones.

How can we find release from the grip of fear and yet maintain a fear that is acceptable and pleasing to God? This is a difficult balance to achieve because, as we've seen, there are sinful fears, prudent fears, and a holy fear. Once we learn how to tell the difference between them we'll be on our way to finding help for our struggle against the fears that trouble us.

Identifying Our Sinful Fears

Because God specifically commands us not to fear, it is clearly sinful for us to succumb to certain fears. That is a hard truth for many of us to swallow. We feel justified in our fears because there are frightening things that could happen to us and our loved ones. Nevertheless, because the One who loves us has told us that some of our fears are sinful, we should seek to understand and deal with the sources of our fears as best we can. The following questions may help you identify the causes of your fears and open the way for you to experience change.

1. What captivates my thoughts when I am tempted to fear?

2. In what ways do I allow fear to paralyze me and keep me from fulfilling my God-given responsibilities?

3. When I am tempted to succumb to sinful fear, what is my

heart craving more than Christ? Am I seeking relief, escape, approval, acceptance, or comfort?

4. Are there ways I have sought to manipulate or control others (friends, spouse, children, coworkers) because of my fears? In other words, are there payoffs I gain for nurturing my fears?

5. What am I believing about God when I'm afraid?

Bravely facing the answers to those questions is the first step to learning to overcome sinful fear. For instance, if I fail to recognize that I love safety more than I love Jesus, then fear will continue to plague me no matter how I might pray against it. Or if I long for the approval of others more than I delight in the approval of God, then I'll continue to fear what others might think of me or say about me. In the times when I give in to that fear, I'll remain a slave to other people's opinions of me rather than live like a free and beloved daughter of the Lord.

Like you, I am a woman who experiences the temptation to give in to a sinful fear. And although I have been significantly freed from the grip of sinful fear so that it no longer controls me, I still find myself tempted to be overwhelmed by it from time to time. When I begin to feel that old, unwelcome guest invading my heart again, I ask myself the five aforementioned questions and remember God's truth.

Although God has given us the ability to experience fear, the Bible teaches that a paralyzing fear of people, things, and circumstances does not come from God. The apostle Paul wrote to young Timothy, a new pastor who was facing grave danger of persecution, "God gave us a spirit *not of fear* but of power and love and self-control" (2 Timothy 1:7, emphasis added). Paul wrote those words from prison, where he was already near death for his faith. Yet he urged Timothy to be strong and not fearful, because such fear is not from God. Because God has given us the spirit of "power and love and self-control," we can face extreme difficulties and trials without fear.

God's Word also teaches us that "love is from God; and everyone who loves is born of God and knows God...There is no fear in love; but perfect love casts out fear, because fear involves punishment, and the one who fears is not perfected in love" (1 John 4:7,18 NASB).

Notice these two truth statements in those verses: "love is from God," and "there is no fear in love." God does not want us to be characterized by our fear, because sinful fear and love for God cannot easily coexist. As we will see later, God's great love for us is part of "fear's answer."

Holy Fear Combats Sinful Fears

But you might say to me, "I have read the Bible, I go to church, I know these things about God, and yet there is still fear in my heart. I can't seem to control myself when it comes to fear." I truly understand what you are saying, and I intend to give you the hope and help you are longing for.

My purpose in writing to you is not to simply give you one more solution to try. If you already know that you are in a struggle against sinful fear, you no doubt have already tried other approaches to gaining control of your life. Some people try psychotherapy; some try antianxiety medication; some try hypnosis; others try Eastern religions or meditation. Many just try to get through each day, hoping that by some miracle they will "get better." But there is another way—God's way. In fact, it is the *only* way to gain complete freedom from fear. If you believe that only God has the answers to your sinful fear, and if you follow in His ways, you will find Him a faithful Savior who will rescue you from sin—the One who redeems your soul from the distresses of life.

Defining Holy Hear

Understanding the *holy fear of God* is the answer to your struggle with *sinful fear*. We already looked at the first part of Psalm 33:8, which says, "Let all the earth fear the LORD." The second part of that verse reads, "Let all the inhabitants of the world stand in awe of him!" Holy and righteous fear will "stand in awe" of the Lord. *This* kind of fear is the beginning of wisdom (Proverbs 9:10). This kind of fear believes what the Bible says about God's character—He is holy, just, loving, powerful, and in control—so that we can view the very difficult circumstances of life through these truths. It is the kind of fear that causes us to trust and obey Him in difficult times because He is God; He is powerful and in control. A holy fear of God means that when we feel afraid, we can say with King David,

> I will rejoice and be glad in your steadfast love, because you
> have seen my affliction; you have known the distress of my
> soul, and you have not delivered me into the hand of the
> enemy; you have set my feet in a broad place (Psalm 31:7-8).

David wrote these words when he was running for his life. Strong and important people were hunting him down, wanting to kill him. His situation was very real and he was in grave danger. But he could still rejoice—and so can you—because of God's steadfast love for His children. God sees our affliction, knows how distressing our trouble is, and has not delivered us into our enemy's hand. Instead, He has placed us where our feet will not slip. God will care for us so that we will not fall while running from the evil that pursues us. What God did for David He also does for us because it is the nature of God to save and rescue all His children.[4]

David fought against sinful fears with holy fear. Holy fear is *reverence for God* based on what God has already done and what He will continue to do for His people. Looking further into Psalm 33, we note the reasons David gave for his holy fear:

> Let all the earth fear the LORD; let all the inhabitants of the
> world stand in awe of him! For he spoke, and it came to be; he
> commanded, and it stood firm…The LORD looks down from
> heaven; he sees all the children of man…Behold, the eye of
> the LORD is on those who fear him, on those who hope in his
> steadfast love, that he may deliver their soul from death and
> keep them alive in famine…he is our help and shield.[5]

Demonstrating a Holy Fear

Having a holy fear or reverence of God also means that you believe and seek to live by everything He has said in His Word, the Bible. God has declared to us that salvation—the rescue and forgiveness we so desperately need—is through His Son Jesus Christ. The apostle John confirmed this for us when he said, "We have seen and testify that the Father has sent His Son to be the Savior of the world."[6] The apostle Peter testified to this same truth in Acts 4:12 when he declared (referring to Jesus Christ), "There is salvation in no one else, for there is no other name under heaven given among men by which we must be saved."

Face it—as busy women we tend to look for a quick fix, a painless solution. It seems too hard to figure out how our salvation in Christ can free us from fear. Our desire for relief overcomes us and we can think of nothing else. But God the Father has declared, "This is my beloved Son; listen to Him!" The answer to your fear is found in Christ, the One who rescues those whom He loves from the grip of sin and frees them from the fears that overwhelm. God's salvation doesn't simply help us feel better. *It assures us that it is safe to rest in Christ because He has demonstrated His love for us on the cross.*

The Answer Is Found in the Gospel

The ultimate answer to your struggle with fear and the development of holy fear is found in the gospel, the good news of Jesus Christ. The good news of the gospel is that saving knowledge of Christ brings complete redemption. We are redeemed not just to escape the oppression of our sin, but to reconcile us to God, from whom we were separated by our sin. The good news of the gospel is that although we deserved the wrath of God, God instead poured out His wrath on His Son Jesus Christ, who became sin for us so that we might become the righteousness of God in Him.[7]

Further, the good news of the gospel is that Jesus Christ has promised to be our hope and help for the sins that enslave us. At heart, all of our fears are rooted in a failure to believe the gospel. The gospel tells us that God loves us so much that He would not withhold any good thing from us (Romans 8:32). We no longer need to fear loss, punishment, or death. He has walked through everything for us already and has promised to bring us safely to Himself. In the meantime, while we continue to struggle with sinful fear, He is able to deliver us and keep us safe. Our faith will not fail even when we are walking through the valley of the shadow of death. He has walked there before us and has promised never to leave us or forsake us. As we meditate on precious truths like these, our holy fear or reverence will grow.

Steps Toward Driving Out Fear

Just knowing that Jesus is our only hope is not enough, however. We must humble ourselves, give up on trying to perfect ourselves, and believe on *Him* to completely save us. How many times have you thought, *I can do this; I can fix myself up; I'll start over again tomorrow and I won't be controlled by sin again,* only to fail again the next day? Today, instead of relying on yourself again, turn to the One who really does save, the Lord Jesus Christ. He is God, and because of His great love He became a man so that He could become the perfect sacrifice for sinners—for those controlled by fear. He lived the perfect life that you and I could never live, and He lived it for us, just as though we had lived it ourselves. On the cross, He took upon Himself God's wrath for our sin. Totally alienated from His eternal Father, Jesus Christ suffered the excruciating pain of crucifixion while God poured out His wrath on Him. It was as though Christ had committed all our sins. What an amazing sacrifice for undeserving sinners like us!

And after Jesus took our punishment, God was pleased with His sacrifice and raised Him from the dead. Our Savior is not dead! He is alive. Because of His resurrection—because He conquered death—we, too, can live in Him! *This* is the hope of the gospel—the help for our poor, helpless, fearful souls. His resurrection proves that we no longer need to fear God's judgment or the failure of our faith. The ascended Lord is watching over every aspect of your life and will not allow anything to destroy you.

Out of reverence for God's great love we need to repent[8] or turn from everything we're trusting in to save us from our fears and trust in Christ's rescue alone. To repent means to stop trying to hide from our fears or manipulate situations so that we need not feel afraid, and instead, seek to discover God's will in every circumstance. Reverential obedience, not to *earn* our salvation but *because* of our salvation, will enable us to conquer our fear. The only power strong enough to conquer sinful fear is a loving, holy fear born out of gratitude for Christ's work on our behalf.

An Example of Driving Out Fear

Perhaps an example will help at this point. Let's say Mary is afraid to drive over bridges. Every time she approaches a bridge her heart beats faster, she feels like she can't breathe, and her palms begin to sweat— even though she hasn't reached the bridge yet. Thoughts of fiery crashes fill her mind. She experiences these feelings of fear simply because she has *imagined* driving over the bridge.

Now, to further complicate matters, let's say her church is located on the other side of that bridge. How will she fight her fear? Of course, she could decide to stay home from church and download the sermons onto her computer, but she knows that cyberchurch is not God's will for her. How will she love and minister to the people God has placed in her life if she gives in to her fear and decides to stay home?

What will enable Mary to overcome her fear? Only this: obedience engendered by loving reverence. This is where her faith in the truth of the gospel will be exercised. She will have to say to herself, *I believe that God loves me and that all His plans for me are good. I know this because I have seen His love demonstrated on the cross. I want to obey Him more than I am afraid of dying. So, I will trust in Him that He will protect my faith and my soul so that even if I am in an accident, I know He'll keep me and use everything for His glory and my ultimate good. My heart might beat fast, but even if it does, I don't have to fear losing Him or that I'll have to face difficulties alone.*

Then, in grateful obedience for all the love God has shown her, Mary can go to her car, turn on her CD or tape player, listen to gospel songs of praise, and drive (even if it's very slowly!) across that bridge. Perhaps she'll have to fight her fear a number of times before it starts to go away. But she can be assured of this: The Lord sees, knows, and loves, and He will deliver her.

Understanding God's Power in You

If you have believed in Christ as Your Lord and Savior, you have been given the strength to resist sin. However, this does not mean you will no longer struggle with sin. It does not mean you will stop experiencing sinful fear. Even as a Christian, there are habitual responses still ingrained in your heart. The difference now is that the *power* of sin is broken in your life.[9] You can begin changing today—even if that change is gradual and halting at first. God's power is at work in you!

The apostle Paul, while describing our salvation, explained how this works:

> God, being rich in mercy, because of the great love with which
> he loved us, even when we were dead in our [sins], made us
> alive together with Christ…For by grace you have been saved
> through faith. And this is not your own doing; it is the gift
> of God, not a result of works, so that no one may boast. *For*
> *we are his workmanship, created in Christ Jesus for good works,*
> *which God prepared beforehand, that we should walk in them.*[10]

God is at work in us—we are His workmanship. Yet He also prepared good works for us to do. So He works…and we work also. Driving over that bridge will certainly seem like work…at least the first few times Mary does it. We are called to work in faith, not to obtain our salvation but to overcome sin. We will have to war against our sin for the rest of our lives. That's why Paul said we are to "put off [our] old self, which belongs to [our] former manner of life and is corrupt through deceitful desires, and to be renewed in the spirit of [our] minds, and to put on the new self, created after the likeness of God in true righteousness and holiness."[11]

Where we once succumbed to sinful fear, we now put on the holy fear of God. Where we once focused on loving and protecting ourselves, we can now love and protect God's reputation and name. This means that we trust Him in the fearful situations of life because He has shown Himself to be trustworthy. He has saved us from the power of sin and lived that perfect, fear-free life that we could never live. We know that He is working in us and that He desires to transform us into His likeness. These are truths we need to know, yet we could never make them real in our lives on our own.

Christ, the Answer to Every Fear

The situation that causes you fear may be like Mary's, or it may be completely different. The truth about Christ, however, is the same. Whatever fears you face, whatever fears have controlled you, whatever fears you have allowed to become sinful…for these, Christ is the answer. Turn to Him and find the help you need.

I leave you with these words from God to His children:

> Thus says the LORD, he who created you, O Jacob, he who
> formed you, O Israel: Fear not, for I have redeemed you;

I have called you by name; you are mine. When you pass through the waters, I will be with you; and through the rivers, they shall not overwhelm you; When you walk through fire you shall not be burned, and the flame shall not consume you. For I am the LORD Your God, the Holy One of Israel, your Savior.[12]

Recommended Resources

Fitzpatrick, Elyse. *Overcoming Fear, Worry, and Anxiety.* Eugene, OR: Harvest House Publishers, 2001.

Mack, Wayne. *Fear Factor.* Tulsa, OK: Hensley Publishing, 2002.

Welch, Edward T. *When People Are Big and God Is Small.* Phillipsburg, NJ: Presbyterian & Reformed Publishing, 1997.

Chapter 8

Help for Overcoming Anger

❦ *Martha Peace* ❦

I vividly remember discipling a young wife and mother we'll call Linda. She and her husband had two young school-aged children and were active in their church. Linda worked part-time out of her home teaching music lessons. They had a nice home, money to pay their bills, and outwardly they looked like a happy family. Unfortunately, there was one significant black cloud that loomed over them all.

Linda came to me for help because she had a very bad temper that would flare up at the most unexpected times and was usually directed at her husband or her children. She and her husband were discouraged over her lack of progress in overcoming it. As I thought about how to help Linda, I realized what she needed first was hope. Then she needed to know what the Scriptures teach about anger and how to apply that learning in practical ways.

There *Is* Hope

One way I gave Linda hope was to use myself as an example. When I was a new Christian I was very much like her. My temper would often flare when others least expected it. My family never knew if they were coming home to a peaceful refuge or a war zone! As a new Christian at age 33, I grieved over my repeated sin. I prayed and begged God to change me. Eventually I learned that even our *thoughts* can be sinful. I also knew that if I confessed my sin God would be faithful to forgive me and cleanse me from all unrighteousness (1 John 1:9). So when I began to *feel* irritated, frustrated, or stressed out, I would confess my anger to God and ask Him to help me. Gradually I began to realize that my *thoughts* were leading to my anger outbursts, so I began the process of changing my thoughts. Although doing that sounds easy, it wasn't easy at all. It was difficult because my angry thoughts flooded my mind like water bursting through a dam. In spite of my habitual sin, though, God gave me grace to persevere in my efforts at mind renewal.

One day upon being provoked, I thought, *Love is patient. I can show love to this person by being patient* (see 1 Corinthians 13:4). God enabled me to react to the circumstance with grace and love toward the other person, and I was delighted as I realized that God was supernaturally working in my heart to grow me toward Christlikeness (Romans 8:28-29).

I reminded Linda that she was like me and that she, too, could experience change. Then I showed her an absolutely astounding promise from God's Word: "No temptation has overtaken you that is not common to man. God is faithful, and he will not let you be tempted beyond your ability, but with the temptation he will also provide the way of escape, that you may be able to endure it" (1 Corinthians 10:13).

I told Linda that no matter what her circumstances, God would never allow her to experience a temptation she couldn't resist. I also explained that He eventually will provide a way of escape. I told her that God is always faithful and will give her grace to "train [herself] for godliness" (1 Timothy 4:7). In other words, she was responsible for controlling her thoughts when she responded to circumstances, but God would supernaturally help her.

After giving Linda hope, I taught her what the Bible says about anger.

Warnings in Proverbs

Probably the most frequently quoted proverb concerning anger is this: "A soft answer turns away wrath, but a harsh word stirs up anger" (Proverbs 15:1). The very next verse continues that idea, comparing the "the tongue of the wise" with the "mouths of fools" (Proverbs 15:2). Someone who is wise will stop and think about *how* she will respond. It is not only our actual words that convey anger, but also the tone of our voice and our facial expressions. Although the Proverbs are not promises, they are general truths. Therefore, the principle is this: If you respond with a kind, soft answer and a pleasant expression on your face, the other person will likely remain calm.

Proverbs describes the angry person as a "hot tempered man" who "stirs up strife" (Proverbs 15:18). And it describes those who are "slow to anger" as having a soothing influence on others (Proverbs 15:18). Another benefit of being "slow to anger" is that it demonstrates you have "great understanding" (Proverbs 14:29). In contrast, "a hasty temper exalts folly" (Proverbs 14:29). A person who is angry acts like a fool.

I explained to Linda that her anger outbursts had the potential to provoke her husband and children to anger. "Make no friendship with a man given to anger, nor go with a wrathful man, lest you learn his ways and entangle yourself in a snare" (Proverbs 22:24-25). Her family had no choice but to be around her and be exposed to her tirades. Instead of provoking them, she should make herself a joy for them to be around.

Linda cried as we went through the book of Proverbs because she so much wanted to be a loving wife and mother. And most of all, she wanted to honor God and give Him glory. So I showed her from the Scriptures how, by God's grace, she could renew her mind and...

Replace Anger with Kindness

I suggested to Linda that she compile a self-talk log. She was to write down her thoughts whenever she *felt* irritated or frustrated. She carried out her assignment for a week and came back with the following thoughts:

- "That makes me so mad!"

- "Leave me alone!"

- "How stupid can he be?"

- "Stop it right now!"

- "I can't take it anymore!"

- "That irritates me!"

- "Hurry up! You are too slow."

- "He doesn't care about me. He only thinks of himself."

Linda stopped adding to the self-talk log when she realized the same kinds of thoughts were recurring over and over again—even when her circumstances were not especially provoking.

Angry people tend to have a sinful bent toward a selfish focus or a lack of compassion for others. Linda had both. As a result, she could almost instantly respond in a screaming rage when one of her children got in her way or her husband did not give her the attention she thought she deserved. When she was in the PMS time of her monthly cycle, everyone knew to stay out of her way!

Linda's sin was worse than she thought it was. Her mind needed renewal and instead of thinking selfish, angry thoughts, she needed to confess her anger as sin and learn to think in terms of loving God and loving others. When asked what the most important commandment was, the Lord Jesus answered, "You shall love the Lord your God with all your heart and with all your soul and with all your mind. This is the great and first commandment. And a second is like it: You shall love your neighbor as yourself" (Matthew 22:37-39).

There is nothing more important for a Christian, in their devotion to God, than to show love to God (by obeying His Word) and love to others (by being kind and compassionate to them). Because Linda was a Christian and her life was "hidden with Christ in God" (Colossians 3:3), she had supernatural grace from God to help her change. The apostle Paul explained it this way:

> Now you must put them all away: anger, wrath, malice, slander, and obscene talk from your mouth...and have put on the new self, which is being renewed in knowledge after the image of its creator...Put on then, as God's chosen ones, holy and beloved, compassionate hearts, kindness, humility, meekness, and patience, bearing with one another and, if one has a complaint against another, forgiving each other, as the Lord has forgiven you, so you also must forgive. And above all these put on love, which binds everything together in perfect harmony (Colossians 3:8,10,12-14).

Linda was not going to stop exploding in anger until she started showing kindness and compassion.

There was one more critical step Linda needed to take to demonstrate true love to God and others. She needed a heart of thanks. The apostle Paul promised that the "peace of Christ" will rule the hearts (Colossians 3:15) of those who "put on love" (verse 14). Then he added, "And be thankful" (verse 15). To emphasize the necessity of a grateful heart, Paul spoke about thanks two more times in the next two verses:

> Let the word of Christ dwell in you richly, teaching and admonishing one another in all wisdom, singing psalms and hymns and spiritual songs, *with thankfulness in your hearts to God.* And whatever you do, in word or deed, do everything in the name of the Lord Jesus, *giving thanks to God the Father through him* (Colossians 3:16-17, emphasis added).

Before Linda could stop venting anger, she needed to show kindness and compassion to others, and a grateful heart to God.

How the Gospel Helps with Anger

Even though Linda had been a Christian for a number of years and she could easily rehearse the truths of the gospel, she had failed to see how the gospel should impact her life and particularly her anger. Because she assumed that the gospel was "a given" for her, she didn't give much thought to what Jesus had done for her. She knew she should ask, WWJD? (What would Jesus do?), but she had forgotten to ask, WDJD? (What did Jesus do?). And because of that omission, she labored under loads of self-recrimination and lacked the proper motivation for change.

Linda needed to realize that the key to change was the good news about the life, death, resurrection, and ascension of Jesus Christ. Whenever she felt anger rising up within her, instead of dwelling on her weakness and feeling guilty about her anger, she began to intentionally think about everything Jesus had done for her. For instance, when a driver in front of her was traveling too slowly on the road, she remembered how Jesus Christ had come to save her, and she had been so very slow to respond to Him. In fact, apart from His grace, she never would have gotten out of the "spiritual slow lane" that was so much a part of her life. She had been just as inconsiderate and slow as the driver in front of her. Just as God had been loving and patient to her, she was to show love and patience to others.

And whenever Linda began to slip down into a miry pit of discouragement and self-pity because she had failed to be patient yet *again*, she remembered how Jesus Christ's perfect record was completely hers. Her heavenly Father continued to view her as completely righteous because Jesus had never gotten sinfully angry with anyone. The resulting sense of freedom Linda felt transformed her heart and made her realize she didn't need to fight for her rights anymore. After all, Jesus had given up His rights for her. She could treat inconsiderate drivers with kindness because she had been treated with kindness herself.

Next, Linda could remember how Jesus' resurrection had broken the power of sin in her life. She was no longer a slave to habitual anger. Instead, Jesus had given her the ability and courage to continue to fight against it. He had set her free!

And finally, Linda could remember that Jesus was her *ascended* King. He was overseeing every part of her life, even this difficulty, so that she would remember what He had already done for her. She could look at this situation—this slow, inconsiderate driver—with new eyes now. She could see the cross and everything it meant to her and she could rejoice.

In light of all that Jesus had accomplished for Linda, Linda's heart was filled with love for Him. And that love was the only agent powerful enough to transform her and help her love her neighbor—even if that neighbor was traveling too slowly on the freeway!

Understanding the Providence of God

Another gap in Linda's understanding was a clear understanding of God's providence. *Providence* is "the continuing action of God by which he preserves in existence the creation which he has brought into being, and guides it to his intended purposes for it."[1] For all of us, including Linda, God's providence means that God is not only sustaining and maintaining all of His creation, but He is also guiding and directing the course of events in our lives to fulfill His purposes. These purposes include bringing glory to Himself and molding us more and more into Christlikeness. In other words, God providentially uses circumstances in our lives to deliberately test us to see if we *are* going to have a grateful heart and honor Him.

For example, instead of thinking, *I hate him!* Linda should think, *This is difficult, but God has a good purpose for testing me this way. Thank You, Lord, that I do not have to go through this in vain. Thank You for reminding me how much I need You. How can I show love to my husband when he is ignoring me?*

Remembering God's providential care and purposes behind every tiny detail in her life greatly helped Linda in her desire to change from an angry person into a woman who loved God and others.

Practical Tips to Overcoming Anger

What else helped Linda? The psalmist said that one way he fought sin was with the help of God's Word. This is how he put it: "I have stored up your word in my heart, that I might not sin against you" (Psalm 119:11). In light of this passage, I assigned Linda several Bible verses to memorize. I encouraged her to repeat them to herself so many times in her thoughts—and when she could, to say them aloud—that she could recite them almost without thinking. Here are the passages:

> Love is patient and kind; love does not envy or boast; it is not arrogant or rude. It does not insist on its own way, it is not irritable or resentful, it does not rejoice at wrongdoing, but rejoices with the truth. Love bears all things, believes all things, hopes all things, endures all things (1 Corinthians 13:4-7).

> Give thanks in all circumstances; for this is the will of God in Christ Jesus for you (1 Thessalonians 5:18).

> Know this, my beloved brothers: let every person be quick to hear, slow to speak, slow to anger; for the anger of man does not produce the righteousness of God (James 1:19-20).

> We do not have a high priest who is unable to sympathize with our weaknesses, but one who in every respect has been tempted as we are, yet without sin. Let us then with confidence

draw near to the throne of grace, that we may receive mercy and find grace to help in time of need (Hebrews 4:15-16).

Do not be overcome by evil, but overcome evil with good (Romans 12:21).

No temptation has overtaken you that is not common to man. God is faithful, and he will not let you be tempted beyond your ability, but with the temptation he will also provide the way of escape, that you may be able to endure it (1 Corinthians 10:13).

Let all bitterness and wrath and anger and clamor and slander be put away from you, along with all malice. Be kind to one another, tenderhearted, forgiving one another, as God in Christ forgave you (Ephesians 4:31-32).

In this [what the Lord has done for you] you rejoice, though now for a little while, if necessary, you have been grieved by various trials, that the tested genuineness of your faith—more precious than gold that perishes though it is tested by fire— may be found to result in praise and glory and honor at the revelation of Jesus Christ. Though you have not seen him, you love him (1 Peter 1:7-8).

After Linda understood her obligation to love God by obeying Him, to love others by thinking kind and compassionate thoughts, to acknowledge God's love and providential care over her in even the tiniest of circumstances, and to guard her heart by memorizing Scripture, it was time to revisit her self-talk log and help her renew her mind away from angry, selfish thoughts to thoughts about loving God and others. We came up with the following chart:

Angry Thoughts	Kind, Tenderhearted, and Forgiving Thoughts
That makes me so mad!	I need to be "quick to hear" because I might have misunderstood (James 1:19). I will remind myself about how Jesus was misunderstood and yet answered patiently.
Leave me alone!	"Love is patient." I *can* show love to him by patiently listening to his request (1 Corinthians 13:4). I will remember that Jesus willingly gave up His throne to help sinners like me. He is Emmanuel, the One who came to live with us.
How stupid can he be?	What he did was wrong. Lord, help me to think of practical ways to "overcome evil with good" (Romans 12:21). Jesus overcame my evil at great cost to Himself by dying in my place. I can love my neighbor because Jesus has loved me.
Stop it right now.	"The anger of man does not produce the righteousness of God" (James 1:20). I will tell him to stop and do so in a normal, kind tone of voice. Jesus deals patiently with me every day.
I can't take it any more.	This is very hard, but God will give me the grace to endure it. Every day that I do endure this I show love to God and my husband, as "love…endures all things" (1 Corinthians 13:7; see also 10:13). Although what I'm going through is difficult, it's nothing compared to what Jesus went through for me. I can ask Him for the same grace to endure this trial and be thankful that He will grant it to me.
That irritates me!	He does not realize that what he is doing annoys me. I will tell him gently because "love…is not irritable or resentful" (1 Corinthians 13:5). Even though it annoys me, he is not sinning, so it is all right if he does not change. I will remember Jesus' great patience with me when I sin.

Angry Thoughts	Kind, Tenderhearted, and Forgiving Thoughts
Hurry up. You're too slow!	"Love is patient" (1 Corinthians 13:4). I can show love to him by waiting.
He doesn't care about me. He only thinks of himself.	He does not know the Lord; therefore, he has no capacity to love me as he should. I will tell him that what he is doing *is* selfish. Even though he is not a Christian, I will show love to him, as love "does not rejoice at wrongdoing, but rejoices with the truth" (1 Corinthians 13:6). The truth is that I always think first of myself, and yet the Lord is patient and kind with me.

The Change God Can Bring

Because Linda truly did love the Lord and wanted to please Him, she worked hard at memorizing Scripture and renewing her mind by thinking kind, tenderhearted, and forgiving thoughts. By God's grace, she took to heart the command to "train [her]self for godliness" (1 Timothy 4:7). She became aware that when she *felt* irritated or frustrated or resentful her thoughts were stirring her toward anger. No longer could Linda blame her anger on others or her circumstances. Because she was more aware of her sin, she confessed it more quickly to the Lord, and if she happened to respond angrily to someone, she asked for their forgiveness. At first she had to ask for forgiveness quite a lot!

Providentially, God tested Linda's faith, but thankfully she grew in her ability to recognize what was happening. She learned that "God gives grace to the humble" and "opposes the proud" (1 Peter 5:5). So, she humbled herself before God and asked her husband and children to tell her when she sounded the least bit harsh or mean. She sincerely thanked God when one of them pointed out her anger, and she thanked her family for loving her enough to speak the truth to her. At first Linda struggled with great frustration and embarrassment when her family alerted her to her behavior. But she knew that God loved her and therefore disciplined her "for [her] good, that [she] may share his holiness" (Hebrews 12:10).

Finally, Linda worked diligently to renew her mind. At first it was easy for her to slip back into her sinful ways of thinking. However, the more humble she became and the more diligent she was, the more grace God poured out on her. The day came when, like me at the beginning of this chapter, Linda realized that her first thought was a God-honoring, grateful, love-the-other-person thought. She, like me, became delighted about how God was supernaturally working in her heart.

Does Linda ever become sinfully angry now? (Or me, for that matter?) Yes, but the Lord has changed us both so much that our anger is rare and much less intense. Both of us, with God's help, simply remember to "confess our sins, [knowing and believing] he is faithful and just to forgive us our sins and to cleanse us from all unrighteousness" (1 John 1:9). God faithfully, wondrously, and providentially continues to work in our hearts for our good and his glory.

> Put on then, as God's chosen ones, holy and beloved, compassionate hearts, kindness, humility, meekness, and patience, bearing with one another and, if one has a complaint against another, forgiving each other, as the Lord has forgiven you, so you also must forgive. And above all these put on love, which binds everything together in perfect harmony (Colossians 3:12-14).

Recommended Resources

Bridges, Jerry. *Respectable Sins.* Colorado Springs: NavPress, 2007.

Jones, Robert D. *Uprooting Anger.* Phillipsburg, NJ: Presbyterian & Reformed, 2005.

Mack, Wayne. *Anger and Stress Management God's Way.* Merrick, NY: Calvary Press, 2005.

Chapter 9

THE DIFFICULT ROAD THROUGH DEPRESSION

Mary Sommerville

A re you unable to enjoy the colors in a sunset, the flavors in your food, or the smiles of your friends? Do you feel like the lights have gone out in your life? Do guilt and feelings of worthlessness consume your every moment? Have you lost the joy of your life with God? Is everything black and hopeless—a living hell? Does reading this chapter take a herculean effort?

When you're depressed, your brain feels like life is going by in slow motion and you are constantly fatigued. You have trouble concentrating on anything and find it hard or impossible to make decisions. Sleep, the one thing you really want to do, escapes you. You are restless and irritable. You have unaccounted-for pain. Perhaps you feel like a child. Or, you don't want to be alone but you also don't want to be around people or have to make conversation.

All of those thoughts and feelings can produce thoughts of death or suicide. They are signs that you are experiencing depression, or what some call the dark night of the soul.

My heart goes out to you, as depression can be excruciating to deal with. In fact, the pain of a major depression may be greater than any other malady you've ever endured. It impacts relationships with your husband, children, friends, and extended family. You feel debilitated, unable to accomplish anything, including your normal, everyday work and ministry.

It's into the midst of this suffering that I would like to speak to you today. In this chapter we will consider some of the meaning in your suffering and I'll share how you can bring glory to God even in the midst of depression. God doesn't promise immediate relief, but He does promise to eventually wipe every tear from our eyes (Revelation 21:4) and make every crooked path straight (Isaiah 40:4). As you deal with both the physical and spiritual causes of your depression, it's possible you may find complete deliverance. Then again, maybe not. But you will *definitely* find that God's grace is sufficient for each day as His power is made perfect in weakness. There *is* hope for you.

The Origin of Depression

The first step toward freedom from depression is to determine all the contributing factors. With depression there are varying degrees of severity from less severe, often referred to as "situational depression," to a major bout, like the kind I've described above. A brief survey of the symptoms I listed makes it obvious that both the inner and outer you are involved.

Where do these symptoms come from? Depression can come from a heart that is hurting, from emotional pain. Sometimes overwhelming grief or difficult circumstances can bring on depression—such as the death of someone close, moving, the loss or change of a job, relationship problems, a church conflict, a marriage breakup, a rebellious child, or severe financial problems. Inward causes can include unconfessed sin, personal failures, and unmet desires and disappointments—hopes that have been crushed over and over again. If your depression stems from your inner pain, you can turn to God and His Word for restoration of the soul. There you will find answers for the inner person.

Other causes of depression may be more physical, having more to do with your physical body than your inner person. These may include exhaustion from years of overwork, serious injury or sickness, chronic pain, a thyroid problem, or lack of sleep. Medications taken for different conditions may also cause depression as a side effect. A diet of fast or junk foods, or eating disorders such as bulimia and anorexia, can also bring on depression. High consumption of caffeinated drinks or alcohol can also contribute to depression.

Hope for Your Body—the Outer You

Sometimes physical factors that lead to depression need urgent attention before the inner causes can be addressed. Note that God ministered to the physical needs of the prophet Elijah before He delved into the deeper cause of his depression by sending an angel to give him food and drink and by letting him sleep (1 Kings 19). God has compassion on us. He knows our frame and He is mindful that we are merely dust (Psalm 103:14).

If you're struggling with depression, you will want to get a thorough physical exam that includes a thyroid test. Also, are you at a transitional time of life in regards to your hormones? Then examine your eating and sleeping habits. Maybe you need to change your diet. Perhaps you need to fix your sleep patterns. Sleep loss can impact your health and mood. Of course, getting proper exercise is important. And finally, are you taking one day a week to rest? Whether you're a strict Sabbatarian or not, this creation ordinance is important and you can experience consequences if you neglect it (Exodus 20:8-11).

We are fearfully and wonderfully made—both physically and spiritually. What happens to our physical bodies impacts our inner person. There is a definite connection between the mind and body. John Piper points this out when he says, "What we should be clear about... is that the condition of our bodies makes a difference in the capacity of our minds to think clearly and of our souls to see the beauty of hope-giving truth."[1]

Our bodies are the temple of the Holy Spirit (1 Corinthians 6:19). Taking care of that temple—through good rest, nutritious meals, exercise, and proper supplements—is a wise course of action and can even help with the affliction of depression. Then you can rest in the knowledge that you are doing all you can physically for restoration to take place. (What about psychotropic medicines? Don't they also help restore emotional balance to the body? Because all chapter 10 deals with this complex subject, you'll want to go there for a more thorough answer.)

While the body is being cared for, how do we care for the soul? We need to look to Jesus, the Author and Finisher of our faith, and tap into the resources in God's authoritative and all-sufficient Word to find the best way for handling depression from a spiritual perspective.

Hope for Your Soul—the Inner You

When you're in the depths of a depression, that's when you need God the most. It's safe to cry out to Him. And it's instinctive to cry out to your Abba Father because you're in Christ and His Spirit is praying on your behalf (Romans 8:26). You can cry out to the One who understands completely what you are going through and who hears you (Hebrews 4:14-16). He loves to hear your cry, even when you feel like you've hardly got enough faith to lift your eyes to heaven.

Part of the pain of depression comes from feeling isolated and alone. You might be thinking that Jesus Christ never felt such loneliness. But He did—and infinitely more! Before He went to the cross, Jesus' soul was very sorrowful, even to death. In the garden, He sweat drops of blood as He faced the prospect of bearing God's wrath for us. He gave Himself up to the will of His Father to die in your place and to drink the cup of suffering so that atonement might be made. On the cross He wailed, "My God, my God, why have you forsaken me?" (Mark 15:34). Jesus Christ was utterly alone. In bearing your sin, He was totally abandoned by God so that you might never have to be completely alone. He was cast off so you could be brought into God's family.

This glorious plan to save you was established in eternity past. The Father decided to love you with such a fierce love that He would pour out his wrath on His Son in your place. The Son, Jesus Christ, would take on flesh, bear your sin in His own body on the cross, be raised from the dead, and ascend to heaven, where He is interceding for you, to the praise of His glorious grace (Ephesians 1:5-6; 2 Timothy 1:9-10). *This* is the gospel—the good news! *This* is the meaning of the universe and of all mankind—God desires to bring glory to Himself through this display of His love and grace, through you, and yes, even through your suffering.

Right now God is not calling you to glorify Him by great and mighty deeds, but by resting in what He has done. In one way, you're like Naaman, a leprous general whose story is told in the Old Testament. Naaman, who had come to Israel to find physical healing from his leprosy, was incensed when God's prophet said Naaman must dip himself in the dirty Jordan River to receive healing. He thought he needed to do some great deed to earn God's blessing. When Naaman was about to leave, his servants asked him, "My father, had the prophet told you to do some great thing, would you not have done it? How much more then, when he says to you, 'Wash, and be clean'?" (2 Kings 5:9-15 NASB). Naaman didn't need to do anything great. He simply needed to believe.

In the same way, you need to believe the good news of the gospel every day. You don't need to accomplish any great feat to earn God's blessing. No, the great feat was already accomplished by the death of the perfect Lamb of God. In the book of Revelation we're told there is a "book of life of the Lamb who was slain." It's not a book about your great works. No, it's a book about His, and that if you are in Christ, your name has been written there from before the foundation of the world (Revelation 13:8). Your greatest need has been met—peace with God. You can know that you're not alone and that He will come to you and sustain you.

God Has a Goal in Your Suffering

None of us need a reminder that we live in a fallen and broken world because of man's sin in the Garden of Eden. We are so conscious of the consequences; we feel them every day. We're groaning in ourselves and all of creation will groan with us until Christ comes to set us free (Romans 8:22). What a hope we have—that there is coming a day when we are no longer subject to sin, pain, and suffering! Until then, we can believe that even our sin and suffering is the raw material out of which God works glory into our lives. This transforms what seems like useless suffering into suffering with hope. God is working in us even now.

God Is the Blessed Controller of All Things

The trials you experience don't come without God's superintending of the events of your life. His design is to use your suffering to make you more like His Son. Your transformation into Christlikeness will bring Him glory. So, even though you feel useless and empty, you can remind yourself that God is working all things together for your good (Romans 8:28-29).

Through our trials, God teaches us to trust in His wisdom, love, and power. We learn to bow before Him as Job, the Old Testament saint, did. After Job had lost everything, he received no answer to his "Why?" questions. By the end of his suffering, Job had learned to put his hand over his mouth when he was tempted to charge God with wrongdoing. He realized that God was God and he was not. As was the case with Job, when we go through suffering as believers, God is treating us as a father who diligently disciplines His dearly loved children (Hebrews 12:7). He is up to something good that we can grasp only by faith. He is drawing us closer to Himself; He is making Himself our only hope. During our times of depression He is holding us, even when our faith is weak and we do not feel like we're His. *Our security rests in Christ and not our feelings.*

God Is Glorifying the Son

When we suffer, our greatest goal is the same as our Father's goal—to magnify Jesus and to bring Him glory. This happens when we express faith in the midst of our pain—even if our faith seems small, the size of a mustard seed. Because of Christ's work on the cross, we are no longer under condemnation for our sins. Instead we are perfectly right before God because Jesus' sinless life has been credited to our account (Romans 8:1). This is the truth we need to dwell on. We are completely free from any condemnation, from any wrath. As we dwell on His work, rather than ours, we can bask in the light of our inheritance in Christ. We have been adopted into God's family and made a fellow heir with Christ (Romans 8:17). We are not alone nor friendless—we're part of His family! God isn't angry or disappointed with us. We're *in* Christ.

The apostle Paul, who knew quite a lot about suffering, helped put our suffering in perspective when he wrote, "I consider that the sufferings of this present time are not worth comparing with the glory that is to be revealed to us" (Romans 8:18). Because Paul taught that God-centered suffering is the pathway to eternal glory, we can petition God to give us hope and an eternal perspective on suffering, even when we're in the midst of it.

Right now, though we may feel like sheep ready for slaughter, we are actually "more than conquerors through him who loved us" (Romans

8:37). That is because we are secure in God's love. Nothing can separate us from it. You may not feel like a superconqueror, but that is what you are as a believer in Christ. Let your weary soul find rest here—Jesus has conquered for you!

As we remember the promises in God's Word, it's a good idea to write them in our own words and post them in conspicuous places around our house. These slips of paper can remind us, "Jesus loves me!—perfectly, sacrificially, eternally, extravagantly"; "God has forgiven me a debt I could never pay"; "I'm His!"; "God is faithful!"; "Jesus died for me to make me His perfect bride"; "Jesus' blood gives me victory over my accuser." Those are the truths we need to remember when our hearts are overcome with guilt, doubt, or shame. We can even place a slip of paper by the clock: "Every time I look at this clock I will remember that God loves me all the TIME."

God's Love Motivates Us to Action

Because God loves us with an immeasurable love and has a goal in our suffering, our response to Him should include the following:

Think about your guilt. Depression and guilt go together. While the truth is that we all stand guilty before the holiness of God and there is no person on earth without sin, we believers can face our sins and guilt because of Jesus. Unlike the secular approach to depression, which tells us we're without guilt, we know that the price has been paid for our sins, and God's great love motivates us to face them and then deal with them. Because we have a great and loving Savior, we are free to examine our lives in light of the cross and repent of any known sin. The guilt of our sin doesn't have to crush us because it already crushed Him.

Scripture tells us that if we confess and forsake our sins we will obtain mercy (Proverbs 28:13). As we come to God and confess our sin, we can know that it is covered by the blood of Christ and we are cleansed (1 John 1:9).

Has guilt over some sin in your life precipitated your depression? King David felt such guilt. He wrote:

> When I kept silent, my bones wasted away through my groaning all day long. For day and night your hand was heavy upon me; my strength was dried up as by the heat of summer. I

acknowledged my sin to you, and I did not cover my iniquity;
I said, 'I will confess my transgressions to the Lord,' and you
forgave the iniquity of my sin (Psalm 32:3-5).

The Holy Spirit's work is to let us know what grieves the heart of
God in our lives. When we put other things in the place of Christ, they
become an idol, as stated in chapter 1 of this book. Though it's often
hard for us to see our own idols, we can ask God to reveal them to
us. Are we treasuring anything more than we treasure Christ? Perhaps
we've idolized beauty or health. Or, maybe we worship being in control
of our circumstances. There are many things that can easily gain higher
priority in our life than Christ—whether intentionally or not. Here are
some questions you can ask yourself to help see if this is the case:

1. Have you sought worldly success at the expense of everything else?

2. Do you seek the approval of people more than approval
   from God?

3. Have your disappointments led to sin in the area of not caring for your body, the temple of the Holy Spirit?

4. What do you think you *must* have in order for your life to
   have meaning again?

5. Are you filled with anger and bitterness, and unwilling to
   forgive someone?

Did you answer yes to any of those questions? If so, you need to
come to the Lord—the One who loves you—with a broken heart over
your sin. Jesus died to set us free from enslavement to sin. His death
made full atonement for it. You don't have to do penance or cower
before Him. Instead, you can freely admit your failure. It is covered
by the blood of the spotless Lamb of God. He wants to free you and
release you to a life of love-motivated obedience.

Seek counsel from a mature Christian who can help you see your blind
spots and make a plan to overcome your sin. Perhaps you have a mature
Christian friend, an elder's wife or biblical counselor, who can help you
as you struggle with the sin that makes you feel so guilty. Ask her to

help you find Scripture passages that apply to specific areas in which you struggle. Pray together for the Holy Spirit's power to enable you to walk in victory as you memorize and meditate on His Word. Ask your friend to show you how to replace the sin in your life with patterns of obedience that will please God. You may need to seek forgiveness, go back and be reconciled to someone, or do other hard things in order to take care of your sin. But God will strengthen you so you can do what is necessary to take steps toward obedience.

Remember that you're in a moment-by-moment battle and a process. If personal sin is not the cause of your depression, your counselor can still help you to know best how to handle, in a God-honoring way, the trials you are facing.

Know that depression is a spiritual battle for your very life. There is more to your struggles than you can see. Scripture says you are wrestling against the rulers, authorities, cosmic powers, and spiritual forces of evil in the heavenly places (Ephesians 6:12). Satan is our adversary and wants to destroy us when we're down. Jesus said that Satan is a murderer and the father of lies (John 8:44). Satan likes to tell you that you are useless and your battle has already been lost. He will tell you that God has abandoned you and that everyone is better off without you. *Don't believe Satan's lies!*

If you have transferred your trust to God through faith in Jesus' death for you on the cross, then you are His forever (Romans 10:9-10). You were chosen before He made the world, and nothing can take you out of His hand (John 10:28; Ephesians 1:4). God has a plan for you that involves this suffering, and He will bring you through, as promised in 1 Corinthians 10:13: "God is faithful...and he will provide the way of escape."

Spend time with the Great Counselor. Take time each day to get into God's Word with pen and paper in hand so you can note the wonderful truths He impresses on your mind (Psalm 119:18). This will force you to pay attention to what God wants to say to you. Ask yourself, *What is in this text that causes me to want to respond in obedience and praise?* Take comfort from the promises of hope that abound and cling to them. God's Word is ultimate truth—an antidote to distorted negative thoughts that lead to hopelessness. You can then journal the lessons you are learning. God's Word renews our minds with the truth and has the power to change our feelings.

Dig into the biblical accounts of godly people who experienced the depths of despair. From the oldest recorded Scripture you can read about Job's response to his severe testing. Who can blame him for saying he longed for death and searched for it more than hidden treasures (Job 3:20-26)? Moses pleaded with God to kill him because his burden was too great (Numbers 11:14-15). Elijah, a great Old Testament prophet, defeated the prophets of Baal then collapsed in exhaustion and asked God to take his life (1 Kings 19:3-4). Jonah was angry at God and prayed, "O LORD, please take my life from me, for it is better for me to die than to live" (Jonah 4:3). Many others have gone before you; you're not alone in your suffering.

Yet even in their misery, these valiant people knew that God was the author of life and it was He alone who had the power and authority to give and take it. To pray for death at God's hands is sometimes understandable, but contemplating suicide is a sin we must run from. Taking our own life is murder, no matter what the circumstances. So, if you're feeling tempted in this way, be sure to tell others and especially those who are closest to you so that they can stand with you against this temptation.

In each of the Bible accounts above, we can also see how God met these people where they were and brought them out of their doubts. He did this through their faith in His promises. He enabled them to continue serving Him. Jeremiah's eyes were a fountain of tears and his heart was faint (Jeremiah 8:18–9:1). But in the midst of his sad lament, he gave one of the greatest expressions of hope found in the Bible. Let this key promise bring you out of the dungeon of despair:

> The steadfast love of the LORD never ceases, his mercies never come to an end; they are new every morning; great is your faithfulness...For the Lord will not cast off forever, but, though he cause grief, he will have compassion according to the abundance of his steadfast love; for he does not willingly afflict or grieve the children of men (Lamentations 3:22-23,31-33).

Voice your sufferings to God, who already knows what you are going through. You don't have to suffer in silence. When you don't know how to express the agony of your soul, consider King David, who spoke of his struggles in the book of Psalms. God allowed David, a man after His own heart, to go through every kind of trial and record the full range of his emotions in song—to shine light into our darkness even three millennia later!

David often confessed that he could not see God. He laid bare his doubts, fears, anxieties, anguish, and sin. Yet God pulled him up out of the miry pit and set his feet upon a rock, making his footsteps firm. God put a new song in David's heart, a song of praise to his God (Psalm 40).

Can you relate to the desperate plea that begins, "Out of the depths I cry to you, O LORD!"? "O Lord, hear my voice! Let your ears be attentive to the voice of my pleas for mercy!" (Psalm 130:1-2). By the end of the psalm we see the despair replaced by hope: "O Israel [O sister], hope in the LORD! For with the LORD there is steadfast love, and with him is plentiful redemption" (Psalm 130:7-8). Why not memorize Psalm 130 and let God use it in your life to remind you of His steadfast love for you?[2]

Thank God for what you know you should be grateful for—His abundant goodness. Add to your journal things for which you can praise God every day, and do it to glorify God because He is worthy, not to raise your spirits. You can follow the examples of Paul and Silas, who sang praises to God even while serving time in prison. You can also use songs written by other Christians who have experienced God in suffering.[3] As you pour out your heart before the Lord in psalms and hymns and spiritual songs, you will find comfort. Choose a good hymn to read or sing every evening before you fall sleep.

Fulfill your responsibilities as much as you can. Live a structured life. When you think you are unable to do what is necessary, ask God for strength (Philippians 4:13). When you don't know what to do, do the next thing you can find to do. Pulling back from meaningful work and activities only adds to depression and complicates the problem. Ask God for help, and He will enable you to persevere.

Ask God for His strength to look outside yourself. When you seek to avoid pressure, your life can become very small and self-absorbed. Pray for and reach out to someone else on a daily basis no matter how you feel. You could make a phone call, visit someone, or write a note of encouragement. If the love of Christ is in you, you will love others (1 John 4:7). You may be surprised by the joy you receive as you take what may appear to be very small steps toward giving to others.

Seek fellowship with other believers both at church and in your daily life. Although you feel like withdrawing, you need to fight for joy. You can do this by utilizing the provision God has made for this very purpose— His church (Hebrews 10:24). This is where you will find strength and encouragement to persevere as others share the comfort they have received from the Lord (2 Corinthians 1:4). Allow those who have been through this valley to tell you their stories and enlighten your way.

The Best Is Yet to Come

Dear friend, above all, don't give up. Someday you too will have the opportunity to share with others your journey through depression and bring them hope.[4] "Weeping may tarry for the night, but joy comes with the morning" (Psalm 30:5). The best is yet to come, when God Himself will wipe every tear away in a place of undiminished joy. There you will place your hand in the nail-scarred hand of the One whose love has brought you there…and you will bask in His love forever!

Recommended Resources

Bridges, Jerry. *Trusting God: Even When Life Hurts.* Colorado Springs: NavPress, 1988.

Fitzpatrick, Elyse M. *Because He Loves Me.* Wheaton, IL: Crossway Books, 2008.

———. *Comforts from the Cross.* Wheaton, IL: Crossway, 2009.

———. *A Steadfast Heart,* Phillipsburg, NJ: Presbyterian & Reformed, 2006.

Fitzpatrick, Elyse and Dennis Johnson. *Counsel from the Cross.* Wheaton, IL: Crossway, 2009.

Piper, John. *When the Darkness Will Not Lift.* Wheaton, IL: Crossway, 2006.

Tada, Joni Eareckson and Steven Estes, *When God Weeps.* Grand Rapids: Zondervan, 1997.

Welch, Edward T. *Depression: A Stubborn Darkness.* Greensboro, NC: New Growth, 2004.

Chapter 10

About Medicines:
Finding a Balance

§ *Laura Hendrickson* §

W hat is it about psychiatric medicine that brings out such strong feelings among God's people? While preparing to write this chapter, I spent some time surfing Internet blogs and discussion forums to see what Christians are saying these days about the use of psychiatric drugs. What an eye opener! Although the discussions I read all began pleasantly enough, many ended in angry interchanges.

Those in favor of psychiatric drugs tended to see emotional pain as solely a physical problem. They argued that the use of medicines is rational, necessary in all cases, and compassionate. As the discussion became more heated, some even implied that those who were opposed to their view were ignorant and uncompassionate.

On the other hand, those who disapproved of the use of such drugs were inclined to see emotional problems as strictly spiritual. They found it difficult to believe that using a medication could ever be right. As the dialogue intensified, they came close to accusing their opponents of being weak, unspiritual, or even in sin.

What struck me about these disagreements was that almost no one said, "Maybe medicines aren't always the best choice." They also weren't saying, "Maybe sometimes medications can be helpful." Perhaps Christians take such strong positions on this issue because they feel that certain principles should not be compromised. And zeal for the truth is a good thing. But harshly judging those who disagree with us can never be the right thing to do.

A Quest for Balance

Sometimes members of the antimedication group can come dangerously close to making a "Job's comforters" kind of mistake. Though they might not actually hurl accusations, they can sound as though they're saying, "You have unconfessed sin in your life. Repent and you'll feel better!" On the other hand, it's easy to understand why members of the promedicine group—who take psychiatric drugs—want to make sure everyone understands their suffering isn't due to sin. But in their zeal, they can sound as though Romans 3:23, "All have sinned and fall short of the glory of God," doesn't apply to them. As we'll see, neither extreme position is consistent with the full counsel of Scripture or with the findings of medical science.

I believe we can agree that our bodies play an important role in our emotions without insisting that all painful feelings are due to a disease. I also don't think that it's a sin or an admission of weakness to take psychiatric drugs. But taking a medication *without* considering spiritual issues may leave a very important matter unaddressed. In fact, it's been my experience, through 20 years of psychiatric and biblical counseling practice, that a medicine-only approach doesn't resolve emotional pain completely or permanently in most cases.

The controversy about medicines hinges upon what the Bible and medical research say about our emotional problems. Do they contradict each other, such that we have to choose one or the other? Or are they in more agreement than we may realize? Let's take a careful look at what each one affirms.

What Does the Bible Say?

The Bible teaches that your human nature is made up of two parts: You have a spiritual inner person or heart, and a physical outer person or body. Your heart is the part of you that thinks, feels, and makes choices. God interacts with you through your heart.

Your body, on the other hand, enables you to relate to the world around you. Your speech, behavior, facial expressions, and tone of voice reveal to others what's going on inside your heart. It's important to note that because the brain is a physical organ of your body, it can't be the source of your thoughts, feelings, and choices. Scripture clearly teaches that these activities take place in your inner person. But because your brain is the "master controller" of your bodily functions, it makes sense to think of it as a mediator that translates what's inside of you into physical form. While the Bible is silent about how this happens, its clear teaching is that your heart is the source of what comes out of you, not your brain (Luke 6:45).

The Bible also teaches that what takes place in your body affects what goes on in your heart. If you're sleep deprived, sick, in pain, or on medicines that make it harder for you to think clearly, you will experience physical changes or consequences that will influence your thoughts and emotions. These changes may even tempt you to make wrong choices.

The prophet Elijah's faith wilted after he confronted the prophets of Baal. Afterward, when Jezebel threatened Elijah, he ran all day long to escape her evil. When he finally stopped, he was physically and emotionally exhausted and very hungry. He asked God to kill him—then promptly fell asleep! Later, after some rest, food, and encouragement, he was ready to return to the Lord's service (1 Kings 18:21–19:21).

Elijah's exhaustion didn't *make* him give up, but it did make the temptation harder to resist. And I think the reason God gave him rest and food before appearing to him was because his body needed to be strengthened so he would be ready to respond in the right way.

What Does Modern Medicine Say?

Generally speaking, medical science confirms what the Bible teaches. Any doctor can tell you that physical stresses strongly affect heart attitude. People who suffer from pain or illness often struggle with depression and anxiety. Some of this may result from the discomfort they feel, and some may result from the side effects of medication taken to treat a given condition. On rare occasions, certain diseases of the body can directly produce confusion, depression, or anxiety. Doctors also agree that renewed physical strength often improves a sick person's spirits.

Research has shown that psychiatric medicines alter the levels of certain chemicals in the brain. While these medicines can help diminish pain, because the brain controls the organs of the body, these drugs can also have powerful unintended effects elsewhere in the body. I'm currently helping two people who have experienced serious side effects from their medications. One developed disfiguring facial tics that didn't go away even after she stopped taking her medicine. The other briefly lost touch with reality after the first dose.

It's also important to realize that some statements you may hear about how psychiatric drugs work are not completely accurate. When television commercials tell you that painful feelings are caused by an imbalance of chemicals in your brain, they are oversimplifying complicated information. It's true that psychiatric medications alter the levels of certain chemicals in your brain, which may make you feel better. *But there is no proof that abnormal levels of these chemicals developed all by themselves, thereby causing your emotional pain.*

Here's a way to think of the brain's role in your emotions that's consistent with what the Bible teaches: The thoughts and feelings of your heart can change your brain's chemical balance. The opposite is also true: Medicines that change your brain's chemical balance can affect the thoughts and feelings of your heart. This view accepts the findings of medical science on the role of the brain *without* insisting that your emotional pain comes solely from your body rather than from your heart, as the Bible teaches.

Putting It All Together

The Bible teaches that your emotions come from your heart, not from your body. It also teaches that improving the way your body feels can change your emotions for the better. Medical science confirms the Bible's teachings. Whether you're taking hormones to help you through PMS or menopause, arthritis drugs for pain, or psychiatric drugs, medications may improve the way you feel. But they won't, by themselves, work the spiritual change that may be needed in your heart.

Remember Elijah's story. Rest and food fortified his body, but they didn't solve his emotional problem. He wanted to give up because he'd decided that his situation was hopeless and his ministry was a lost cause.

Elijah's hunger and tiredness didn't do this to him, and food and rest alone couldn't solve it. It took an encounter with God's truth to set Elijah's heart right.

Satan understands very well the connection between your physical condition and your spiritual struggles. That's why he waited until Jesus was weakened by hunger, when He was fasting in the wilderness, before launching a spiritual attack (Matthew 4:1-11). How did Jesus resist Satan? He countered each lie with truth from God's Word, simply stating, "It is written…"

In the same way that food and rest revived Elijah, medications may improve the balance of chemicals in our brains. But by themselves they can't solve complex spiritual problems. We need to hear God speaking truth to our hearts as Elijah did. We also need to actively use God's Word, as Jesus did, when we're struggling.

The great Protestant reformer Martin Luther, who himself struggled with the temptation to become depressed, understood this truth. He urged his followers not to think depressed and anxious thoughts, "for our adversary, the devil, walks about, seeking not only to devour our souls but also to weaken our bodies with thoughts of the soul." He encouraged his followers to correct their thinking with truths from Scripture.

The prominent nineteenth-century British preacher Charles Spurgeon struggled with depression off and on throughout a long and fruitful ministry. He taught his students that we often experience painful feelings when we're physically weak or under the pressure of circumstances. In his own case, Spurgeon suffered painful gout, kept up a grueling ministry schedule, and struggled with feeling at fault when several people died after false cries of "Fire! Fire!" caused a large crowd to panic and trample over each other when he preached at the Surrey Gardens Music Hall. But because he understood that suffering is a normal part of the Christian life (1 Peter 4:12), he wasn't surprised when he experienced seasons of sadness. Instead, he saw difficult times as opportunities to draw closer to God in faith.

The Bottom Line

We don't have to reject the Bible's teachings about our nature to agree that taking medicines may help us with painful feelings. But we also should understand what we're doing when we take a psychiatric drug. In the vast majority of cases, we aren't treating an illness. We're simply giving a boost to our bodies by changing the balance of chemicals in our brains. But because the Bible teaches that our feelings come from the heart, this strictly physical improvement can't, by itself, solve our emotional problems.

These drugs are never medically *required* unless you're so discouraged that you're thinking of taking your own life, or so confused that you can't think clearly. In fact, because they can produce their own serious physical problems, psychiatric medicines should never be the first option. Instead, Bible truth should be your primary source of help. If you're having difficulty applying Scripture to your struggles, your pastor or a biblical counselor[1] are specially trained to help you understand yourself and your struggles in the light of God's Word.

What About Difficult Cases?

Even as we uphold Scripture as a fully sufficient source of answers for every problem (2 Peter 1:3), we should remember that there is much that we don't understand. In my years as a biblical counselor, I've sometimes been puzzled when a godly person just can't seem to make full use of Scripture's truths to solve her emotional troubles.

I'm comforted to realize that Jesus, in His time on earth, helped different people in different ways. For instance, I can count five distinct ways that He healed blind men. Jesus showed Himself to be the ultimate "heart doctor." He perfectly understood each blind man's spiritual condition, and tailored His actions to meet each one's deeper need. Two men needed to say they believed before their sight was restored (Matthew 9:27-29). Jesus saw faith already present in another, and confirmed it by speaking an immediate healing (Mark 10:52). Two men instantly received sight by Jesus' touch on their eyes (Matthew 20:34). Another's vision improved gradually (Mark 8:22-25). And Jesus healed a man's physical *and* spiritual blindness progressively as He spat on the ground, made mud, anointed his eyes, sent him to wash, and then ordained events to deepen his faith as he testified to others (John 9).

So why are we surprised that the Lord doesn't solve everyone's painful feelings in the same way today? We're told that one of Martin

Luther's faith struggles was settled instantly by reading a single Bible verse. Similarly, in my experience, some counselees grasp right away what God's Word has to say about their problems and recover their emotional balance quickly. But others, no less godly or committed, may toil slowly in counseling for many months.

Some individuals come to me in so deep an emotional hole that it seems best to recommend the physical boost of psychiatric drugs in addition to the ministry of God's Word to restore them. Others come to me already on medications, having already spent many months in counseling, but still grappling with painful feelings. And finally, a few people have diseases that have required continued medical treatment as well as biblical counseling to help them remain emotionally stable.

In John Bunyan's famous allegorical work titled *Pilgrim's Progress*, Hopeful crosses the final river easily, while Christian, who has no less faith, struggles desperately to keep his head above water. Charles Spurgeon commented, "I note that some whom I greatly love and esteem, who are, in my judgment, among the very choicest of God's people, nevertheless travel most of the way to heaven by night."[2] I don't know why the Lord deals with one person differently than another, but I know that He is good, and He works everything together for good for His people (Romans 8:28). My confidence as I come alongside suffering counselees is this: Jesus, who healed the blind men five different ways, still provides what each of us needs to increase our faith and restore us.

We who love this wise and compassionate Lord should have the same attitude toward one another. Let's not judge our sisters' faith by the quantity or difficulty of their trials, and not make the same mistakes as Job's friends when they wrongly judged him. Let's also resist the temptation to offer easy answers, whether they be "Just trust God," or "Just take medicines." Instead, as we seek to be skillful women discipling women, let's imitate the Lord's gentleness and patience for those whose sufferings we can't fully understand, because only He knows their hearts (Jeremiah 17:10).

Recommended Resources

Fitzpatrick, Elyse. *Because He Loves Me: How Christ Transforms Our Daily Life*. Wheaton, IL: Crossway, 2008.

———. *Idols of the Heart: Learning to Long for God Alone.* Phillipsburg, NJ: Presbyterian & Reformed, 2001.

Fitzpatrick, Elyse and Laura Hendrickson, M.D. *Will Medicine Stop the Pain?* Chicago: Moody, 2006.

Welch, Edward T. *Blame It on the Brain? Distinguishing Chemical Imbalances, Brain Disorders, and Disobedience.* Phillipsburg, NJ: Presbyterian & Reformed, 1998.

Part 3

A Woman and Her Relationships

Chapter 11

SINGLE WOMEN AND THE TEST OF LONELINESS

⸱⸱ *Joan Kulper* ⸱⸱

I have always wanted a family of my own. I wanted someone to love and to love me. I want what my parents had, and I'm afraid that I will never be able to have that. I've made many wrong choices in my life trying to fill that void. My friends mean well, but they seem to be on an endless quest to match me with that perfect guy. Sometimes I feel like they think there's something wrong with me because I can't seem to find 'Mr. Right.' When I'm alone I think, *Maybe I weigh too much,* or *Maybe I need a nose job.* I wonder what I can do to get guys to notice me. Most of my friends have significant others in their lives—why not me? I don't feel like I fit in anywhere and I'm lonely."

A woman we'll call Kathryn, an attractive 28-year-old, sat in my office feeling lonely, without direction and without purpose in her life. She had already experienced several failed relationships, and each year that passed she felt more pressure to find a husband. It seemed that most of her friends had found "soul mates," while she still went home to an empty house. It was easy for her to think that a husband could fill her feelings of emptiness and provide for all of her needs. Kathryn had taken advice from well-meaning friends, magazine articles for lonely hearts, TV talk-show hosts, and radio psychologists, but none of it seemed to make a lasting difference.

If you can identify with Kathryn, or you know someone who can, her story probably sounds very familiar. We are all influenced by what

others think and say. There are many outside influences that promote
the idea that a single woman cannot experience happiness. Many parents feel that when their daughters marry, their job of parenting is
finally over and, without meaning to, place undue pressure on young
single women to marry. They see marriage as a sign of adulthood and
maturity and completion. Dating services fill the airwaves with commercials that promise to deliver "the perfect match." And, to add insult
to injury, there is no end to comments and jokes about the "biological
clock." All these send messages that tend to make single women even
more anxious about their singleness, and they have influenced the way
people view singleness.

God's Word Has Answers

The Bible has answers that we can count on in every circumstance.
Psalm 19:7 teaches us, "The law of the LORD is perfect, reviving the soul."
We can trust in the truth of the Bible to change our perspective and give
us happiness and satisfaction. Verse 8 goes on to say, "The precepts of
the LORD are right, rejoicing the heart." God does want us to be happy,
but He has designed us to experience the most joy in life when we are
obedient to Him. "The commandment of the LORD is pure, enlight-
ening the eyes" (Psalm 19:8). Without the Word of God, life makes no
sense at all. And finally in verse 9, "The fear of the LORD is clean, enduring forever." Everything in life changes, but not God's Word. It is relevant to our life yesterday, today, and always. The Word of God speaks
to our feelings of loneliness and gives us direction and purpose.

In the Beginning

The desire for relationship is written on the hearts and minds of all
men. In the beginning God created man in His own image. The record
of Adam and Eve in Genesis, the first book of the Bible, shows us that
man was created to have an intimate personal relationship with God,
and also with others. It says in Genesis, "It is not good that the man
should be alone" (2:18). Man is different from other creatures in that
God has given him the ability to communicate his ideas and emotions
at a deeper level of intimacy with his Creator and with other humans.

At creation, everything was made perfect, and God declared that everything was good (Genesis 1:31). Adam and Eve were given freedom within God's spoken law (Genesis 2:16-17), but man decided that his own thoughts were more important than obedience to God. As soon as man acted upon the temptation to disobey God, he immediately felt the fear and pain of separation from his Creator (see Genesis 3). Because of this act of disobedience, which God's Word defines as sin, all people now experience loss, fear, guilt, and separation from God.

The sin of Adam and Eve not only separated them from God, but also from one another. Instead of love and openness, they felt fear and shame for disobeying God's clear command to not eat of the tree of the knowledge of good and evil. They were unable to communicate in transparent truthfulness: Eve blamed Satan, and Adam shifted blame first to Eve, then ultimately to God. Together Adam and Eve were responsible for breaking the trust they had with God. Guilt stood between man and woman, causing a loneliness that all men would feel the effects of from that time forward. All of the God-given qualities of human relationship were now broken.

The good news is that God never intended to leave man in such a lonely, fallen condition. From the beginning God had a plan to bring man back into a personal relationship with Him, and ultimately to restore the broken relationship between man and woman (Genesis 3:7-8). God planned that His Son, Jesus Christ, would pay the penalty for our disobedience. The Son of God gave up His life on the cross to reconcile us to God. For those who are called by God there is a promise of new life—not only in eternity, but in this life as well. When we come to the Lord and confess our rebellious and disobedient thoughts and deeds, placing them at the foot of the cross, we are returned to God's good favor and are given a new relationship with Him. With that new relationship comes a new understanding of our relationships with one another.

Earthly Solutions: Our Never-ending Turmoil

Because we live in a fallen world, we often try to solve our problem of loneliness using earthly solutions—that is, our own solutions instead of God's. The feeling of loneliness is tied to the desire for intimacy with God, and that desire is often misunderstood as merely a desire for a spouse. Single women often try to overcome loneliness through dating, sometimes one guy after another. This emotional merry-go-round keeps us in turmoil and clouds our judgment of what a real relationship looks like.

We often believe that marriage will fix us and make us feel whole, that a husband will provide comfort, security, and love. This way of thinking will ultimately bring us disappointment and failure. In counseling I have seen the devastating results of believing that loneliness can be resolved through marriage. It doesn't take long for women to realize their mistake. They take their wrong ideas into the marriage relationship, and soon there are two people who, though living together, are still very much alone.

The pattern for family is written on our hearts, and it is a good and desirable thing to obtain, but the model for marriage has been corrupted. It is not wrong to desire a husband, but it becomes wrong when that desire is more important than loving God and developing a personal and intimate relationship with God's Son, Jesus Christ. God's Word teaches that wholeness comes only through faith in Christ Jesus. The apostle Paul wrote in Colossians, "In Him you have been made complete, and He is the head over all rule and authority" (Colossians 2:10 NASB). There is nothing we need, apart from Jesus Christ, to make us complete.

Godly Solutions: Our Identity in Christ

If I were to ask you to identify who you are, what would you say? Most women would describe themselves based on their occupation or their role in life. They might say they are a secretary, a teacher, a mother, or a single woman. But does that explain who they are at the deepest level?

What you do only describes the *role* you are performing at present, and that will change as you go from one stage of life to the next. There will come a time when you are unable to continue in the role that you are now performing. You might marry, retire, have an accident, become ill, or become a widow. As the circumstances in your life change, they do not affect who you are at the deepest level. God has made you with an internal identity that is lasting, regardless of your circumstances. As God's child, you have an identity that is written on your heart that will sustain you through life. You are not defined by what you do, but with whom you are connected—specifically, Jesus Christ.

You may be living alone for now, but you need not be lonely. All children of God are adopted into the family of God. Your identity, your confidence, and all that you are as a person is tied to Jesus Christ. Therefore, you need not fear about your future. As the apostle Paul wrote in Romans 8:15, "You did not receive the spirit of slavery to fall back into fear, but you have received the Spirit of adoption as sons, by whom we cry, 'Abba! Father!'"

Out of love for our Lord, we have an obligation—as His creatures—to learn more about Him and to seek to know Him. We can pray today that God will give us the desire to know Him personally through His Word. "You will seek Me and find Me when you search for Me with all your heart" (Jeremiah 29:13 NASB).

Friendship and the Family of God

Single women often rely on their friendships to fulfill the need for human companionship. It is important to develop a network of friends who are trustworthy and able to help you grow in your relationship with God. If you are a Christian, then the best place for this to happen is in the context of a local body of believers, the church. It is important for you to find a church that teaches the truth of God based solely on the Bible, and where the people have a heart for serving one another and the community.

Also, do not confine yourself to only meeting other singles. The whole body of Christ—people of different ages, circumstances, and backgrounds—ought to be part of all our lives. Paul wrote in 1 Corinthians 12:12, "Just as the body is one and has many members, and all the members of the body, though many, are one body, so it is with Christ."

When we are part of the body of Christ, we are no longer alone, for we are Christ's adopted sons and daughters. Jesus said concerning this, "'Who are my mother and my brothers?' And looking about at those who sat around him, he said, 'Here are my mother and my brothers! For whoever does the will of God, he is my brother and sister and mother'" (Mark 3:33-35).

Singles should develop a network of friends within the church who are willing to help them in times of need, and whom they can also help. As Christians we are part of a larger family in Christ. You should never feel timid about asking for help from those who are part of the family of God. They are your first priority, and you theirs. We were made for companionship and close relationships, and that includes singles. In Romans, Paul wrote,

> Love one another with brotherly affection. Outdo one another in showing honor. Do not be slothful in zeal, be fervent in spirit, serve the Lord. Rejoice in hope, be patient in tribulation, be constant in prayer. Contribute to the needs of the saints and seek to show hospitality (12:10-13).

Love and Service

We should make sure we never see the church as merely a place where we go to have *our* needs met. Rather, we go to become more like our Savior, Jesus Christ. When Jesus was asked which was the greatest of the commandments He said,

> You shall love the Lord your God with all your heart and with all your soul and with all your mind. This is the great and first commandment. And the second is like it: You shall love your neighbor as yourself. On these two commandments depend all the Law and the Prophets (Matthew 22:36-40).

One of the ways we show our love for God is by helping other people. All women have been given an opportunity to serve in areas where they are uniquely gifted, and singles are more free to do so than married women. God designed all women to be nurturers, teachers, and caregivers to the underprivileged and weak. The period of singleness is an ideal time to develop and use those God-given gifts and womanly characteristics before one is faced with the added responsibility of family. In 1 Corinthians, Paul suggested it is fine to remain single so you can devote your life to serving God. He wrote,

> I want you to be free from anxieties...And the unmarried or betrothed woman is anxious about the things of the Lord, how to be holy in body and spirit. But the married woman

is anxious about worldly things, how to please her husband.
I say this for your own benefit, not to lay any restraint upon
you [about marriage], but to promote good order and to
secure your undivided devotion to the Lord (1 Corinthians
7:32,34-35).

Your single state provides you more opportunity to find out where
you stand in relationship to God. When you make an effort to see your
circumstances from God's point of view, He will provide you with
opportunities to grow and mature in your identity as His child. If, by
God's grace, He wills that you marry, you can then carry this identity
into your new role as a wife, friend, companion, and mother.

The Dating Game

When we meet a new single man for the first time, we might quickly
wonder, *Is this the one?* Yet we want to be careful about how we view the
opposite sex—especially when it comes to dating. With that in mind,
let's look at what God has to say about this subject.

The Principles from Scripture

It is important to have friends of all kinds, including men, women,
and children of all ages. Companionship is one of God's good gifts to
mankind, for it is not good for man to be alone. Single women need
to begin, however, by thinking of all single male friends as brothers in
Christ instead of potential husbands—serving them as they would the
rest of the church family. The focal point that should draw us together
as friends, companions, and neighbors is Jesus Christ and His way for
life and godliness.

When it comes to dating, it is not wise to date a man who isn't saved
or is supposedly *almost* saved. This is often called "missionary dating."
Do not deceive yourself into believing your influence will bring an
unbeliever to Christ. The Word of God is very clear about those whom
we can consider as a potential mate: "Do not be bound together with
unbelievers; for what partnership have righteousness and lawlessness,
or what fellowship has light with darkness?" (2 Corinthians 6:14 NASB).
Instead, choose someone whose life shows that he loves God and that
he has a heart for serving and loving others.

Of course, we too need to have the same kind of evidence in our lives. As a sister in Christ, we should stand ready to encourage a man in a way that shows we are looking out for his purity and spiritual growth. Paul wrote,

> If there is any encouragement in Christ, if there is any consolation of love, if there is any fellowship of the Spirit, if any affection and compassion...Do nothing from selfishness or empty conceit, but with humility of mind regard one another as more important than yourselves; do not merely look out for your own personal interests, but also for the interests of others (Philippians 2:1,3-4 NASB).

God's principles will also guide you in making a judgment about how others view you. If you are dating someone who is unwilling to help protect your sexual purity, that is a clear indication this man is immature in his understanding of God's good purpose for friends in Christ. True love involves more than romantic feelings—it puts the needs of others above self (John 15:13; 1 Corinthians 13:4-7).

If the relationship begins to develop into a romantic possibility, based on mutual love and devotion first to God and then one another, continue to stay on guard. Check your motives and ask yourself hard questions such as these from pastor and author John Piper:

> Why is there marriage? Why does anything exist? Why do you exist? Why does sex exist? Why do earth and sun and moon and stars exist? Why do animals and plants and oceans and mountains and atoms and galaxies exist? The answer to all these questions, including the one about marriage, is: All of them exist to and for the glory of God—all things exist to magnify the truth and worth and beauty and greatness of God in people's minds toward [that] reality.[1]

Go ahead and enjoy friendships with men as brothers in Christ. And guard your heart against selfish motives and behavior.

The Perils of Internet Dating

Rapid advances in technology are changing the way that we view and respond to life. They have touched every aspect of our modern culture, including dating. Matchmaking Web sites promise to deliver the husband of our dreams. No longer is it a story of boy meets girl and they fall in love, but "You've got mail."

One common problem for Christian women is finding a suitable, eligible Christian man. It is not that they are not out there; rather, the issue is where can they be found? Dating services promise to solve this problem; however, it is important to understand that such a service cannot replace our church community. God provides the church family for the purpose of nurturing your spiritual growth, offering encouragement and godly counsel, and giving protection through teaching wisdom and right living.

The Internet has some very real dangers. It is impossible to know a person's motivation for getting onto a site, and to make sure what that person says is true. An Internet contact can lie about his identity, beliefs, and other things. The Internet can give false hope for a loving relationship. One young woman reported that online dating services gave her the hope she might find someone to marry. She went on to say, "When I was feeling lonely, I'd get online and write the whole country…You meet someone, you date, it doesn't work out, and then you go back and try again."[2]

The better option is to participate in activities within the context of a church family. One of the problems of cyberspace interaction is that *it robs us of time we could spend developing relationships with real people who are in need of our love and service.*

A Counterfeit Intimacy

There are some single women who desire the love and companionship of marriage and, out of their loneliness, substitute a counterfeit love based on sexual lust. Our society has taught us that it is fine to explore our sexual self, and that there is nothing wrong with having one physical relationship after another. But what does the Word of God have to say? The apostle Peter wrote,

> As children who are under obedience, don't shape your lives by
> the desires that you used to follow in your ignorance [before

you knew Christ and His Word]. Instead, as the One Who called you is holy, you yourselves must become holy in all your behavior (1 Peter 1:14-15).[3]

God made us sexual beings so we could enjoy a satisfying and intimate relationship *inside the bounds of marriage*. Remember, God said that what He created was very good. And He created sex for more than the obvious reasons of producing children and growing closer to a spouse. He also gave it so we can show love and give satisfaction to our spouse. When done unselfishly, within a marriage, physical intimacy is one of the best ways of deepening the emotional and spiritual relationship between husband and wife. God created sex as a self*less* act of love, not a self-*serving* one.

When single women indulge in sexual activity, they may experience a temporary closeness. But in the end, self-gratification does not deliver what it promises in terms of intimacy. Casual sex is never thought about or acted upon in a vacuum. It always hurts and defrauds you and your partner. In the beginning it gives false hope of commitment and a lasting relationship, only to later bring shame, guilt, regret, and disappointment. Single men and women have found this to be true whether they end their physical relationship or carry it on into a marriage.

The good news is that Jesus understands the temptations that we face, and has provided a way of escape. Paul wrote,

> No temptation has overtaken you that is not common to man. God is faithful, and he will not let you be tempted beyond your ability, but with the temptation he will also provide the way of escape, that you may be able to endure it (1 Corinthians 10:13).

The fourth chapter of the Gospel of John tells the story of Jesus' compassion toward a Samaritan woman who was living in consistent sexual sin. Jesus lovingly confronted her about her life of sin, including the five husbands she had had and the boyfriend she was living with. He offered her forgiveness that would cleanse her from her past sinful behavior. Thank God for such a loving Savior! If you have lived a life like that of the Samaritan woman's, there is great hope in Jesus

Christ. In Proverbs 28:13 we read, "Whoever conceals his transgressions will not prosper, but he who confesses and forsakes them will obtain mercy."

God Satisfies Your Deepest Longings

Loneliness in our lives is often translated as pain and suffering. We find ourselves pleading with God to take us out of our circumstances and give us the desires of our hearts—in this case, marriage. When we focus only on our own desires and do not acknowledge that God is working in us something greater than we can immediately see (2 Corinthians 4:16-18), then we can find ourselves pushing against God and His greater plan for us.

All women were created for a deep spiritual relationship with God that cannot be satisfied through marriage or children. That doesn't mean it's wrong to desire marriage—not at all. Marriage is a great blessing from God, and allows you to serve God by serving your spouse. Yet if your motivation is to cure your loneliness through marriage rather than through a loving relationship with God, your loneliness will follow you into marriage. If you are a daughter of Jesus Christ, your first desire must be for Him. When you desire something more than your relationship with Jesus Christ, that something is an idol. A relationship that is more important to you than your relationship with God will fail to bring you contentment or relieve your loneliness.

With God, whether you are single or married, your happiness will never have to depend on another human being. Jesus alone provides the strength and power to live a rich, productive, and purposeful life. That does not mean you will cease to struggle with loneliness—all people struggle—even married people. But your identity will never be tied to your role in life or to any one person. Rather, it will depend on your personal relationship with Jesus Christ. He is the only One who truly understands the pain of loneliness. He willingly laid down His life and faced the penalty of our disobedience—completely alone—so that you would never face the future without His presence.

Recommended Resources

Brownback, Lydia. *Fine China Is for Single Women Too*. Phillipsburg, NJ: Presbyterian & Reformed, 2003.

Elliot, Elisabeth. *The Path of Loneliness*. Grand Rapids: Revell, 2001.

————. *Passion and Purity*. Grand Rapids: Revell, 2002.

Farmer, Andrew. *The Rich Single Life*. Gaithersburg, MD: Sovereign Grace Ministries, 1998.

Harris, Joshua. *Boy Meets Girl: Say Hello to Courtship*. Sisters, OR: Multnomah, 2005.

————. *Not Even a Hint: Guarding Your Heart Against Lust*. Sisters, OR: Multnomah, 2003.

Mahaney, C.J. *Sex, Romance, and the Glory of God*. Wheaton, IL: Crossway, 2004.

McCulley, Carolyn. *Did I Kiss Marriage Goodbye?* Wheaton, IL: Crossway, 2004.

Piper, John and Justin Taylor, eds. *Sex and the Supremacy of Christ*. Wheaton, IL: Crossway, 2005.

Chapter 12

Way Beyond the Man of Your Dreams: Help for Single Moms

Lynn Denby

W hen Cherie finally made it into bed, she collapsed from exhaustion. She didn't know how she and her children would make it. This was all just too much. There were overdue bills, the bathroom sink was barely draining, the car engine check light had just turned on, her son wanted to join Little League, and her daughter needed new shoes for school.

How could she possibly be both mother and father for her children? What had happened to her dream of raising a family together with her husband? It had already been two years since the divorce, but she still was not coping much better than right after David announced he was leaving her for someone else. At times she was consumed by anger and resentment over being left to raise the kids alone. She just wanted some time for herself without all of this responsibility. Was that asking too much?

Gabrielle, too, struggled with being a single mom. She thought she and her boyfriend would be together forever, but they split up when the fighting got to be too much. She felt guilty for shuttling the girls between two homes and often felt envious when she saw what appeared to be happy couples together. The lives of others looked so much easier to her than her own.

Latoya, a successful career woman, purposely chose to become a single mother, but raising a child alone had proven to be more challenging than she had imagined. Between working full-time and caring for her son, she had little time to spend with friends or pursue her own interests, and she felt so lonely, starved for adult companionship.

Amber found herself in a situation she had never imagined. She and her husband had been happily married for 15 years when he was suddenly killed in a car accident. Her life was shattered. She was consumed by fear and worry as she tried to support her three children. How would she ever earn enough money and where would she find the time to give each child the attention they needed? She often found herself wallowing in self-pity as she trudged along facing what seemed like impossible demands on her.

Struggling Single Moms

Cherie, Gabrielle, Latoya, and Amber are all struggling. The feelings they wrestle with are feelings common to many women. Yet the fact they are all single mothers makes their struggles much harder. Whether by divorce, the death of a spouse, the break-up of a relationship, or by choice, single mothers face a difficult task. In the midst of raising their children, they may grapple with loneliness, guilt, grief, self-centeredness, anger, resentment, fear, worry, envy, and self-pity.

At times these emotional responses are God-given human reactions to life experiences. God made us to feel guilt when we break His law, to feel fear when our lives are in danger, and to feel righteous anger when we see evil. Grief and loneliness can also be normal responses to loss and isolation.

However, sometimes our sinful nature takes what God has given for our good and turns it into self-oriented, sinful responses. We can become angry and worried when we are not getting our way. We might feel guilt over shortcomings or wrong actions or struggle with envy when we see others getting what we want. These self-oriented, sinful responses, however, can be turned into the fruit of God's Spirit (joy, hope, peace, etc.) as we learn how to trust in God and change our thoughts, especially when we change what we think about God Himself.

You Are Not Alone

As a single mom, you need to know that you are not alone in your struggles. God is with you, ready to help, support, guide, strengthen, and encourage you. He wants to be, and can be for you, way beyond any "man of your dreams." God is faithful, loving, involved, and supportive of His children. God can be trusted to be with you and for you (Romans 8:31-39). But, as in any relationship, we can only trust someone to the point that we know them, so we need to get to know God better (2 Peter 3:18).

What Do You Really Know About God?

What people know about God most often comes from what they were taught as children or how God is portrayed in the media. You may wonder if God is even real if you've been taught all your life that God does not exist. You may have heard people describe God as a cosmic killjoy or a stern judge who is waiting for you to have fun or make a mistake so He can zap you. Or do you think of God as being disinterested, more like the way Morgan Freeman portrayed Him in the movie *Bruce Almighty*, wanting to take a break and leaving the universe in the hands of someone like Bruce?

Our human ability to comprehend God is limited (Isaiah 55:8-9). We must be careful to not create a "God of our own understanding," but instead to seek to know the true God as He is revealed to us in His Word, the Bible. While some qualities about God are visible in His physical creation (Romans 1:19-20), most of what we can know about God comes from the Bible. It is filled with descriptions about God. You might find yourself surprised by what the Bible has to say about who God is and what He is like.

God Is Knowable

God is knowable because He has chosen to stay involved with His creation (Acts 17:27-28). The Bible is the story of God reaching down to communicate to His creation the truth about Himself. In the Bible, we can learn about what God has done and about His character. This allows us to know Him, learn to trust Him, and live lives that please Him.

We learn about God and get to know Him as we read His Word and live by faith, trusting He will do and be what He has said. Our faith in God can only be as strong as what we know about the character of

God. The stronger our faith, the more we will experience God's peace, joy, and hope, as opposed to being ruled by sinful responses such as fear, anger, and envy. But before we look at specific character qualities found in God, it is important for us to understand how our thought patterns can affect us.

Why Does It Matter What We Think?

Our Thoughts Affect Our Feelings

What we think about greatly impacts what we do and how we feel. It is *not* our circumstances that lead to our feelings; it is what we are *thinking about* our circumstances that produces feelings. Perhaps that is a new thought for you. So again, what you *tell yourself* about your circumstances will determine *how you feel* about your circumstances. As you look at your circumstances through the lens of who God says He truly is, you will view them differently, and then begin to feel differently.

Feelings Are Not Facts

We frequently live as though our feelings are *facts*, but our feelings are *not* facts. It is possible for us to feel something that is based on a lie. For example, you may *feel* God could not possibly forgive you for some of the things you have done in your past. Yet that is a lie, because God's Word clearly tells us that when we confess our sin God is faithful to forgive us and to cleanse us from *all* sin (1 John 1:9). Because our thoughts influence our feelings and our feelings so often affect how we live, it is essential for us to make sure we are thinking only those things that are true (Philippians 4:8).

Changing Our Feelings

Our feelings can change when we change our thoughts. While it is natural for us to think about the people and events connected with our circumstances, thinking about our circumstances can often lead to negative emotions. Negative emotions produce confusion, indecision, panic, and bad decisions, and keep us from positive, God-centered emotions and attitudes such as peace, joy, contentment, and thankfulness.

Choose to Think About God

We must choose to turn away from negative thoughts and instead focus our thoughts on who God is and what He is doing in our lives. This may feel like a battle at times (Galatians 5:16-24), but we're not alone in this battle. We can ask God to help us change what we think about. The Bible tells us to "take every thought captive to obey Christ" (2 Corinthians 10:5). We are to "set [our] mind on things that are above, not on things that are on earth" (Colossians 3:2).

Right Thinking About God

With the help of the Spirit of God, we can turn wrong thinking and sinful responses into right thinking and the peace and joy we long for. As we think about God more than about our circumstances, we can grow in hope, encouragement, trust, and understanding. We can work at putting our focus onto the facts of God's presence, God's purposes, and God's person.

God's presence: As a single mom, you need to remember that you are not alone in your struggles. God is always with you. All that God is and all of His character qualities are always present with you. Remember, He wants to be and can be way beyond what any "man of your dreams" could offer.

God's purposes: Seek to remember God's purposes for your circumstances. God uses suffering and difficulties in your life to develop your character, to provide what you need, to mature and complete you, and to make you useful to others so you can bring honor to Him (Romans 5:1-5; 2 Corinthians 1:3-4; James 1:2-4; 1 Peter 1:3-9).

God's person: Think about what God is like. God is loving, involved, and supportive of His children. You can trust God to stay with you and care for you (Romans 8:31-39).

The more you know about God, the more you will want to follow Him, trust Him, choose His ways, and rest in Him, because you will see His love for you and His wisdom and power on your behalf. As you turn your thoughts to God by faith and obedience, you can rejoice in His presence, purposes, and person even in the midst of painful trials. You can begin to view your situation as a gift from God that allows you to learn more about yourself and about God than you would be able to do otherwise. This kind of faithful obedience is pleasing to God.

If you want to work at changing your thoughts about God and turning your self-oriented sinful responses into God-centered thoughts and actions, you will need to learn more about God from the Bible. Let's take a look at some of what the Bible says about God and how knowing more about God can make a difference in how you face your struggles as a single mom. Along the way, you'll find verse references that allow you to look in the Bible for yourself and see what it says about God.

How Knowing About God Can Help You

When Facing Loneliness

Raising children alone can consume all the time you have. The loneliness you feel may not come so much from a lack of having people around you, but rather a lack of close companionship with someone whom you can share your life with. You may feel isolated, unconnected, and invisible. When you struggle with loneliness, remember God is always with you, and He desires to have a close relationship with you.

REMEMBER GOD IS ALWAYS WITH YOU

God did not create this world and then leave us alone to fend for ourselves. He created us and has stayed close by. He is close enough to see you, hear you, and help you (Psalm 34). God is close enough to not only see what is going on around you, but to also "see" what is going on inside of you (Psalm 139:1-4).

You can count on God to stay close: "My father and my mother have forsaken me, but the LORD will take me in" (Psalm 27:10); and, "I will never leave you nor forsake you" (Hebrews 13:5). Before leaving His disciples here on earth, Jesus comforted them with these words: "Behold, I am with you always, to the end of the age" (Matthew 28:20).

REMEMBER GOD WANTS A CLOSE RELATIONSHIP WITH YOU

The Bible tells us that God is not only near to us, He has also made Himself accessible to us (John 14:23; Romans 5:1-2). The Old Testament speaks of us being able to dwell in His presence (Psalm 16:11;

23:6; 65:4). God has made it possible for us to have a relationship with Him through Christ (John 14:6; 1 Peter 3:18), and we can draw near to God with boldness (Hebrews 4:14-16).

In John 15, Jesus makes it clear He wants us to abide with Him or stay closely united with Him. When you find yourself feeling lonely, remember you are never alone, for God is always with you. The God of all creation wants to have a close relationship with you and give you all that He knows you need.

When Wrestling with Guilt

As a single mom, you may feel guilt over how you became a single mother, not having a father in the home for your children, or not having enough money or time. Whether you feel guilty because of wrong you have done or because you feel inadequate, remember that God is compassionate and forgiving, not wanting you to live overwhelmed with guilt.

REMEMBER GOD IS COMPASSIONATE AND MERCIFUL

God does not sit back and wait for you to mess up so He can pounce on you. God is described as being "rich in mercy" (Ephesians 2:4) and "compassionate and gracious" (Psalm 103:8). For God to be compassionate or merciful means that He feels concern for you and desires to help you in your difficulties, even if you might be to blame for some of the problems in your life.

Jesus illustrates the compassion of God in the story of the prodigal son. Despite all the wrong things the son had done, the father longingly waited and watched for the son, running out to greet him and celebrating when he returned (Luke 15:11-24). That God is compassionate means you can trust Him to stick with you and tenderly help you.

REMEMBER GOD IS FORGIVING

God, who is merciful, made possible our forgiveness through the life, death, and resurrection of His Son (Ephesians 2:4-7; Colossians 2:13-14; Titus 3:4-7). To *forgive* means to remove our sin from us. We are told about God's forgiveness in many places throughout the Bible, such as Psalm 86:5, 103:8-12, 130:3-4, and 1 John 1:9.

When you are wrestling with guilt, remember that it is God's forgiveness, and *only* God's forgiveness, that can take away your guilt. Go to God, confess your sin, and receive God's compassionate forgiveness. Then continue to remember He has mercifully forgiven you.

When Working Through Grief

Single mothers frequently deal with the death of a dream—the dream of raising their children with their father. If this is true for you, when you are working through grief, remember that God is your loving, faithful comforter.

Remember God Is Loving

We are told in the Bible that "God is love" (1 John 4:8). *Loving* is not something God *does*, but is something God *is*. The Bible tells us that God loves His children (1 John 3:1; 4:16). This great love God has for you is a constant and enduring kind of love—nothing can separate you from Him (Romans 8:31-39).

God took the initiative to love you when you were unlovable (Romans 5:8). His greatest act of love for you was when He sent His Son to pay the penalty for your sin (John 3:16; 1 John 4:9-10). God's love draws you to Him (Jeremiah 31:3), and it is His love that is the basis for everything that He does for you (Romans 8:31-32).

Remember God Is Faithful

God is a faithful God (Deuteronomy 7:9; 1 Corinthians 10:13; 2 Timothy 2:13). To be *faithful* means that God is dependable, reliable, and trustworthy. God never changes (Malachi 3:6; Hebrews 13:8; James 1:17), and God never lies (Numbers 23:19; Titus 1:2). If God has said it, He will do it. You can absolutely count on Him.

Remember God Is Your Comforter

The Bible declares God to be the "God of all comfort" (2 Corinthians 1:3). It also describes God as comforting His children like a mother (Isaiah 66:13) and a shepherd (Psalm 23; Isaiah 40:11). God can comfort you in your pain and sadness because His Son, Jesus, can "sympathize with [your] weaknesses." He's intimately acquainted with all your sorrows because He lived as a man on earth for over 30 years and experienced sorrows Himself (Hebrews 4:14-16).

When you are working through grief over the losses in your life, remember to turn to God for His loving, faithful comfort. While the people and circumstances of your life may be unreliable and continually changing, God is not. You can depend on Him to stay with you and help you. He will follow through and do what He has said in His Word. You may feel great sorrow, but God is with you to soothe your pain and give you the courage and strength you need to face your trials.

When Battling Self-centeredness

The inherent self-centeredness of our own hearts is encouraged by our culture, which tells us to put ourselves first. But God did not create us to be the center of our own lives. When battling with self-centeredness, remember that God is our Creator and worthy of our worship.

REMEMBER GOD IS YOUR CREATOR

Your thoughts about God must begin at the beginning. The first words in the Bible are, "In the beginning, God created…" (Genesis 1:1). God is your Creator, and you are His creation: "Know that the LORD, he is God! It is he who made us, and we are his; we are his people" (Psalm 100:3).

As Creator, God is to be the center, the focal point of everything in our lives. As Romans 11:36 says, "From him and through him and to him are all things. To him be glory forever. Amen." Recognizing God as your Creator will change how you live. The world and your life are not random happenings but instead have purpose—*His* purpose (Isaiah 43:7; Ephesians 2:10). Seek out what God says in the Bible about how you are to live as His creation.

REMEMBER GOD IS WORTHY OF YOUR WORSHIP

Being our Creator makes God the one most worthy of our worship. To be *worthy* is to have value. The Creator, by nature, has more value than His creation. God's value is demonstrated to us by all He does on our behalf (Psalm 18:1-3). This seems so obvious, yet we do not readily live out these truths.

We most often live self-centeredly, as though *we* are the creators of our own lives, and that our lives are *for us* and for *our* purposes and desires. Yet such self-centeredness is *self*-worship. God tells us plainly why He created us: for His glory (Isaiah 43:7; 1 Corinthians 10:31). To *give glory* to God is to give God the attention, respect, adoration, and devotion He so deserves.

When you are battling self-centeredness, remember that your life is not about you, or what you want, need, or think you deserve. Your life, as the creature, is to worship your Creator. Psalm 95:6 calls you to worship "the LORD, [your] Maker." Only when you turn first to worship and honor God as your worthy Creator will you be able to turn away from a self-oriented life.

When Filled with Anger and Resentment

You may feel anger and resentment toward your children's father, toward your children, or toward others who are not giving you the help you so desperately need. When filled with anger and resentment, remember that God is in control of everything in this world and He is good.

REMEMBER GOD IS IN CONTROL

As the Creator, God is the sovereign ruler over all things (Psalm 103:19; Daniel 4:17). What happens in your life does not happen by chance. No one is able to surprise God or in any way mess up His perfect plans for your life (Job 42:1-2; Proverbs 16:4,9). In the Bible, we see how God is in control of all that happens—even in the worst circumstances. For example, Joseph was sold into slavery by his brothers. Then he ended up in prison. After years of adversity, God then raised up Joseph as a ruler under the Pharaoh of Egypt. This made it possible for Joseph to help his people when famine struck the Middle East. Joseph recognized that while his brothers had meant him harm, God was in control and had directed the painful circumstances in his life in order to work out His purposes (Genesis 50:20).

REMEMBER GOD IS GOOD

This God who is in control over everything is also good (Psalm 86:5;

100:5). It is not at all in His character to harm us. You can know that His involvement in your life is for your benefit even when you cannot understand what He is doing.

When you feel angry and resentful over what is happening to you, or when you are not getting your way, remember that God, who is good, is in control. No situation or person (not even your ex!) can interfere with God's good plans for you (Ephesians 1:3-12). Though you might not get your way, you can be assured that God is getting *His* way. You can take comfort by remembering "that for those who love God all things work together for good" and that God's best good for us is that we would become more like His Son (Romans 8:28-29).

When Overcome by Fear and Worry

Whether from real threats or from what you think might or could happen, fears and worry can overwhelm you as a single mom. You can fear for your children's safety or worry about how you will pay all of the bills. When you are fearful and worried, remember that God is your powerful protector.

REMEMBER GOD IS POWERFUL

God rules over His creation by His great power (2 Chronicles 20:6; Psalm 66:7). He has the power to accomplish whatever He wills (Jeremiah 32:27; Matthew 19:26). He demonstrated His power when He created the world (Jeremiah 10:12; 27:5) and when He raised Jesus from the dead (Ephesians 1:19-20).

REMEMBER GOD IS YOUR PROTECTOR

In the Bible, God is described as our fortress and our refuge (Psalm 18:2; 91:2). A *fortress* is a military structure used for protection and defense against enemies. A *refuge* is a shelter of safety away from danger. Psalm 46 tells us that because God is our refuge and helper, we need not be afraid (verses 1-3).

When you are overcome by fear and worry, think about the power God used to create the universe. Then remember that He will use that power to do whatever He knows is right and good for you. Turn to God as your place of protection and safety from whatever causes your fears.

When Struggling with Envy and Self-pity

Life is difficult. The extra challenges you face as a single mom can make life even tougher. It may seem like others around you are enjoying a much easier life, and you may find yourself struggling with envy and self-pity.

Envy is feeling deprived when you see others having what you feel you deserve to have yourself. Envy can easily lead to fault-finding, discontentment, rivalry, and hatred. When filled with envy, our eyes are blinded to all that we *do* have, and we can only see what we are lacking. We also focus only on those who have more than we do, rather than those who have less.

To feel *self-pity* is to indulge in thoughts about how terrible your life is and about how unique and alone you are in your suffering. Self-pity asks, "Why me? Why this? Why now?" It comes out of a heart that is self-centered and ungrateful. When you find yourself simmering in envy and self-pity, remember that God is your just and wise provider.

REMEMBER GOD IS JUST

God is fair and does not play favorites (Deuteronomy 32:4; Daniel 4:37). God does not judge by appearance or by personal preferences (Deuteronomy 10:17-18; Ephesians 6:9). When you find yourself thinking, *This is not fair!* remember that God truly *is* fair—although He only treats us kindly because He was unfair to His Son. What may appear as unfair to you is part of God's purpose. Remember what Isaiah 55:8-9 tells about God: His thoughts and ways are not like our thoughts and ways.

REMEMBER GOD IS WISE

Our wise God (Job 9:4) knows everything (Job 37:16). God knows all things because He *created* all (Job 38–41), He *is everywhere* (Psalm 139:7-10), and He *sees* all (Psalm 33:13-15; Proverbs 15:3). There is nothing hidden from God; nothing is in the dark to Him (Psalm 139:11-12; Hebrews 4:13).

REMEMBER GOD IS YOUR PROVIDER

Scripture paints the picture for us of God as our tender, sufficient provider: "The LORD is my Shepherd; I shall not want" (Psalm 23:1). God alone is the source of all we need because He is the source of all life. God is generous in His provision. We are told that He "graciously gives us all things" (Romans 8:32). Jesus came so we could "have life and have it abundantly" (John 10:10). God is "able to do far more abundantly than all that we ask or think" (Ephesians 3:20).

When you are struggling with envy and self-pity, remember that God *knows* what you need, *can* provide what you need, and *will* provide what you need because of His wisdom, power, and love for you. When you are feeling left out or you must do without what others have, remember that God is wise and knows even better than you what you truly need, and He does not play favorites. He is not keeping back from you what you need to live joyfully before Him. When you struggle with envy and self-pity, think about how God is at work in ways you cannot see. When you cooperate with Him, God will use the trials and struggles in your life to provide for you in ways beyond what you can imagine (2 Corinthians 9:8; Ephesians 3:20).

Growing Closer to God

There is great hope for single mothers like Cherie, Gabrielle, Latoya, Amber, and you. God wants to come alongside you and be the primary relationship in your life. God is your compassionate forgiver, your loving and faithful comforter, your good ruler, your powerful protector, and your just and wise provider. He's way beyond "the man of your dreams," isn't He?

Here are some suggestions for using your thoughts about God to turn your self-oriented responses into God-pleasing fruit of His Spirit:

- *Pray* and ask God to help you change your thoughts.

- *Mark* your Bible whenever you read something about God's character.

- *Study* the character qualities of God, beginning with the verses in this chapter.

- *Keep* a list of the qualities of God and write down the verses for those qualities.

- *Carry* an index card with you that lists specific qualities of God that are relevant to your present situation.

- *Memorize* verses about key qualities of God.

- *Remember* that your feelings are *not* facts.

- *Say* the qualities of God out loud when you find your thoughts focusing on your circumstances instead of on God. For example: "God, I know that You are good and that nothing that is happening to me is meant to harm me." Or, "God, You are powerful. You are forgiving." Or, "Thank You, God, that You are compassionate. Thank You, God, for being right here with me in this situation."

- *Sing* worship songs about the character of God.

- *Meet* regularly with other Christians for worship and Bible study.

Recommended Resources

Bridges, Jerry. *Trusting God: Even When Life Hurts.* Colorado Springs: NavPress, 1988.

George, Elizabeth. *Loving God with All Your Mind,* 2d ed. Eugene, OR: Harvest House, 2005.

MacArthur, John. *Our Awesome God.* Wheaton, IL: Crossway, 1993.

Pink, Arthur W. *The Attributes of God.* Grand Rapids: Baker, 2004.

Tozer, A.W. *The Knowledge of the Holy.* New York: HarperCollins, 1961.

Chapter 13

DOES ANYONE HEAR ME?
FACING LONELINESS IN MARRIAGE

§ Venessa Ellen §

It is Christmas Day, 2008. The jarring sound of the alarm clock jolted me awake. It was supposed to be raining and very cold, a miserable day, but as I awoke and stepped outside to get the newspaper, I saw hints of blue peeking through the clouds. I immediately knew that the weather reporter had gotten it wrong again. Just another thing in this life that had not turned out the way I thought it would. Just like my marriage. Indeed, it was cold, but the rain had stopped and the clouds looked thin and nonthreatening.

Somehow I knew the first order of the day should be to go back inside, open my Bible, and see what the Lord had to share with me this morning. As I walked on the hardwood floors and headed for the study, the sound of my bare feet echoing step after step was deafening. Or was it really just the loneliness in my heart? The bitter words of the argument from the night before were weighing me down—the emptiness I felt was more than I thought I could bear.

My Bible would have to wait a little longer; the thunderstorm of tears would not allow my eyes to see the words on the page, and the disappointment in my heart and the loneliness of my soul would not allow me to comprehend God's message for me this morning. Jeff had stormed out of the house. Would he ever come back? And if he did, would I continue to feel so alone?

I had always thought that my marriage would be joyful and sweet. But this was something different. Of course I had expected times of discord, disappointment, hurts, and pains. But this had gotten so bad that I was tempted to throw in the towel. There are few things more difficult than being married and feeling the brutal pain of loneliness, especially when arguments end with a spouse storming out of the house or threatening to leave.

I imagine you're reading this chapter because, if you allowed yourself to be honest, you would have to admit that although you put on a happy face your heart is hurting and you feel as though you may suffocate from the loneliness that grips you and threatens to take your breath away. Some couples choose to stay together in a relationship that feels lonely because of the children, for appearance's sake, or possibly to avoid change. Thus, you live under the same roof, you sleep in the same bed, you even eat at the same table as your spouse; yet in reality, you and your husband are merely roommates. Even when he is home, you still feel alone and often wonder to yourself about God's purpose in marriage. Know this: There is hope for you, there is an answer. There is a way to live happily even after your wedding day despite the circumstances or feelings that cause you to have a lonely heart.[1]

I, too, understand the terror of a lonely heart. There was a season of loneliness in the early days of my marriage. Many nights of heartache would come flooding back to my memory when I would find that I had again awakened with a watery, tear-stained pillow after falling asleep with thoughts of another argument on my mind. One day, I found myself at the crossroad—you know the crossroad of which I speak—the place where you decide whether you should go on or give up. Maybe you are approaching this same crossroad and feel like you absolutely have to make a decision about your marriage. But before you consider thoughts about leaving your marriage, please continue reading. As a woman once said to me, when you get to the end of your rope, tie a knot and hang on. My hope for you is that what you read over the next few pages will inspire you to go on. Journey with me for just a moment; seek to open your mind to the possibility that there just might be hope for your situation after all.

What Is Loneliness?

June Hunt, in an article on loneliness, writes that it is "the state of sadness that comes from feeling alone, isolated or cut off from others."[2] Although we may define loneliness in different ways, most often women describe loneliness in terms of their unique feelings. The description of loneliness varies from person to person. One woman's description of her feelings may differ greatly from those of the woman sitting next to her. You may not agree with either description because they don't sound like your situation at all. One resource describes loneliness as

> a feeling of emptiness in the pit of your stomach when some-one you love has deserted you and you feel no one really cares anymore. You feel unwanted or unneeded…as if you are all by yourself, though people surround you. You may experience loneliness and feel isolated even in the midst of a crowd.[3]

Though descriptions of loneliness vary, the feelings are very real. The reason for the differences in our experience of loneliness is that our thoughts and actions vary in response to the many difficulties we face.

Some women experience loneliness because their husband has left them. Or perhaps their husband is still in the home, but has deserted their wife for the television, sports, or even pornography. Maybe the husband has even had affairs. When a wife is faced by such circumstances, she will not only feel lonely, she'll feel inadequate. She'll be tempted to assume that if she could just make herself more attractive to her husband, she wouldn't feel so alone. The problem, however, is that a wife's personal beauty or attractiveness will not guarantee that her husband will not give in to sin, ignore her, or shut her out of his life. Husbands and wives are both responsible for their own choices, no matter what their circumstances.

Why Do I Feel So Lonely?

All of us have the ability to make choices, whether good or bad. Just as some husbands choose to violate their commitment to their marital vow, some women choose to give in to loneliness and despair. And sometimes there's more to our loneliness than we initially realize. If we take time to examine the reason for our loneliness, we might come to see the problem is deeper than we thought. Our assumptions about the source of our lonely feelings might not be accurate.

Sometimes we feel lonely because we believe that happiness comes from obtaining what we think we need. If we believe that all we need ultimately comes from our husband, we will feel let down, unhappy, and lonely when he doesn't measure up. If your joy and contentment depends on the thoughts, words, and actions of your husband, then there is a sense in which your husband has become the god of your life. You're expecting him to be your savior, to be the source and reason for your very life. Of course the truth is that he is but a mere man, unable to truly fulfill your desires. Even if your husband is willing to do all he can to please and satisfy every void in your life, he will fail in this pursuit. There is only one person that can do that, and His name is Jesus Christ.

Why Am I So Unhappy?

Where do you think happiness comes from? Often we are unhappy because our husband makes decisions that we feel are not wise or because he does not give us what we want. When we cannot obtain what we think will make us happy, a sense of emptiness and sadness can fill our hearts. These feelings of loneliness should act as the "check engine" light of our soul; they should warn us of dangerous attitudes or responses that may lurk in our hearts: selfishness, bitterness, or idolatry.

As you evaluate your feelings and thoughts of loneliness, perhaps you will began to discover that the root of the problem is selfishness. Of course, I am not saying that wanting a good marriage; a faithful, kind and gentle husband; and marital fulfillment is wrong. But the idea that these things will satisfy you at your deepest level, to the extent that you will never feel lonely again, is a fallacy. Even the best husband cannot fulfill all of a woman's hopes and dreams. God never designed for that to happen. Your husband is not meant to be your Savior. He's there to help you grow in Christlikeness and to teach you about Christ's love for His bride, the church. But he cannot bring you complete fulfillment. To expect him to do so is idolatry because you are expecting him to do what only God can do.

Here is a checklist of ideas for fighting your feelings of loneliness. Mark those that seem most pertinent to you, then ask the Lord to grant you the grace to understand how you should respond.

✓ Your feelings of loneliness may stem from your faulty analysis of your marriage or your husband. Are you expecting something of him that only the Lord can supply?

✓ Your feelings of loneliness may begin to decrease if you focus more on loving your husband and less on getting what you want from him. What concrete action could you take today that would demonstrate an attitude of Christlike service?

✓ You may be physically alone but that does not automatically mean you have to feel lonely. Although your husband may spend all of his time on the computer, on the golf course, or in front of the television, you don't have to feel lonely. You can continually remind yourself of the Spirit's presence in your life and you can reach out to others who may need comfort.

✓ You need to manage your loneliness carefully because your feelings can open the door to sinful temptations such as adulterous relationships. Have you talked with your husband about your loneliness? If he is not interested, have you confessed your problems to a mature, godly woman who can hold you accountable?

✓ When you reduce your life to always having what you want, what you think you need, or what you believe is right, you are sure to feel lonely because your life has become all about you. Have you asked your husband how you might serve him or suggested ways that you two can spend time together? Have you willingly laid down all your expectations and demands at the foot of the cross and found Christ's joy there?

Late afternoon, Christmas Day 2008
I sit here now completely numb, wondering how in the world the devil could have stolen so much on a day like today. I still can't believe it. But my mind is racing ahead and I'm thinking about tomorrow. Will he call me? He is the most stubborn, proud man I have ever known. It could be days before we talk about this. I am the Christian in this marriage and I

certainly played into Satan's hands. I let my anger run away with me. My thoughts range from refusing to let him come back home until he gets counseling to worrying about him not coming home at all. I think about how my father walked out on us and wonder what is it about me that drives people away. I feel so alone. No one understands me…I wonder if anyone will ever love me.

Your Relationship with Your Husband, Your Relationship with God

In the Bible we find hope and an explanation for our loneliness. King Solomon wrote that two are better than one (Ecclesiastes 4:9), but long before Solomon addressed the issue, God had already set a plan in motion. In the beginning God created the heavens and the earth (Genesis 1:1); then He created man (Genesis 1:26). Man entered into a love relationship with God that was perfect and good. God saw that there was no one for Adam to relate with on earth, so there was a sense in which Adam was alone. God Himself decided that Adam's aloneness was not good—Adam did not come to that conclusion. Adam was the only being like him in all creation, but he was not lonely because of his relationship with God. "Adam had no human person-to-person relationships, so God made a 'companion who [would] help him' (Genesis 2:18), one who was nearly a mirror image of him. God created a woman to be his companion created from Adam's side. Adam and the woman became husband and wife, in a wedding performed by God himself."[4]

On my wedding day the minister stood before our guests, inhaled deeply, then exhaled, and began by saying that there would be no wedding. Guests squirmed in their seats, and several family members looked anxious as tension quickly formed in the air. After achieving this desired effect, the minister continued, "There can be no wedding between two people unless there is a marriage between three." You see, a marriage includes a relationship between the husband and the wife as well as a relationship between God and the husband and God and the wife. All too often a woman has expectations in marriage that her husband cannot meet—certain expectations only God can fulfill. Continually expecting your husband to fulfill desires that only God can fulfill will spark the embers of loneliness and fuel the fires of disappointment.

The Prerequisite to Fulfillment

You must have a love relationship with Christ before you can hope to have a fulfilling relationship with your husband. Without the vertical relationship with Christ, virtually every horizontal relationship you develop, including your marriage relationship, will leave you feeling lonely and wanting much more than any husband could ever supply. Only Jesus can give us the ability, wisdom, and skill to love the unlovable. Only Jesus can enable us to love the selfish, self-centered, and enslaved because that's what He does. Only He can enable us to see the good when our perceptions see only what is bad and difficult. You cannot treat your husband properly without the love of God flowing through your heart. That means you must place your trust in Jesus Christ, the one and only living God (1 John 3:16).

But even having this kind of relationship with Jesus Christ will not guarantee that you will never feel rejected or lonely in this life. The reality is that some husbands will leave their wives, physically or emotionally. Others will forsake their marital vows for moments of pleasure with pornography or other women. By contrast, God will never leave or forsake you (Hebrews 13:5-6). His marriage vow will comfort and keep you even when your husband hasn't fulfilled his. Without Christ, not only is marriage difficult, but life itself becomes one tedious trial after another that offers little peace and even less hope of improvement. With Christ as your bridegroom, your life can become an adventure of faith, and even a lonely and difficult marriage can turn into a fulfilling relationship.

If Your Husband Is an Unbeliever

Marriage is precious in the sight of God. Within the context of marriage, a woman can find companionship and an intimate partnership that can last for a lifetime. But when a husband has not trusted Christ as his Savior, that can make a marriage relationship more difficult. In such a situation, the Christian wife will yearn for what the Bible says is to take place between a husband and wife, but the reality of her marital experience will be quite different. In the Bible, the apostle Peter talked about how a wife should act toward her husband even if her husband does not act toward her as he should (1 Peter 3:1).

Placing biblical expectations on an unbelieving spouse is as unwise as playing in the middle of a busy street. Sooner or later you will get hit with such disappointment and disillusionment that it could severely test not only the relationship but also your faith.

So, whether you're married to a believer or an unbeliever you can continue to seek to glorify and please God and serve your husband whether or not he responds in godliness, faith, or gentleness (2 Corinthians 5:9; 10:5; Philippians 4:8; Colossians 3:2). Many women struggle with loneliness because their husbands fail to help them or care about their needs. As long as you are focused on what you want, you will remain discouraged and lonely. So, rather than thinking about how your husband should serve you, follow in the footsteps of your Savior and seek ways to serve him.

In addition, many women desire an open and honest relationship with their spouse but are not willing to confess the ways they have failed in the marriage. Although it seems counterintuitive, confessing your shortcomings may actually open up a door of communication with your husband. As you begin to understand God's plan for your marriage you'll be more able to love and serve the Lord and others with joy, rather than continuously remembering all the ways your husband has let you down. Realize that God's plan for marriage is not simply to make you happy. It's to make you holy and wean your heart away from all those things you think you need aside from Him.

July 4, 2010

As I walked around with my coffee cup in hand, I began to think back to that horrid day when my husband and I fought and he threatened to leave. What had started the argument? I had wanted a specific gift from him for my birthday, and he had forgotten. Even though he had always been faithful to remember my birthday, that was never enough for me because I thought I needed signs of his love more than anything else. What could I have been thinking? I had forgotten that the Lord had given me the most beautiful sign of His love—a sign I could never deserve and one that fills my heart with gratitude. It turns out that I didn't really need that gift from my husband because I had been given the gift of Calvary—the most beautiful sign of all. Things are well now. The orange sunset fills the sky, the smell of B-B-Q still lingers in the air. "Father, I thank You for Your provisions of food, clothing, and shelter. And most of all I thank You for giving me the strength to trust You and the knowledge that I will never be alone because You are always with me."

Emotions are ever changing, and husbands and wives inevitably have ups and downs, but the Lord is ever *unchanging* and *always* with us (Malachi 3:6; Hebrews 13:8). God may not solve all our problems the way we anticipate, but He will give us peace in the midst of our situation, peace that we cannot get from having a good marriage. It comes only from God. His peace will surpass our understanding and will shine a new light on our situation (Philippians 4:6-7).

God Understands Loneliness

Know this: No matter how you define or describe your feelings of loneliness, the true and living God—the God who sent His one and only Son to die a very painful death on a scornful cross just so that you would never be alone again—knows what you feel.

When I accepted God's plan for marriage, I stopped expecting something from my husband that was only available from God. I decided to love my husband unconditionally and believe that my marriage was greater than our arguments despite the disappointments, hurts, and pains. This decision was not devoid of the feelings of loneliness from which I struggled to free myself, but rather, it was based on the love and commitment that had to come out of the very depth of my soul. I decided to press on despite what I was feeling.

You, too, can press on regardless of the many fires that are fueling your feelings of loneliness. Yes, it is possible to do what seems most impossible—to go on. I will never forget that I was a sinner in need of a Savior. I would never have turned from a life of sinful pleasures and selfish agendas to follow a Holy God if He had not first loved me and saved me from sin bringing me into a right relationship with Him and a life that I could not have dreamed. I am now free to serve God and love others. I am now committed to a thankful attitude toward trials and tribulations that arise in my marriage.

We should not feel lonely, but when we do, we can fight against our feelings by cultivating a grateful heart (1 Thessalonians 5:18). By deliberately focusing on the many precious blessings and promises we have because of our inheritance in God's kingdom, we strengthen the vertical perspective of our relationship and that will drive away doubt and fear. When we seek Him first, His promise to provide all that we need can become a reality (Matthew 6:33), but it begins when we cultivate that all-essential vertical relationship. When seeking God becomes an earnest pursuit, then gratitude for what He has done, is doing, and will do will fill your heart to overflowing. You do not have to trust me on that, dear sister—it is written in His Word. It is His promise to you.

Recommended Resources

Burroughs, Jeremiah. *The Rare Jewel of Christian Contentment*. Mulberry, IN: Sovereign Grace, 2001.

DeMoss, Nancy Leigh. *Lies Women Believe*. Chicago: Moody, 2002.

Ellen, Nicolas. *Happy Even After: Biblical Guidelines for a Successful Marriage*. Mustang, OK: Dare 2 Dream, 2007.

———. *With All Your Heart: Identifying and Dealing with Idolatrous Lusts*. Mustang, OK: Dare 2 Dream, 2008.

Fitzpatrick, Elyse. *Helper by Design: God's Perfect Plan for Women in Marriage*. Chicago: Moody, 2003.

Hunt, June. *Loneliness: How to Be Alone but Not Lonely*. Dallas, TX: Hope for the Heart, 2005.

Mahaney, C.J. *How Can I Change: Victory in the Struggle Against Sin*. Gaithersburg, MD: People of Destiny International, 1993.

Wiersbe, Warren W. *Lonely People*. Grand Rapids: Baker, 2002.

Chapter 14

Healing for Hidden Wounds from Verbal Abuse

§ *Debra Gentry* §

Many of us, when we were children, can remember a chant we would give in response to others who picked on us or called us names: "Sticks and stones may break my bones, but words will never hurt me." But even as children we knew this chant was not true.

In reality, words do hurt and the pain they cause can be intense. As adults we also experience words that hurt and leave wounds and scars in our lives. These wounds and scars are mostly unseen by others and many times hurled at us by those who are close to us. We find ourselves in relationships characterized by anger, hateful words, manipulation, blaming, slander, name-calling, harshness, mockery, and criticism. Society labels this behavior as abusive when it becomes habitual, destructive, and controlling. The Bible condemns such behavior as sin. We are commanded to "let no corrupting talk come out of [our] mouths" (Ephesians 4:29). Verbal abuse is unwholesome, nasty, harmful, controlling, and destructive words spoken repeatedly in order to exert power over another person.

As common as verbal abuse is, many people are unsure whether they are being verbally abused. Perhaps you can relate to this story about someone we'll call Brenda. On the outside, Brenda and Tom's marriage seems perfect. Tom is successful in his job and they live in a nice neighborhood. The couple has three beautiful children and is involved in the local church and community. In public, Tom is attentive and loving to

Brenda, but inside their home—behind closed doors—Brenda walks on eggshells.

It wasn't always this way in their marriage, but over the last several years, Tom has become increasingly angry and sarcastic. Brenda does not know what to expect from Tom when he comes home from work. One day everything will be fine, and she has done everything right. The next day, Tom will be irrationally mad at her for everything. Many nights he follows her around the house, cursing her and saying hurtful things. It is at these times that Tom attacks Brenda personally. He makes fun of her appearance and tells her she is fat.

She works all day on the house to have it clean and organized like he wants it, only to have him find fault with it. He demands the reason for her not doing the errand he had asked her to do. When Brenda tries to explain that she does not remember him telling her about the errand, he questions her intelligence. Brenda then begins to wonder if Tom is right and if she is losing her mind.

Their conversations keep her feeling off balance. She is uncertain of exactly what she has said that was wrong and has set Tom off. She constantly reviews their conversations in her mind, trying to understand what she is doing wrong. When Brenda tries to talk to Tom about their relationship, he acts surprised that she would think something is wrong with their marriage. He acts hurt and tells Brenda that he is trying to be a good husband and provider. Brenda then becomes convinced that the problem is with *her* attitude and expectations. Brenda hopes that their relationship will improve—once she can understand Tom and he can understand her.

Lately, Brenda has been feeling increasingly discouraged and miserable. She wants relief from her misery and unhappy marriage but does not know what to do. She considers divorce but does not know how she could support herself financially. She also fears for the children's well-being if there is a divorce. Brenda believes she cannot go on much longer without help for her marriage. She needs to know how to respond to Tom.

Can you relate to Brenda? Perhaps your story involves a relationship that is characterized by control. At first, you think that someone taking control of your time, friends, and daily activities is a sign of caring and wanting the best for you. However, as time goes by, you begin to feel as if you have absolutely no control over your own life. You are not allowed to have your own opinions or experiences. You are told that if you would just obey your husband, your life together would be happy. You are constantly feeling worthless and powerless.

So what do you do if you find yourself in a relationship that can be described as verbally abusive or controlling? The first response is usually to ignore or pretend that it isn't happening, try harder to please, or resign yourself to the abuse. You may enjoy having someone to depend upon and love you. Perhaps you find yourself tired, hopeless, feeling trapped, miserable, and desperate for help from someone who can understand your situation. Proverbs 18:14 states, "A man's spirit will endure sickness, but a crushed spirit who can bear?"

The Bible offers help and hope through the person of Jesus Christ, as well as responses that can guide you through the turbulent waters of a verbally abusive relationship. The first and most important response a person in such a situation can make is to God's offer of salvation through Jesus Christ.

Respond to God's Offer of Hope

While God never intended for people to use hurtful words and treat one another in such cruel ways, the world in which we live, as well as each person's heart, is corrupted by sin. Even Jesus Christ, while He was on the earth, had to deal with those who hurled insults and cruel remarks at Him. The religious leaders of that day slandered Him and plotted against Him. The common people treated Him with respect one moment and disdain the next. The government belittled and blamed Him for crimes He did not commit. The soldiers mocked Him unmercifully—"they came up to him, saying, 'Hail, King of the Jews!' and struck him with their hands" (John 19:3). The prophet Isaiah described Jesus as one who "was despised and rejected by men; a man of sorrows, and acquainted with grief" (Isaiah 53:3). Jesus willingly took the anger, abuse, and wounds so that He could provide a way for us to have hope in this sinful world.

God loves us so much that He sent His Son to earth to die for us on the cross. Though God knew the pain and agony Jesus would endure on our behalf, He sent Jesus to provide a way of salvation for those who would believe in Him and receive new life and hope. "God so loved the world, that he gave his only Son, that whoever believes in him should not perish but have eternal life" (John 3:16). God looked at the world and saw the sin in people's hearts that prevented a relationship with Him (Romans 3:23). In love, He provided a way for us to be forgiven of our sins. The penalty for our sins is death (Romans 6:23). The wonderful news is that Jesus lived a sinless life and died on a cross as a substitute for those who would believe in Him. He took the punishment for our sins. This means God accepted Jesus' payment on our behalf; and now it is as if we have never sinned and we have always obeyed God. In order to receive this free gift, we must personally respond in faith to Jesus Christ. The Bible gives us the words of Jesus:

> Come to me, all who labor and are heavy laden, and I will give you rest. Take my yoke upon you, and learn from me, for I am gentle and lowly in heart, and you will find rest for your souls. For my yoke is easy, and my burden is light (Matthew 11:28-30).

Jesus is saying these words to *you* personally. He asks you to admit that you are a sinner who has disobeyed God's laws, and then trust in Him for forgiveness of your sins. This requires a deep sorrow for your personal disobedience to God and a sincere commitment to turn from sin and now live your life in obedience to Christ, which is true repentance. When you come to Jesus in repentance and faith, He promises forgiveness of your sins and eternal life.

After Christ died on the cross, He rose again in three days. He showed Himself to many people before ascending back into heaven, where He lives today. Christ's victory over death gives you, as a believer, all the spiritual resources you need to live the Christian life (Ephesians 1:3). When you realize all that Christ has done for you, a deep joy and love motivates you to respond to circumstances in your life in a way that imitates Christ and pleases Him.

As a Christian, the love of Christ controls you. The apostle Paul, a leader in the early church, wrote, "Because we have concluded this: that one has died for all, therefore all have died; and he died for all, that those who live might no longer live for themselves but for him who for their sake died and was raised" (2 Corinthians 5:14-15).

As a Christian, with Christ living in you, you can learn to respond biblically as Christ did when verbal abuse comes your way (Philippians 4:13).

Respond by Sharing Your Situation

When it comes to responding to verbal abuse, first it is very important that you are involved in a local church where you can share about your situation with a trusted counselor or pastor. Perhaps you feel ashamed and you are isolating yourself from sources of support because you don't want others to know what is going on. You may also want to prevent others from thinking negatively about your abuser. Yet God tells us to "bear one another's burdens" (Galatians 6:2). God knows that we all need help when it comes to enduring the trials that come into our lives. You need the support of your church to help you and help the abuser change his behavior.

God has given instructions in Matthew 18:15-17 for situations in which the abuser is part of a church. The ultimate purpose of the process of church discipline is not to punish the offender, but to restore him to Christlike behavior. In situations where the abuser is not a Christian, the wife can still turn to her church for help, seeking encouragement and counsel on how to respond to her husband. She has the promise in 1 Peter 3:1-2 that even if her husband fails to hear the gospel through her or the church, he can see the gospel lived out through her responsive and godly service to him.

Respond with Prayer

One of the most important things you must learn is to run quickly to God when you are hurting, confused, angry, or feeling weak or hopeless. Prayer fills this need. Prayer is personal communication with God. You don't have to pray for God to know what you need; the Bible tells us that God already knows what you need before you ask Him (Matthew 6:8). However, God wants you to pray because in choosing to pray, you are expressing your trust in Him. God wants you to depend on Him, love Him, and enjoy your relationship with Him.

When you pray, God responds. The Bible is full of prayers by those who found themselves in distressing situations. Whenever you feel emotionally overwhelmed because of harsh treatment from an abuser, read some of the prayers found in the book of Psalms. Remind yourself of God's love, care, and protection.

> I call upon you, for you will answer me, O God;
> incline your ear to me; hear my words.
> Wondrously show your steadfast love,
> O Savior of those who seek refuge
> from their adversaries at your right hand (Psalm 17:6-7).

> In you, O Lord, do I take refuge;
> let me never be put to shame;
> in your righteousness deliver me!
> Incline your ear to me;
> rescue me speedily!
> Be a rock of refuge to me,
> a strong fortress to save me! (Psalm 31:1-2).

> Give ear to my words, O Lord;
> consider my groaning.
> Give attention to the sound of my cry,
> my King and my God,
> for to you do I pray…
> But let all who take refuge in you rejoice;
> let them ever sing for joy,
> and spread your protection over them,
> that those who love your name may exult in you
> (Psalm 5:1-2,11).

Are you feeling as though God has let you down in the past when you prayed? You may have asked God to take away the pain of your verbal abuse, or to make your abuser understand his hurtful ways and stop the attacks, but nothing has happened. The Bible tells of a similar situation in the life of Paul:

> A thorn was given me in the flesh, a messenger of Satan to
> harass me, to keep me from becoming conceited. Three times
> I pleaded with the Lord about this, that it should leave me. But

he said to me, "My grace is sufficient for you, for my power is made perfect in weakness." Therefore I will boast all the more gladly of my weaknesses, so that the power of Christ may rest upon me. For the sake of Christ, then, I am content with weaknesses, insults, hardships, persecutions, and calamities. For when I am weak, then I am strong (2 Corinthians 12:7-10).

Paul prayed three times and asked God to remove a "thorn" from his life. This thorn could have been a person who tormented Paul. Whatever this thorn was, God allowed this painful assault to continue in Paul's life to keep him humble and dependent on God. Paul went to God in his pain, and God heard Paul and answered his prayer, but not by removing the "abuser" from his life. Instead, God gave Paul "relief" from his pain by giving him the grace and help he needed to endure it. Like Paul, you can endure your trial of an abusive relationship with grace and help from God.

When it comes to life's difficulties, we are given this assurance in Hebrews 4:15-16:

We do not have a high priest who is unable to sympathize with our weaknesses, but one who in every respect has been tempted as we are, yet without sin. Let us then with confidence draw near to the throne of grace, that we may receive mercy and find grace to help in time of need.

Christ will help you if you cry out to Him for wisdom and strength when you are verbally attacked.

Finally, the Bible commands us to pray for those who persecute us. "I say to you, Love your enemies and pray for those who persecute you" (Matthew 5:44). In whatever kind of relationship you find yourself, Jesus commands us to love and to pray. Our hearts draw near to God as we pray for the person who is making our life miserable. As we love our enemies and pray for our persecutors, we're walking in the footsteps of our Savior. In doing so we'll find peace in knowing that we are being obedient even in our suffering.

Respond by Overcoming Evil with Good

Another way the Bible plainly teaches us to deal with evil is to respond with doing good. As Christians, we are to aggressively fight against evil and seek to overcome it with good. How this plays out in each situation will be a day-by-day decision, but we should commit to being obedient to this command in the Bible.

> Bless those who persecute you; bless and do not curse them…
> Live in harmony with one another…Repay no one evil for
> evil, but give thought to do what is honorable in the sight
> of all. If possible, so far as it depends on you, live peaceably
> with all. Beloved, never avenge yourselves, but leave it to the
> wrath of God, for it is written, "Vengeance is mine, I will
> repay, says the Lord." To the contrary, "if your enemy is hun-
> gry, feed him; if he is thirsty, give him something to drink; for
> by so doing you will heap burning coals on his head." Do not
> be overcome by evil, but overcome evil with good (Romans
> 12:14,16-21).

One practical way to do good in response to your abuser's evil is by choosing your words carefully. "Bless and do not curse" makes it clear that your natural response to being cursed is to curse in return. It is much easier to curse than to bless an abuser. Remember that God never asks His children to do anything without giving them the power to do it—and it is the Holy Spirit who enables us. Think ahead so that the next time you find yourself at the receiving end of a verbal attack, you can respond by giving a blessing. One way to bless is by respond-ing with a soft answer to the other person's anger. "A soft answer turns away wrath, but a harsh word stirs up anger" (Proverbs 15:1). Bless by not retaliating and saying hurtful words back to your attacker. Bless by saying kind, good, and helpful words.

Besides responding with kind words, you can overcome evil by lov-ing the abuser and putting his interests ahead of your own. Jesus says in Luke 6:27-28, "Love your enemies, do good to those who hate you, bless those who curse you, pray for those who abuse you." If you focus only on you and your pain, it is almost impossible to return good for evil. When your concern is only your hurts, it is likely you will feel self-pity and depression. In order to love your enemy and do good to him, you must think about his needs. Think about the sin in his life and his need for God. Pray for him, asking God to do good to him and show mercy to him in spite of what he has done to you. Ask yourself what you can do for your abuser and how you can respond to him in a way that does him the most good. This type of thinking enables you to return good for evil.

As you continue to return good for the evil that your abuser gives you, you will "heap burning coals on his head," as Romans 12:20 says. This phrase refers to an ancient Egyptian custom in which a person demonstrating public contrition would carry a pan of burning coals on his head. This represented the burning pain of his shame and guilt. Likewise, as you love your enemy and genuinely seek to do good to him, you will shame him for his hatred and abuse to you. When you meet his needs, you are pouring coals—or good deeds—on him. In doing this, you may become an instrument in bringing him to salvation in Jesus Christ—or at least your actions may modify his evil behavior.

Respond Wisely to Manipulation

Most often when we think of verbal abuse, we think of name-calling, cursing, profanity, and mocking. However, because verbal abuse can also include the use of manipulative words intended to control, influence, confuse, or intimidate someone, you should understand the process of manipulation. The manipulator will use words designed to get an emotional response such as guilt, fear, or shame. When this happens to you, carefully plan how you will respond. The book of Proverbs gives two wise guidelines for dealing with a fool or manipulator:

> Answer not a fool according to his folly,
> lest you be like him yourself.
> Answer a fool according to his folly,
> lest he be wise in his own eyes (Proverbs 26:4-5).

The first two lines of the proverb teach us not to answer back in anger, self-defense, or manipulatively. In other words, do not act like your abuser. The next two lines teach us what to do instead. Answer or respond in such a way as to expose what the manipulator is seeking to do and show him his responsibility.

Manipulation can take many different forms. For example, the manipulator may attempt to pressure you into doing something he wants. A manipulative comment like "If you really love me like you say you do, then you'll tell my boss I'm sick on the day I'm going golfing with friends." You can respond by telling your husband you do love him, but it is *his* responsibility to deal with his boss about getting time off. You do not mind if he uses a day to golf with his friends, but you will not lie to his boss for him. The Bible says that lying lips are an abomination to the Lord (Proverbs 12:22).

Another form of manipulation is to impose guilt on another person. For example, suppose your husband wants to buy an expensive boat. You know that you are in considerable debt and struggling to pay the bills each month. You express your concerns to your husband and point out that your budget cannot handle the purchase of a boat. Your husband says that you never support him nor want him to have things that bring him happiness. Because he works hard every day, he deserves some pleasure in life. Then over the next several days he speaks to you only when necessary. And usually he includes a comment about how he sacrifices everything for you, yet you object to him spending money on himself this one time.

How should you respond? Show understanding to your husband, but remind him of his responsibility to provide for the support of his family (1 Timothy 5:8). Your objection to the purchase of the boat is not to deny him happiness, but because it's not a wise expense on account of your financial situation (Proverbs 1:5; 22:7; Ecclesiastes 5:5).

While your response might not stop the manipulation, at least you have exposed the manipulation and responded in a Christlike manner. You must have your emotions under control to make sure you respond without sinning. (See chapter 5 for more about controlling your emotions.) You need to make sure you are thinking clearly so you can show love to the other person and help him see his responsibility. Pray and ask God to give you strength and help so that you can respond firmly but lovingly.

Be aware that manipulation takes on many forms, such as sweet talk, begging, accusations, and threats. Be prepared and recognize the manipulation for what it is, and then speak the truth in love. Remember that love is an action.

Love is patient and kind…not arrogant or rude. It does not insist on its own way; it is not irritable or resentful; it does not rejoice at wrongdoing, but rejoices with truth. Love bears all things, believes all things, hopes all things, endures all things (1 Corinthians 13:4-7).

Respond by Trusting God

Living in a relationship characterized by abuse can be overwhelming and exhausting. So it's vital to remember that your strength comes from your relationship with God. Jesus loves you and sympathizes with your weaknesses and pain—He is "one who in every respect has been tempted as we are, yet without sin." Because He completely understands your trials, you can "with confidence draw near to the throne of grace, that [you] may receive mercy and find grace to help in time of need" (Hebrews 4:15-16).

Christ will help as you cry out to Him for power and strength when you are being verbally attacked. Trust Christ and the promises in the Bible. "Trust is not a passive state of mind. It is a vigorous act of the soul by which we choose to lay hold of the promises of God and cling to them despite the adversity that at time seeks to overwhelm us."[1]

To trust God through the painful circumstances of life, you have to see your life through eyes of faith. You must believe that God is in control and He loves you perfectly. When you are being verbally assaulted, you must acknowledge that nothing happens in this life that God did not make or permit to happen. "Who has spoken and it came to pass, unless the Lord has commanded it? Is it not from the mouth of the Most High that good and bad come?" (Lamentations 3:37-38). The circumstances in our life are not accidental. They flow from sin and evil, but evil is held within the hands of a God who is all-powerful and good. Evil cannot touch God's children unless He permits it. We may find ourselves questioning God's control because we do not understand what He is doing. But our lack of understanding does not change the fact that God is all-powerful and all-loving. All suffering in our life has meaning and purpose in God's eternal plan, which is all about our ultimate good and His glory (Romans 8:28-29).

An example in the Bible of a man who trusted God through many difficult life circumstances is Joseph. Joseph was betrayed by his brothers and forced to live in a foreign country far from his family. Later he was framed by a woman who accused him of attacking her sexually and was imprisoned. For years Joseph continued to experience injustices, but he remained faithful to God and trusted Him. Years later, Joseph looked back on his life and acknowledged that what others had done to him was meant as evil, but God used it for good in his life and the lives of many others (Genesis 37–50). The next time you feel overwhelmed and want to give up, do as Joseph did—trust God and cling to the promises of Scripture. Remind yourself of what you know about God from the Bible. Do not listen to thoughts of hopelessness, but instead talk to yourself and remind yourself of the promises of God's care, love, provision, faithfulness, power, and compassion.

Respond by Taking Responsibility for Your Responses

As you live each day in a relationship that is characterized by anger, criticism, manipulation, and control, you must first make the decision that you are going to take responsibility for your responses. You cannot change the other person's behavior. You can influence him and invite him to change, but just as you cannot make him sin, you cannot make him change.

As for yourself, you can seek to stop old behaviors that prevented you from responding to abuse in a confident, loving, straightforward, and godly manner. As you struggle with your sin and unbelief, you can confess to God your habit of responding in a wrong manner to your abuser. As you fill your mind with truths from the Bible, you can train yourself to respond in a new way that imitates Jesus Christ (Ephesians 4:22-24).

Our union with Christ is a living relationship that enables us to overcome sin and live a life that is obedient to the Bible and pleasing to God. "We know that our old self was crucified with him in order that the body of sin might be brought to nothing, so that we would no longer be enslaved to sin" (Romans 6:6).

Also, know that change is a process that takes time. With consistent effort and a conscious effort to make right choices each day, seek to obey the Bible whether you feel like it or not. Then God will enable you to change how you respond to verbal abuse.

Respond Knowing that God Is Faithful

You may feel overwhelmed and frightened by the responses you have been encouraged to make in this chapter. Perhaps you are tempted to give up because the situation seems hopeless and you don't know how you can respond in this way to abuse. But remember that you are not to make this journey alone. Reach out to leaders in your church and ask for help. A verse that has provided encouragement to many Christians through the ages is 1 Corinthians 10:13: "No temptation has overtaken you that is not common to man. God is faithful, and he will not let you be tempted beyond your ability, but with the temptation he will also provide the way of escape, that you may be able to endure it." In every situation in your life, God will show you His power and grace. Place your hope in God and His faithfulness—and with courage, face your relationship and know that you can change and respond biblically to verbal abuse.

Recommended Resources

Adams, Jay. *How to Overcome Evil.* Phillipsburg, NJ: Presbyterian & Reformed, 1977.

Bridges, Jerry. *Trusting God: Even When Life Hurts.* Colorado Springs: NavPress, 1988.

Peace, Martha. *Damsels in Distress.* Phillipsburg, NJ: Presbyterian & Reformed, 2006.

Vernick, Leslie. *The Emotionally Destructive Relationship.* Eugene, OR: Harvest House, 2007.

Chapter 15

Faithful Parenting: Reaching Your Child's Heart

§ *Barbara Scroggins* §

While grocery shopping, how many times have you noticed a mother losing the battle for control over her children? Have *you* ever been that mother?

I remember a day at the grocery store when my two children were ages four years and nine months. It was one of those busy days when I was pushing my kids' patience so I could accomplish my agenda for the day, and the grocery store was the last thing on my to-do list. The store where I shop is smaller than the average grocery store, with small carts and narrow aisles. My baby girl was sitting in the front of the cart while I was ineffectively trying to corral my four-year-old son by hastily throwing out commands like "Don't touch that!" "Stay by the cart!" and "Don't stand on the cart!"

At one point I was having trouble finding a particular item while maneuvering between all the other carts in the busy little store. So I parked my cart to one side and stepped around the corner to go to the produce table. As I did so, I heard a crash followed by loud crying. It took only an instant to recognize the cries—they were coming from my children! As I stepped back around the corner, I was horrified to find my children on the ground with the cart tipped over on top of them. Apparently my son had climbed up the side of the wobbly little cart, casuing it to tip over. I was filled with a rush of emotion: concern for my children, anger at my son, and embarrassment because of all the people who were now watching me.

I can laugh about it now, but I wasn't laughing then. It was another opportunity for God to reveal the condition of my heart and teach me to trust Him. My immediate response toward my son was anger—he had disobeyed me and hurt himself and his sister in the process. But later, when I reflected on the incident, I realized that I was the one who had failed miserably—not my son. In my busyness to pursue my own agenda, I had not taken the time to consistently train my son and build my relationship with him. Instead, I had thoughtlessly barked out orders whenever I noticed him doing something that was not to my liking, and then I had neglected to enforce my commands. Finally, I failed by provoking him. We had already had a busy day, and it was nearing nap time. But I had overlooked my children's needs so I could accomplish my goals. I was focused on me, and my children suffered the consequences.

A Different Type of Parenting

Parenting is hard work. It can be physically, mentally and emotionally draining—with no breaks or vacation time. In the midst of all the demands of parenting, we have problems because both parents and children are sinful (Romans 5:12). Our children are born sinful (Psalm 51:5) and the sin in their hearts comes out early in life, creating conflict in our relationship with them and stirring sinful responses in us at times.

Often we spend so much time caring for the physical needs of our children that we have no energy left for training their hearts and minds. When we are inconvenienced or irritated by our children's behavior, we *react* by trying to change or control that behavior at that moment. We overlook the fact that the undesirable behavior is oozing from the child's sinful heart.

God has called us to a different type of parenting. He wants us to *proactively* consider our children's hearts and train them in a way that honors Him. And He has graciously provided us with the perfect parenting resource: the Bible. The Bible has the answers we are looking for in our parenting (2 Timothy 3:16-17; 2 Peter 1:3).

The Bible and Parenting

God is the author of life and He is also the designer of the family. In the Bible, He has provided us with instructions for how our families are to function and the goals that we are to pursue in parenting. The Bible teaches us the bleak reality that we are all sinners (Romans 3:23) and are condemned to death because we have violated God's perfect standards (Romans 6:23). But it also provides us with great hope in that God loved us so much He sent His Son, Jesus, to die in our place (Romans 5:6-8). Our responsibility is to repent of our sin and believe in the saving work of Jesus (Romans 10:9-13).

Because of Jesus' work on the cross, we can have the confident assurance of spending eternity with God. If you do not have that confident assurance, I encourage you to read about how you can get it in Appendix Two.

God's plan is for parents to pass the gospel message on to their children. In the book of Deuteronomy we read, "You shall love the LORD your God with all your heart and with all your soul and with all your might. And these words that I command you today shall be on your heart. You shall teach them diligently to your children" (Deuteronomy 6:5-7). God wants parents to communicate to their children the truth about our sinful condition and His way of salvation. Our goal as parents is to teach our children to know God and love Him.

A Mother's Example

Children love to imitate others. From a young age, they look to those around them (primarily their parents in the early years) to learn from and follow their example. Even infants try to copy the facial expressions and mouth movements of their parents.

Your children learn how to live life by watching you and imitating the things you do. In the same way, they learn how to love God by observing *your* love for God. Notice in Deuteronomy 6:5-7 that the first command is directed to the parents: "Love the Lord your God with all your heart and with all your soul and with all your might." *Loving God is a prerequisite for teaching others to love God.*

In our culture today, relational love is thought of as an emotion, a feeling that comes over you. But biblical relational love is more than just a feeling—it is a commitment. The *feeling* of love, even love for God, may come and go throughout life. But a *commitment* to love God is enduring and is demonstrated by obeying Him. In John 14:15 the Lord says, "If you love me, you will keep my commandments." You can know God more and love Him more as you regularly read the Bible, see how He has first loved you, listen to and live out its teachings, and commit to obeying its commands.

As you seek to live a God-loving life before your children, I want to encourage you not to lose hope in the times that your example does not honor God. Being a Christian means that we have been saved from the eternal consequences of our sin, but that does not mean we are perfect and sinless in this life. As long as we live in this world, we will have to battle against the sin in our hearts. By God's grace, sometimes we will be successful, but sometimes we will not. When we falter in that battle, we can remember that our relationship with God does not change. Our obedience does not secure our salvation; Christ already secured that for us. Although we want to show our children how to love and obey God, we don't have to pretend we are perfect. It's all right for our children to see that we struggle to obey, just as they do. And in that struggle we can show them that we are completely dependent upon God to work in our lives.

A Mother's Mandate

The apostle Paul, in his letter to the Ephesians, gave some practical commands for daily living. One of these commands was about how parents are to raise their children. Ephesians 6:4 states, "Fathers, do not provoke your children to anger, but bring them up in the discipline and instruction of the Lord." Although the language is directed to fathers, the command also applies to mothers. Parenting is a joint effort between father and mother, and though God has given the father the primary leadership role in the home, this passage also applies to mothers as they care for their children under the leadership of their husbands (Ephesians 5:22-24).

Ephesians 6:4 gives clear direction as to how God wants you to parent your children. First it says what *not* to do with your children— you are not to provoke them to anger. Then it gives instruction for what you *are* to do with your children—bring them up in the discipline and instruction of the Lord. Through the remainder of this chapter, we will look at how to live out that command in our parenting on a daily basis.

Act as an Agent of God's Authority

Before Paul gave his instruction to parents, he first commanded children to obey their parents (Ephesians 6:1). As a mother, God has given you authority over your children—meaning that God has made you a steward, or a manager, of their lives. God is your child's ultimate authority, but He has given parents the responsibility to exercise authority on His behalf for the purpose of bringing children up in the discipline and instruction of the Lord (Ephesians 6:4). You are not your child's authority because you are bigger than he is, or even because you are older and more experienced. You are his authority because you were appointed to this position by God.

Your job is to teach your children how to obey. God is in charge; you are to obey God and your children are to obey you. Your children learn to obey God as they learn to obey you, so it is your duty to train your children in obedience. Obedience is "the willing submission of one person to the authority of another...It means doing what [one] is told—without challenge, without excuse, and without delay."[1]

Do Not Provoke Your Children to Anger

A parent's authority is from God, and we must be careful not to abuse that authority by provoking our children to anger. To provoke someone is simply to make them angry. The idea here is that of repeatedly pushing a child to the point of anger.

Generally speaking, children are provoked to anger when a command is unreasonable or unclear, when they perceive hypocrisy in an authority figure, and when they are disciplined outside of a loving relationship. If we think back to the grocery store scene I mentioned earlier, we can see how this is played out. I should have prepared my son in the car, before entering the grocery store, by speaking to him face to face, on his level, about how I wanted him to behave in the store. Then, if he disobeyed in spite of my clear directions, I should have left my cart and taken him to the car to deal with his rebellious heart in a setting where I could focus on him alone—and not on my self-image in front of all the other shoppers. Finally, by barking out commands as we went through the store, I failed to maintain a loving relationship with him. I was trying to control his behavior for my own prideful benefit, when I should have focused on influencing his heart attitude.

When we as parents are not faithful about teaching our children to obey, we are provoking them. And when we tolerate repeated disobedience, which usually invites further disobedience, we may end up responding with heated words that are given quickly, without thought, and in an elevated tone. Words spoken harshly don't invite respect or heart obedience; rather, they push our children to anger, as Proverbs 15:1 says: "A soft answer turns away wrath, but a harsh word stirs up anger."

Both our words and the tone in which they are spoken have a great impact on our children. We can use our words to draw them out and develop a loving relationship with them, or to condemn them and provoke them to anger. When we make the choice to speak with self-control and gentleness, then we are loving our children and teaching them by our example.

If you have acted in a way that has provoked a child to anger, don't despair over it—you can mend your relationship with that child. To do that, humbly go to the child and confess your sin of parenting in a way that was harsh and unkind. Then ask the child to forgive you for sinning against him and let him know that you want to change that pattern by choosing to lovingly instruct him instead of provoke him.

Bring Them Up

So how do we work toward lovingly instructing children instead of provoking them to anger? The next instruction Paul gives is to "bring them up" to maturity by training our children with a tenderhearted nurture. This is done through a combination of discipline and instruction.

Bring Them Up in the Discipline of the Lord

When Paul tells us to bring up our children in the discipline of the Lord, he is referring to providing them with training and correction that will lead them to maturity. The goal of biblical discipline is to change the heart, not just the behavior, through the use of verbal correction and physical discipline.

Verbal correction occurs as we calmly and gently communicate to our children how they have sinned (Ephesians 4:29). We can do this by explaining God's standard to them and then asking them questions that help them understand how they disobeyed God. When they do not meet God's standard, it is sin. Use their sin as an opportunity to communicate God's grace to them. Their sin condemns them to death, but God sent His Son Jesus to die for their sin if they will repent (go in the opposite direction of their sin) and believe (that they need salvation and it can only come through Jesus). God uses the Scriptures to convict us of sin, so it is important that you use the Bible to point it out (2 Timothy 3:16).

But don't stop there! Then you also need to show your children that God will forgive them of their sin if they will make the choice to turn away from it (1 John 1:9). Finally, help your children practice obedience to God's Word by telling them how they should have responded, and then acting out that response so they can see what it looks like.

Here's how these principles might have played out with my son when we were in the grocery store: I could have provided verbal correction to him by stopping what I was doing and either quietly pulling him aside to talk, or going to the car to talk. While talking with him, I would have asked him what God's Word instructs him to do. We have taught him Ephesians 6:1, which says, "Children, obey your parents in the Lord, for this is right," so I would expect him to answer that he needs to obey me. Then I would ask him if he did obey me. Finally, I would tell him what he should have done to be obedient (stay by the cart without climbing on it). Then I would have given him the opportunity to practice obedience before resuming my shopping. By providing my son with verbal correction immediately following his disobedience, I would have trained him how to obey.

Biblical discipline requires not only verbal correction, but also physical correction. "The rod and reproof give wisdom, but a child left to himself brings shame to his mother" (Proverbs 29:15). Proverbs 22:15 says, "Folly is bound up in the heart of a child, but the rod of discipline drives it far from him." Your child's heart is filled with foolishness.

He does not want to obey you because he would rather foolishly follow his own desires. God instructs you to respond to his foolishness with a spanking (Proverbs 23:13-14) so that your child submits to your authority, and thus God's authority.

The concept of spanking your child may be foreign or even horrifying to you. There are many who have perverted the practice of spanking so that it has become a cultural taboo in our society and is often associated with child abuse. But this is not what spanking is! I want to be clear that *the Bible does not promote or encourage any type of child abuse.* When the Bible refers to the use of spanking for the purpose of bringing a child up to maturity, it mandates that spanking be used in a controlled and loving way (Proverbs 3:12; 13:24; 1 Corinthians 13:4-7). When spanking occurs in anger or for your own selfish purposes, it is *not* biblical or godly! The goal of biblical discipline is to reach the heart, not to inflict harm. Discipline that is not thoroughly biblical will serve to provoke your children to anger rather than to change their hearts.

Here are a few guidelines for applying biblical physical discipline:

Biblical physical discipline begins with loving verbal correction. Before you spank your child, it is critical that he know why he is receiving a spanking. This means you must communicate to him what he has done wrong and why your obedience to God requires that you give him a spanking. Then ask him questions to make sure he understands why he is going to receive a spanking.

Biblical physical discipline must be given for the purpose of correcting the heart, not just punishing the behavior. You do not have the freedom or the right to spank your child for your own purposes. Spanking is a tool provided by God to reach the heart of a child and teach him that his sin is wrong. It is not meant to punish him for acting in a way that frustrates or embarrasses you. When you are more concerned about correcting his heart than you are about punishing his behavior, then you will discipline in a calm, careful, and controlled manner.

Biblical physical discipline must be consistent. Consistency in discipline is critical. You need to discipline every time wrong is done, and you need to discipline lovingly and fairly. You must communicate to your children that obedience is always necessary. Therefore, you must always discipline your children for their sin. You do not have the option to skip discipline one time just because your are too busy or it is inconvenient. If you discipline only when it is convenient, then you are not obeying God, and you are confusing your children with changing standards. God's standards never change; therefore, we must always enforce God's standards with our children.

Being consistent with regard to *how* we spank our children guards us against unbiblical discipline and lets our children know what to expect. A consistent method of spanking includes identifying the reason for the discipline, stating the number of spanks to be given, and giving firm, evenly spaced spanks that are not rushed or harmful.

Biblical physical discipline will restore the relationship that has been broken by sin. The end result of physical discipline should be restoration to a loving relationship between you and your child. He will know that what he did was wrong and that wrong actions mess up his relationship with you. But he will also know that once his sin is dealt with, his relationship with you can be restored through forgiveness. Ultimately this teaches him that sin separates him from a loving relationship with God and that he needs to seek forgiveness from God to make his relationship with Him right. Properly administered, discipline will bring your child to humble submission, not angry defiance.

There is a great deal more that can be said about the issue of biblical discipline. Please refer to the resources listed at the end of this chapter to gain a more full understanding of the various methods of biblical discipline.

Bring Them Up in the Instruction of the Lord

The final part of Paul's instruction to parents is that they are to bring their children up in the instruction of the Lord. *Instruction* refers to educating our children with words. This is the act of building up our children through wise communication. As we already read in Proverbs, our children are born with foolishness in their hearts. It is with discipline that we remove their foolishness, and as it is removed, we need to build wisdom in its place. We build wisdom in our children by teaching and training them with wise words—and it is the Bible that can provide these words of wisdom.

The Bible says that wisdom is gained by learning to fear the Lord

(Proverbs 1:7). As we study the Bible and learn truths about God for ourselves, we can then pass those truths on to our children with ongoing communication about what we are learning. When we use our communication to point our children to the greatness, love, and mercy of God, then we are teaching them who He is and what He is like.

In addition to teaching our children about God, we must also train them to do as God commands. Training occurs through continual, repetitive instruction about how to do something. God gives one specific command to children: They are to obey their parents (Ephesians 6:1). So our training needs to focus on training our children in obedience, and enforcing that training with discipline. Here are a few suggestions about training we can work on as we train our children in obedience:

Train Them to Obey Immediately

We are to train our children to obey at once, without repeating a command. It is not necessary to repeat our instructions if we are clear and follow through with loving discipline when they fail to obey right away. If we give them three warnings before we enforce obedience, then we train them to obey only after we have given three warnings. As they learn to obey our instruction the first time, they learn self-control, and ultimately, they learn to obey God right away.

Train Them to Obey with a Joyful Heart

When our children submit to our instruction yet do so with a bad attitude, that is not obedience. Obedience is not merely going through the motions. Attitudes are a reflection of the heart and our goal is to reach our children's hearts, not just control their behavior. We must use loving discipline to enforce our training.

Train Them to Obey Without Being Told Why

Young children frequently ask, "Why?" because they are curious. But when you give your children a command, you need to train them to obey your instruction without being told why. Even though this may seem to be overly authoritarian, it is the right course to take, especially with younger children. A five-year-old doesn't need to know the reason you are calling her to come to you—she simply needs to hear your voice and obey. When they want to know why before they are willing to obey, they are seeking control over the situation. They will obey only if the reason you give is acceptable to them. However, this is not real obedience. You must train them to obey without knowing why by employing loving discipline if they fail to obey. When our children learn to obey us without having to know why, they will be better prepared to obey God during the difficult times of life when they do not know the "why" behind His commands.

A Mother's Love

"Children are a blessing and a gift from the Lord" (Psalm 127:3 CEV). When God gave you children, He gave you a great blessing. As a mother you are to delight in this blessing (Titus 2:4). This delight will flow out in a relationship expressed with affection and fondness for your children. In this loving relationship they will know that you delight in them. And when they know you delight in them, they will want to follow your example and submit in obedience to your authority. Here are three ways to develop a joyful, loving relationship with your children:

Spend Time with Your Children

As a mother, God has given you authority over your children, but that authority does not exclude your need to build relationships with them. Such relationships are built through years of spending time with your children, engaging them and interacting with them daily at their level. Let them know you love them by expressing to them the joy that you receive from being with them. Expressing joy and excitement in what they do shows them you delight in them.

Listen to Your Children

Do you enjoy listening to your children? Building a relationship requires that you not only *talk* to your children, but also *listen* to them. Children learn about the world around them by asking questions. If you want to influence them toward God, then you must establish a pattern of listening to them. When your children speak, they are opening their hearts to you. It is your job to pay attention to what they are saying.

Praise Your Children

Praising your children expresses your joy in them. While biblical parenting does require consistent discipline, you don't want all of your interaction with your children to be corrective. Therefore, you must work diligently to use kind, encouraging words of praise. It *is* necessary for you to say no to them on occasion, but if the majority of your words are negative, your children will not want to listen to you. So work hard at saying yes as often as possible. Children love to be praised and encouraged in what they are doing.

Our Faithful Heavenly Father

God has bestowed on us the responsibility to train our children. It is through this responsibility that we have the privilege of influencing the next generation. If we neglect this responsibility, the world is ready and willing to influence our children according to its own standards and values. Moses instructed the Israelite parents who were about to enter the Promised Land to teach their children so that the next generation would not forget Him. If we want our children to know and love God, then everything we do in parenting our children must be focused on that goal.

As you seek to fulfill this goal, continue to remember God's grace. As an imperfect mother, I rely on His grace every day. Like that day in the grocery store, there are times when I am so focused on myself that I fail to discipline and delight in my children in a way that honors Him. Thankfully, God is perfect. He is merciful and gracious and loving. When I fail, He is there to gently show me my sin and to forgive me, reminding me that He sent His Son Jesus because I simply can't obey Him on my own. I can continue to persevere in my parenting because God has promised that He will make my efforts fruitful (Galatians 6:9).

God has promised that He is in control of our parenting and our children for the good: "We know that for those who love God all things work together for good, for those who are called according to his purpose" (Romans 8:28). As you choose to know God more through reading the Bible and seek God in prayer for wisdom and guidance in your parenting, you can trust that He will faithfully fulfill His promises to you (2 Timothy 2:13).

Recommended Resources

Elliff, Jim. *How Children Come to Faith in Christ* [sound recording]. Little Rock, AR: Family Life Today, 2006.

Plowman, Ginger. *Don't Make Me Count to Three!* Wapwallopen, PA: Shepherd Press, 2003.

Priolo, Lou. *Teach Them Diligently.* Woodruff, SC: Timeless Texts, 2000.

Tripp, Tedd. *Shepherding a Child's Heart.* Wapwallopen, PA: Shepherd Press, 1995.

Chapter 16

THE PERFECT MOM SYNDROME

Connie Larson

The room was packed with more than 100 women, all mothers of preschool-age children. On the stage was a whiteboard on which I was furiously writing their answers to the question, *How would you describe a perfect mom?* It started slowly with one woman volunteering, "Her kids behave perfectly." Then another chimed in with, "She never gets angry or yells at her kids." And another said, "She's always kind and disciplines with gentleness." Others started getting the idea and the image of the perfect mom grew before our eyes. She is well-organized; a great teacher; has a well-decorated home; is fit, friendly, and fun to be around; and a good lover to her husband. The descriptions continued to fill every inch of the whiteboard with the words *creative, calm, nurturing,* and *kid's advocate* written around the edges and squeezed between the lines.

Our image of the perfect mom is larger-than-life. There is no such woman. She is a myth, an illusion. And yet her image looms large in every mom's heart and mind. When I mention the Perfect Mom Syndrome, there are very few moms who question whether it exists—for the awareness of it resonates deep in a woman's soul. My image of the perfect mom is going to be different than your image, but our images will likely share many similarities that are promoted by our culture, espoused by our friends, and taught in our churches. We are different in that our history, personality, and values play a big part in our images of the perfect mom. I may value creativity and think the perfect mom lets her kids finger paint, play in the dirt, and help bake cookies. But you if value order and organization, you might consider the above activities too messy and chaotic.

When we step back and look at the magnitude of our expectations for the perfect mom, it is no wonder we as mothers get overwhelmed. Almost every mother I know reacts to the idea of a perfect mom in one way or another. Some of you grab the bull by the horns and try to do it all. Others feel like a failure from the start. The Perfect Mom Syndrome is the drive to fulfill the expectations that make up your image of the perfect mom. It is the compulsion to do those things expected of you by others so that you will appear to be a perfect mother in their eyes. It is allowing the myth of the perfect mom to rule and determine your thoughts, actions, and words.

Some questions invariably arise as we consider this topic. Is anything wrong with wanting to be perfect? Isn't this God's desire for us? Doesn't He want us to be "perfect and complete, lacking in nothing" (James 1:4)? Aren't we responsible for training our children and making sure they have every opportunity to succeed? Shouldn't we push them to excel? Is anything wrong with high expectations? Those are great questions. Before we can come up with answers, we must gain an understanding of the problem and get God's perspective on it. Then we will look at some practical solutions for excelling as mothers.

Let's get a better idea of the Perfect Mom Syndrome (or PMS—in this chapter, not to be mistaken for premenstrual syndrome) by looking at some of its characteristics. As you read along, put a check next to the ones you struggle with.

- *Overcommitted and overbusy*—You want to do it all or think you should do it all. You don't want to miss any opportunity, and think your children should experience all that they can. You struggle with feeling overwhelmed, stressed, behind, or frantic.

- *Unrealistic or exceptionally high standards for yourself and/or your children*—You base your worth and success as a mom on how well you and/or your children do at measuring up to your standards and fulfilling your expectations. This may include no misbehaving, no messes, no mistakes, perfect performance, perfect scores, and trying to do it all and do it well. Those you live with may see you as pushy, demanding, and hard to please. You may struggle with anger because others are not doing things according to your standards or timetable.

- *Rarely satisfied, happy, or joyful*—When you have unrealistic goals and high standards of achievement for yourself or your children, you may experience a constant, overall feeling of never doing well enough or being good enough.

- *Driven to overachieve, overdo, or be hypervigilant*—You live with the fear that there is always something more you should do, or more information you could find. Nicole had recently quit work as a computer analyst to become a stay-at-home mom. She acknowledged her tendency to treat motherhood as a career, doing endless research in her mothering responsibilities. When it came time to select a preschool for her three-year-old daughter, she interviewed ten preschools out of fear of making the wrong choice.

- *Driven by pressure from others*—When other people express their desires or expectations for you, you feel obligated or pressured to do what they want—or guilty when you don't. You often make decisions based on other people's opinions.

- *Desire to make everybody happy or not let people down*—Your image of the perfect mom might include having a household in which there is no conflict. You will do whatever it takes to accomplish that goal, including giving in to the desires and demands of your children.

- *Measure yourself and/or your children by comparing with others*—When we compare ourselves to others, we will often feel a sense of inadequacy or failure. Jackie was working hard at homeschooling her three boys and was struggling to get them to pay attention and work their way through the basic material. Each time she heard of another home-school mom who was doing more or having an easier time, she felt defeated. Homeschooling is a worthwhile endeavor, but because of the added responsibility of overseeing their children's education, many homeschooling moms are likely to struggle with PMS.

- *Suffer from anger, anxiety, depression or fatigue*—These are common responses to the overwhelming task of trying to live up to the expectations of PMS. If any of these conditions have become a constant in your life, and you have come to the conclusion that it's because you have PMS, you will want to keep reading and carry out the action steps provided along the way.

So, What's a Mother to Do?

I don't think any of us start out thinking we need to be a perfect mom. We just want to do what needs to be done and we want to do the best we can. Most women put a lot of effort into raising their family because they care. But along the way something happens. The Perfect Mom Syndrome kicks in. We become women who are driven to do more, do it better, or try harder. We feel trapped in the busyness and stress of life, anxious about how our kids will turn out and fearful that we might do the wrong thing. For some, the black hole of depression may loom ever closer as they give in to the impossibility of it all.

Sally, a mother of three children under age eight, had an anger problem. She worked part time in the evenings as a nurse at the local urgent care center. She wanted to keep her foot in the job market and help bring in some extra income. She was involved in a mom's group at church and a couples' Bible study on her night off. Her eight-year-old daughter was in a soccer league with twice-a-week practices and a game on Saturday, had piano lessons once a week after school, and took karate lessons. In order to get everything done, Sally had everyone in the family on a tight schedule. Whenever anyone in the household didn't cooperate and stick to the schedule, she would blow up. Yelling and screaming became such a common occurrence that she became fearful she might lose control and hurt one of her children one day.

Another mom, Jennifer, was sure she was having what felt like a nervous breakdown. The boys' war whoops as they ran down the hall and the baby's crying made her want to pull her hair out. She was trying to homeschool the two older boys, but when her toddler got sick and she had several sleepless nights, she just couldn't keep up with the demands. She really wanted to send the boys to public school, but she worried about what her friends would think if she gave up. She felt like such a useless failure of a mom.

Sally and Jennifer are among the many who are caught in the trap of PMS. The blessed news for them—and for you—is that it's possible to break free from the burden and weariness of PMS and have a life of joy and peace.

Out of the Trap

The way out is through a relationship with Jesus Christ. He came to save us from our heartache, trouble, sinful ways, and desperate situations. That is why He is called the Savior. If you don't know Jesus or how He can save you, please turn to Appendix Two on page 321. When you are done, then you can come back to this chapter.

You may be saying, "I do believe in Jesus, but I still struggle, so how do I get that joy and peace you are talking about?" It's amazing how gradually, subtly, and easily we can slip from living a life committed to God and His ways to a life without much thought of God in it. It happens to me, especially when I get busy.

Principle of Drift

I grew up in a sailing family, and one definite principle about safe sailing is that if your boat isn't tied up securely to a dock, or anchored to the bottom of the ocean, it will drift. The wind and the waves will push it further and further away from where you want to be. This same principle is true in the Christian life as well. If you don't make a point to draw near to God and make sure you have a tight connection with Him, then drift will occur. And when you drift away from God, you will find your independent spirit wanting to take over. You'll find yourself neglecting to ask God for help, strength, guidance, and wisdom. You'll become like a two-year-old child who shouts, "I can do it myself." And before you know it, you will find yourself weighed down by life, overwhelmed by commitments, angry that no one is cooperating, and weary of the demands and expectations on you.

Your Invitation

A common problem for mothers with PMS is that most of us try to live our lives independently of God until our own strength runs out. When we get to the end of our abilities and energy, we finally give up. If you are in this place—depleted, overwhelmed and weary from the burden of PMS—then Jesus has an invitation for you:

> Come to Me, all who are weary and heavy-laden, and I will give you rest. Take My yoke upon you, and learn from Me, for I am gentle and humble in heart, and you will find rest for your souls. For My yoke is easy, and My burden is light (Matthew 11:28-30 NASB).

It's plain and simple. Jesus is inviting you to join with Him (take up His yoke), follow His lead, hear what He has to say, and let Him carry your load. What could be simpler? While it is simple, it's not easy. It requires giving up control of your life and handing the reins over to Jesus. Why is this so hard when the benefits—rest for the soul and a lightened load—are so wonderful? Do we think we can do things better or that we know better than God what is good us and our children?

At the end of most invitations are the letters RSVP, for *repondez s'il vous plait*, which is French for "please reply." Jesus desires a reply to His invitation. If you want rest for your soul and a lighter burden, then go to Him. You can't see Him, but He is very near you right now. Tell Him you are done trying to be a mother in your own strength and with your own goals, and that you are ready and willing to learn from Him. This is a most important step in overcoming PMS.

Good News

Are you despairing right now, thinking there is no hope for you, that you are beyond help? I've got some good news for you.

First, *God is in this with you.* We have a faithful, loving God who promises to be with you, stay with you and give you a way out of life's difficult situations (1 Corinthians 10:13; Hebrews 13:5-6). He also promises to be gentle: "He will tend his flock like a shepherd; he will gather the lambs in his arms; he will carry them in his bosom, and gently lead those that are with young" (Isaiah 40:11). He's not merely trying to be a perfect parent, and getting frustrated in the process. No, He *is* the perfect parent, and He's *not* frustrated at all.

Second, *God is in the business of change.* "He who began a good work in you will bring it to completion at the day of Jesus Christ" (Philippians 1:6). Even though there is no such thing as a perfect mom or child this side of heaven, the moment we receive Jesus and believe in Him as Savior and Lord, the process of making us more like Him begins (Romans 8:29, 2 Corinthians 5:17). We are called God's workmanship, a living work of art sculpted by God (Isaiah 64:8; Ephesians 2:10). Trust Him to do a work of change in you.

Third, *God gives us everything we need to do the job of mothering in a way that pleases Him and gives Him glory* (2 Peter 1:3). He has given us the Bible as our instruction manual for living. So turn to God's Word, and see what He says (2 Timothy 3:16-17). He has also given us the Holy Spirit to guide, help, and strengthen us. He enables us to walk by the power of the Spirit each day as we ask for His help in controlling our tongue and emotions (John 16:13; Galatians 5:16-23). He tells us we can call on Him anytime in prayer and ask for help, wisdom, or whatever we need. So take Him at His word and ask for help (Hebrews 4:16; James 1:5). And God has also given us the body of Christ (other believers in the church) to teach us, encourage us, pray for us, and counsel us. You can ask an older Christian woman to mentor and teach you the ways of God so that you can grow as a mother and wife.

With His Strength You Can Do the Hard Things

God doesn't expect you to do everything, or do it perfectly. It takes courage and inward determination, but you can actually change the pace and focus of your life so that you can enjoy it and your loved ones more. Change is not always easy—it will require taking a hard look at your life, your heart, your thinking, your motives, your commitments and your decision making. If you are overwhelmed, stressed, or depressed, then you need to take steps to change that. So get ready to make choices that will require effort on your part.

HEART CHECK ASSIGNMENT

At the beginning of making biblical changes in your life, it is important to take a good, hard look at yourself. Get yourself a notebook to do the assignments. Then do the following:

- On page one of your notebook, write Matthew 11:28-30, then write a prayer in reply to Jesus' invitation. Ask Him to help you make changes in your life.

- On the second page of your notebook, draw a line down the center and divide the page into two columns. On the left-hand side list all the commitments, activities, and responsibilities you have this week. If an item on your list causes you stress or anxiety, put a check mark next to it.

- In the right-hand column, next to each commitment, write why you are doing that particular activity. What is driving you to do this? This is not an easy exercise, so before you start, pray the prayer in Psalm 139:23-24 and ask God to search your heart and help you to understand the motives and intentions behind the choices you make.

Some questions you can ask as you do this are:

- Who am I trying to please? My mom, my friends, God, myself, my kids, or...?

- Am I trying to impress others or get them to admire me?

- Am I doing this because everyone else is doing it?

- Am I trying to gain God's love or approval?

- Do I think I don't need God and that I can do life without Him?

- One major reason we find ourselves entrapped by PMS is that we don't trust God. It sounds crazy, but our actions may indicate we think we can do our job better than God. We want control. We think if we don't take matters into our own hands, nothing will get done, or it won't get done right. You may think it is up to you to determine your child's future and make sure he or she gets a certain class, opportunity, teacher, or college. But the account about the mother of two of the disciples—who told Jesus she wanted her sons to sit next to Him in the place of honor in His kingdom—shows that God is responsible for your children's destinies, not you (Matthew 20:20-23; see also Romans 8:28-29; Ephesians 2:10).

- Make it your goal to learn to trust in God and let Him make your paths straight. Memorize Proverbs 3:5-7 and begin the practice of praying about your decisions, commitments, desires, and daily schedule. I like to write all these things in my notebook and say to God, "This is what I'm thinking, but I want Your will, Your agenda, Your wisdom, and Your plan."

- Learn about God, His characteristics, and all that He has done for you in Jesus. Do this as you read your Bible each day. You may want to begin in a book like Philippians, John, or the Psalms. Before you read, ask the Lord to teach you. Write in your journal one thing you learn each time you read. As you learn more about God, you will *know* you can entrust yourself and your children to His loving, wise, caring, and all-powerful hands.

Another key reason we become enslaved by PMS is that we *fear people*. Proverbs 29:25 tells us that the fear of people brings a snare to our lives. This occurs when you let others control you (whether they are trying to or not), or you try to live up to their expectations (or your perception of their expectations). Both are exhausting. I've heard women say, "I'm tired of trying to make everybody happy. I just can't do it anymore."

- Why do you do what you do? The right motive for everything you do is to show love to God in response to His love for you. In Matthew 22:37 we learn we are to love God with our whole heart. Rather than focus on pleasing others, we need to focus on pleasing God. Make it your ambition to please God (2 Corinthians 5:9). The desire to please God flows out of a realization of His amazing love for us, not because we are afraid He will punish us.

- What should we do when we feel the pressures or expectations of others? This may sound trite, but pray about it. Ask the Lord about your involvement at your child's school, team, or scout troop. Ask God how and where He wants you to serve at church. Don't just say yes to everything that comes your way (and don't say no solely because you are busy). Make God's desires a priority for you. I'm amazed when I ask God for wisdom and direction regarding my decisions and commitments. He will let me know, in some way or other, what I should do.

- One way God clarifies His plans is through our husbands. God tells wives to be submissive to their husbands (place themselves under the husband's authority) in everything and to respect them. God also makes it clear our submission is not conditioned on whether we have a good Christian husband or he is in agreement with us (Ephesians 5:22,33; 1 Peter 3:1). This is not easy to do, but before you do something, ask your husband what he thinks when it comes to making commitments and plans. Many moms think they know what is best for their kids and themselves and that their husbands don't have a clue. You should give your husband enough information to clue him in. Then go with what he says (unless he is asking you to sin). Maybe you won't like his answer, but if you desire to honor the Lord and His commands, then submit to and respect your husband.

- Yet another reason we struggle with PMS is because we are trying to prove ourselves, please ourselves, or do everything ourselves. We feel the need to validate our worth by our performance as a mother or by the performance of our children. We want to prove that our kids are better than other kids, or that we are better than other moms. We struggle with being self-sufficient, proud, and selfish.

- If you see this pattern in yourself, then address your pride and self-sufficiency by acknowledging your total dependence upon God. This has been a major area of growth for me over the years, and I know I am not alone. Memorize John 15:1-5, and study 2 Corinthians 3:4-6 and James 4:6-10. Confess your sin of pride to the Lord and ask Him for help, strength, wisdom, and direction on a daily basis. Remember that you are to focus on making the Lord's name great, not your own.

- If selfishness is an issue for you, study what Scripture says about loving others in Matthew 22:37-39, Philippians 2:3-4, and 1 Corinthians 13:4-7. Mothers are known to be sacrificial and give generously of themselves for their kids, so it is hard to think of mothers as selfish. But *sacrifices are made only for something you truly want*. So check your motives. Are you staying up until all hours of the night getting a project done so you can impress others? Is your reputation more important to you than God and His desires for you?

- Is it possible you are harried by PMS because you *love the ways of the world too much?* One of the difficulties of being a mom in today's world is that there is so much world to love and pursue: things to have, fame to aspire to, education to seek, and appearances to keep up. Again, we need to check our motives. Are we loving the world and the things in the world (1 John 2:15-16)? Are we allowing the world to conform us (Romans 12:2)? Are we keeping busy pursuing the things of the world and missing out on what is important to the Lord?

- Ask yourself the tough questions: Do I want something *too* much? What priorities and values am I communicating to my kids by the choices I make? Am I seeking God first (Matthew 6:33)? Is it always bad to be busy? No, but why are you busy? Is it wrong to pursue excellence? No, but are you doing it in a way that honors God (1 Corinthians 10:31; Colossians 3:23)? Are you are choosing to love the world more than you love the Lord?

- Check your thinking. Change begins in the mind, in your thoughts. Memorize Romans 12:2 and begin the process of not being conformed to the world, but transformed by the renewing of your mind.

- Make it your goal to bring up your children in the discipline and instruction of the Lord (Proverbs 6:20-23; Ephesians 6:4) so they will choose to love God and walk in a manner worthy of Him (Ephesians 4:1).

The Confident Mother

The way to overcome the Perfect Mom Syndrome is to love God above all else—to love His ways and live to please Him. And, love your children and teach them the wisdom and instruction of the Lord. Remember that their faith and character are more important than their accomplishments, and your faith and character are more important than your accomplishments.

Trust God to give you everything you need to be a godly mother. And entrust your children and their future into God's hands, and you will find joy and peace.

Recommended Resources

Bridges, Jerry. *Trusting God: Even When Life Hurts.* Colorado Springs: NavPress, 1988.

Fitzpatrick, Elyse. *Idols of the Heart.* Phillipsburg, NJ: Presbyterian & Reformed, 2001.

————. *Overcoming Fear, Worry, and Anxiety.* Eugene, OR: Harvest House, 2001.

Mack, Wayne. *Anger and Stress Management God's Way.* Merrick, NY: Calvary Press: 2004.

Priolo, Lou. *Pleasing People.* Phillipsburg, NJ: Presbyterian & Reformed, 2007.

———. *Teach Them Diligently.* Woodruff, SC: Timeless Texts, 2000.

Younts, John A. *Everyday Talk.* Wapwallopen, PA: Shepherd Press, 2004.

Chapter 17

RAISING CHILDREN
WHO ARE CHALLENGED

❧ Laura Hendrickson ❧

Blessed with a different child? That might not be the word that immediately comes to mind as you think about the challenges involved in raising a child with autism, a physical disability, or a developmental delay. It may not describe how you feel about parenting a child diagnosed with ADHD or OCD, either. Of course you love your precious child just the way he is, but the message our society often sends is that he's inferior because he's different.

In contrast, the Bible teaches that *all* children are a blessing—not just those who are free of disabilities or health concerns. "Behold, children are a heritage from the LORD, the fruit of the womb a reward. Like arrows in the hand of a warrior are the children of one's youth. Blessed is the man who fills his quiver with them!" (Psalm 127:3-5).

What's more, Scripture tells us that all our children are "fearfully and wonderfully made" (Psalm 139:14), not just the ones without disabilities. In fact, God personally supervised your child's development in the womb and had a detailed plan for his life even before he was conceived!

> You formed my inward parts; you knitted me together in my mother's womb. I praise you, for I am fearfully and wonderfully made. Wonderful are your works; my soul knows it very well. My frame was not hidden from you, when I was being made in secret, intricately woven in the depths of the earth.

> Your eyes saw my unformed substance; in your book were
> written, every one of them, the days that were formed for me,
> when as yet there was none of them (Psalm 139:13-16).

The Bible clearly affirms the value of every child's uniqueness, and we're called to believe this. But that's not always an easy truth to accept.

First, You Cry

I'll never forget the day the doctor told me that my two-year-old son had autism. He said that Eric was mentally retarded, had an IQ of 50, and that he would probably never learn to speak. I'd dreamed of a son who would glorify God as a pastor or missionary. My dream died that morning, and I wept to think Eric might never achieve independence, get married, or give me grandchildren.

At that time, I didn't rejoice over this blessing! I also didn't appreciate the significance of Eric's exceptional characteristics at first. In fact, I wondered if God was punishing me. Although I knew that Jesus has already taken all the punishment I deserved for my sins on the cross, it was hard to remember this in the grip of my sorrow. Furthermore, I wondered how to reconcile this painful news with God's promise that "for those who love God all things work together for good, for those who are called according to his purpose" (Romans 8:28).

I also blamed myself for Eric's condition. I had needed to take pain medications during my eighth week of pregnancy. The doctor had told me that they wouldn't hurt the baby. But what if he was wrong? Why had I taken them? I should have known better! And I blamed myself for being so selfish as to try to conceive so late in life. As a doctor, I should have realized that, given my age, I was more likely to give birth to a child with a disability.

What I didn't realize at the time was that, by blaming myself, I was painting God out of the picture of my life. In effect, I was punishing myself for failing to be the all-knowing, all-powerful "god" of my own pregnancy, who could and should have ensured a positive outcome. My heartbreak temporarily blinded me to what should have been obvious: The Lord is God, and I'm not. He's perfectly wise and good; I'm sinful by nature and make mistakes. Even if I'd had the ability to make my pregnancy turn out the way I had wanted it to, I'm not wise and virtuous enough to know what Eric and I really needed. The Bible teaches that God is the only one powerful enough to control everything, and the only one righteous enough to always do what is best.

Ultimately I came to realize that the only way I could experience God's peace was to believe what Scripture said about Him and look to Him in faith. I needed to remind myself that although I couldn't control the outcome of my pregnancy, the Lord could, and had. Now it was time for me to trust that He would bring about good in Eric's life and mine, even in the midst of this difficult circumstance. God had a plan and a purpose when He created Eric the way He did, and it was a plan to bring benefit, not harm, into our lives (Jeremiah 29:11).

What Is God Doing in My Child's Life?

I started my journey as the mother of a child with autism believing that the central truth about Eric's condition was that he had "deficits"— that is, he was missing qualities that had to be replaced so he could become as much like other children as possible. And it's true that one of my jobs as Eric's mother was to help him to develop in the areas in which he was weak. But because I was so focused on his limitations in those early days, I completely lost sight of what Scripture says is the central truth about Eric: He was made in the image and likeness of God (Genesis 1:27). This meant that he, like all other children, had been born with the ability to have a relationship with the Lord, to glorify and enjoy Him. I thought I needed to somehow fix Eric so he could know God and glorify Him. Later I came to understand that Scripture teaches that Eric reflects the Lord's glory just by being who God created him to be. And that's true for all children who have disabilities.

Please don't misunderstand me. I'm not saying we should just resign ourselves to leaving our different children the way they are, and not help them to develop in every way possible. The point is that the Bible says their value comes from their status as human beings made in God's image and likeness—*not* from what they're able to do. At first this was a hard concept for me to wrap my mind around. But as I came to understand this truth, it changed the way I saw Eric and tried to help him.

Not a Walking Elephant

Soon after his diagnosis with autism, Eric became obsessed with the Dumbo the Flying Elephant ride at Disneyland. Every time we visited the theme park, he wanted to ride it over and over again. Because Eric wasn't speaking much yet, I had lots of time to think. So as we rode silently in circles, I thought a lot about Dumbo. You remember the story: Dumbo was a baby elephant who was born with ridiculously large ears. Every time he started walking, he tripped over his ears. One day, Dumbo discovered that his ears—which seemed to be holding him back from having a normal life—were large enough to act as wings. It turned out that Dumbo wasn't born to walk. Rather, he was born to fly!

In those days, the Dumbo ride at Disneyland had a motto painted on its crown: "Believe, and Soar." That was inspiring, so I began praying, "Lord, I believe that You can do anything. Please let Eric soar." I thought that just as Dumbo's big ears had once been a handicap but ultimately turned out to be an asset, perhaps there was something about the way God made Eric that could lead to his glorifying Him in an equally unexpected way one day.

We placed Eric in an early intervention program, and there, he learned how to speak. Over time it became clear that the doctor who had diagnosed Eric had been wrong about his intelligence. Eric gradually improved over the years, and today he's a college student majoring in linguistics and Chinese. Yes, the boy who had to be taught his native language has turned out to have a gift for languages!

Eric tells me that he first became fascinated with languages while trying to understand the subtle differences between one word and another, back when he was learning to speak. I believe that God planned all along for Eric to develop this interest, and used Eric's differences to produce an unusual ability in his life. What's more, I also believe that God intends to use the challenges in *your* child's life to glorify Himself. Your physically active, impulsive son who doesn't pay attention at school may be a future man of action. One day your fearful little girl, who takes forever to clean her room and worries about germs, may find her attention to detail to be an asset in her work. Granted, none of this is going to happen all by itself. But if you can get a vision for what God may be doing in your child's life, and start asking Him to fulfill it, who knows what might happen?

What if your child has a severe handicap like Eric's but doesn't develop the way Eric did? Does this mean he can't glorify God? Of course not! The whole point of people being made in the image and likeness of God is that each of us reflects a different facet of the Lord's character and ways. A child with a serious challenge still reflects God's glory—just by being who the Lord created him to be.

For example, I think of my friend Randy. He's a young adult with the mental age of a four-year-old, and he *loves* the Lord. You should see his face light up when his parents read from the Psalms to him, as they do every night before bed. If he's upset about something, reading Scripture to him calms him down. He reflects the peace of Christ as he listens, and it's a beautiful thing. I look forward to meeting Randy at the end of time, when he will rise from his grave in a perfect body, with no disability and no more struggles with sin. But even now, Randy's humility and dependence upon God (two traits I struggle with daily) are an inspiration and encouragement to me.

I'm also reminded of Mark and Jonathan. Neither of them will ever attend college, but they're both making unique contributions to their worlds. Mark has autism, and a gift for art. He's not able to live independently, but he partially supports himself through his painting. Jonathan is just an ordinary guy with autism who has a sheltered job in a typical workplace. His special contribution is his kindness to others, and his faithfulness to his job—he has never taken a sick day.

There are many ways such people can make a difference in our world. God has given each of our children a distinctive way to reflect His character. Our calling as parents is to try to understand what God is doing in their lives and be a part of that. Come to think of it, this is an assignment that *all* parents receive—not just the parents of different kids!

Training a Different Child

So how do you go about helping your different child become all that the Lord intended? A classic parenting scripture, Proverbs 22:6, says, "Train up a child in the way he should go; even when he is old he will not depart from it." Usually when we cite this verse, we do so to emphasize the need to train a child while he's young, and rightly so. But the Amplified Bible renders the passage this way: "Train up a child in the way he should go [and in keeping with his individual gift or bent], and when he is old he will not depart from it." This is also accurate because the original Hebrew text reads, "Train up a child *in his way.*"

I believe Proverbs 22:6 contains a powerful child-training principle. Each child, as uniquely designed by God, has his own individual way—a learning style, talent, or manner—of relating to the world. If we can understand what makes a child distinctive, we can learn to work with, instead of against, his natural inclinations. So often we parents of different children spend all our energy on trying to make our kids more like the others, when this shouldn't be our goal. Instead, we should focus on being the Lord's instrument in their lives. We should help them grow into the strengths God intended to produce in them when He designed their bodies and planned their life stories.

For example, if your child is naturally physically active, inattentive, and not interested in schoolwork, you shouldn't try to change his basic temperament. God created him the way he is for a reason. But he still needs an education. Working with his nature instead of against it might include things like letting him practice his reading with books that appeal to his innate interest in excitement and action instead of the reader the school uses, and giving him frequent exercise breaks to help him get through his homework.

But you also shouldn't fail to get to the heart of your child's inattention. Though he probably has real physical traits that make him different, he also has a sinful nature just like the rest of us. While he finds it hard to pay attention, he also wants to do what interests him and tends to resist what he doesn't enjoy. So as you try to help him get the homework done, you also need to confront him with the claims of Christ on his life. Jesus lived His whole life for others, giving up the right to reign in heaven for a time so we could join Him there one day. God calls us to have the same attitude that Jesus had (Philippians 2:4-8). We all must learn to die to our own desires and live for God's glory instead. Even little ones can be motivated to do things they don't like if we teach them to do it in responsive love for the Lord, who has given so much to them.

Dealing with Your Temptations

Your child isn't the only one who needs to die to his desires. As you walk with your child in this way, you can be sure God will use the relationship to expose not just your child's weaknesses and sins, but your own as well. This certainly happened to me.

When Eric was little, life was so hard for him! Literally nothing was quick or simple. I wanted so badly to make his life easier. Sometimes I made excuses for him when what he really needed was more support so he could follow through on what was required of him, even if it was hard. At times I overprotected him. You may remember from Dumbo's story that his mother was locked up as a "mad elephant" when she responded in vengeful anger toward those who were picking on her precious baby. Under pressure, I too was capable of becoming a mad elephant! On occasion I lashed out at kids who picked on Eric, or chewed out teachers who I thought expected too much of him.

Sympathy for Eric wasn't the only reason I sometimes made wrong choices. Not only did I want to make life easier for Eric; I also wanted to make it easier for myself. Sometimes I cut corners in my discipline just because I was tired of dealing with a child for whom everything was a big deal. His behavior also frequently embarrassed me. I wanted to control his conduct because there were times when he made me look bad. I yearned to get him to stop having meltdowns not because his behavior was not glorifying God, but because his behavior wasn't glorifying me. Sometimes I was harsh with Eric because getting him to conform was, at that moment, more important to me than winning his heart for Christ and His kingdom.

I learned that I needed to constantly cry out to the Lord and ask Him to enable me to be gentle and patient with Eric. I asked for the grace to spare no effort in teaching him to honor God not only with his heart, but also with his behavior. I tried to remember that, while Eric had a real disability that made doing the right thing so much harder for him, God had commanded me to teach Eric to obey Him—and I needed to be faithful in doing that.

People sometimes would say, "It's okay. He can't help it" when Eric would misbehave. But I knew that wasn't really true. Yes, it was harder for Eric to do the right thing, but it wasn't impossible, because he sometimes did it. He just needed much more help and support than most kids. My job was to offer that help and support consistently, gently holding him to God's standard for his behavior and being patient with his failures. This meant I needed lots of grace!

I asked God to enable me to love Eric the way that Jesus loved people when He lived among us. He had great sympathy for those struggling with their sins and other limitations, and His compassion shines from every page of the Gospels. But Jesus also loved people enough to confront them with their sin. His kindness never tempted Him to tell those who needed to change that they were fine the way they were. And He never, ever sinned in the ways that I sometimes did—valuing comfort, convenience, or reputation over His Father's glory.

I Wanted a Miracle

But I didn't start praying like that right away. When Eric was little, I begged God over and over for a miracle. I wanted an instantaneous change so that Eric could become all the things I'd dreamed of when I was expecting him. It would be great! No one would think I was a bad mother anymore because he would obey me—at least as well as other kids did. My life would be easier, too. I could go out for coffee with my girlfriends once in a while and leave Eric with a babysitter. Oh, how I wanted to be delivered from the challenge of living patiently and lovingly, day by day, with a child who was so hard to handle!

Please don't misunderstand me. Not all my motives were selfish. I passionately wanted Eric to have a more normal life for his own sake, too. I even persuaded myself that his healing would be the best thing for *God*, because it would show everyone how great He was. Just imagine if one day Eric had suddenly become a typical kid! Everyone would have to know that the Lord had done it.

And just think of how much more useful Eric would be for God's kingdom. He could be that pastor or missionary that I'd dreamed he would become. Surely many people would want to follow the Lord when they heard about the great miracle God had worked for him!

But I prayed and prayed, and nothing like that ever happened. I didn't understand why God didn't seem to realize how much better things would be if He just gave me the desire of my heart!

God Shows His Strength in Weakness

The Bible tells us that the apostle Paul asked for a miracle, too. He had what he called a "thorn...in the flesh" (2 Corinthians 12:7). We don't know what this thorn was, but it must have been unpleasant because he asked the Lord three times to take it from him. At first, Paul might have struggled with the same kinds of thoughts that I had. After all, the thorn was probably getting in the way of his ministry. He thought he could be much more productive as a missionary without the thorn. And think of the testimony his healing would be to the people he was trying to win to the Lord!

God intended to glorify Himself another way, however. When Paul asked the third time, the Lord replied, "My grace is sufficient for you, for my power is made perfect in weakness" (2 Corinthians 12:9). God was saying He wanted Paul to remain weak. Why would He want that?

When I'm feeling strong and capable, I often don't recognize my need for God's grace. But when I know I'm completely incapable of doing what I need to, I pray fervently for His grace. And when I receive it, I know beyond a shadow of a doubt that my ability came from God.

Paul has the same testimony: "Not that we are sufficient in ourselves to claim anything as coming from us, but our sufficiency is from God" (2 Corinthians 3:5). He concluded the account about his thorn by saying that he had learned to remain content in all kinds of weaknesses and afflictions because "when I am weak, then I am strong" (2 Corinthians 12:10). He even went so far as to say,

> I have learned in whatever situation I am to be content. I know how to be brought low, and I know how to abound. In any and every circumstance, I have learned the secret of facing plenty and hunger, abundance and need. I can do all things through him who strengthens me (Philippians 4:11-13).

What an amazing statement—and it came as a result of God's *not* removing Paul's thorn!

Obviously, God sees limitations differently than we do. In fact, Scripture tells us that God has deliberately chosen weak, foolish, and despised people to become wise, righteous, holy, and redeemed by uniting them to Christ by faith (1 Corinthians 1:27-31). And when that happens, God gets the glory, because it's clear that God did something for those people that they couldn't do for themselves.

In the early days of walking with Eric in his way, when I thought about glorifying God, I imagined I'd do it through some amazing achievement. When I thought about Eric glorifying God, I dreamed of a dramatic healing that would remove the weakness that limited his life in so many ways. But God didn't work in our lives that way. As I look back on those years now, I see that every time I thought I had the answers, God humbled me again to show me that I couldn't live this life apart from His provision. And every time I cried out to Him for strength and wisdom, He provided the grace we needed to move forward in whatever new challenge we faced.

Now that Eric's a man, one of my chief joys is to see him beginning to understand what it took me so long to recognize—that God is glorified in his weakness. He doesn't have to be ashamed of his differences or try to hide the things he still struggles with. And neither do I. I don't need to present myself to you as a mother who did everything right. Instead, I can boast in my weakness like Paul did, and glorify God by telling you that although I messed up in so many ways, the Lord was still faithful to bring His healing into our lives.

God didn't do it the way I wanted Him to. Instead of an exciting healing for Eric, He slowly healed the broken places in *both* of us as we lived in relationship with one another day by day while looking to Him in faith. Today, the most important thing about Eric isn't that he speaks, or that he's attending college, or even that he has friends. It's that he's learning to trust the Lord with his weaknesses, and so am I.

God will do this for you and your child as you walk with him or her. I sincerely hope that your autism spectrum son speaks one day, and goes on to make awesome progress in school. I'd be thrilled to hear that your daughter, who won't stay in her seat at school, goes on to become a professional athlete. How wonderful it would be to celebrate your obsessive child's triumph as his attention to detail gained him success as an engineer as an adult!

But whether or not God is pleased to grant your child that kind of temporal achievement, you can be sure that He will use the challenges in her life to conform her to the image of His Son. You also can be confident that He will cause you to grow in faith as you come to Him with your own weakness and brokenness and ask for grace. Look to Him, dear sister, for He is faithful!

Recommended Resources

Fitzpatrick, Elyse and Jim Newheiser, with Dr. Laura Hendrickson. *When Good Kids Make Bad Choices.* Eugene, OR: Harvest House, 2003.

Hendrickson, Dr. Laura. *Finding Your Child's Way on the Autism Spectrum.* Chicago: Moody, 2009.

Hubach, Stephanie. *Same Lake, Different Boat: Coming Alongside People Touched by Disability.* Phillipsburg, NJ: Presbyterian & Reformed, 2006.

Langston, Kelly. *Autism's Hidden Blessings.* Grand Rapids: Kregel, 2009.

Chapter 18

Training Teens
in the True Faith

§ *Jan Steenback* §

No doubt you have heard stories like this one: A young man who was born into a Christian home, attended church, and was active in the church's youth group has chosen to go a different route. His new direction has him running with the wrong crowd. He no longer cares about church and the *boring* Christian life. Despite the sacrificial love of his family and church, he walks away from his Christian environment. The youth who once sang in the choir and participated in mission trips has gone prodigal.

Other variations are the young lady raised in a loving and supportive Christian home who breaks hearts as she chooses a lifestyle of sex and drugs. Or the pastor's son or daughter, who finds a "soul mate," moves out of the house, and will not commit to marriage. Or the high school student who graduates, moves off to college, and though he doesn't practice an immoral lifestyle, Christian fellowship and worship are no longer a priority to him. He is too busy to get involved in church.

Circumstances vary, but the stories have common threads. These teens come from God-fearing families, churches, and perhaps Christian schools. At one time, they were praying, reciting verses, participating in church activities, and sharing the gospel with others. Then for some reason or other, they transform into "someone else." Relationships are strained and broken. Expectations and hopes crumble into pieces that seemingly can never be put back together. And the parents and church members who watched these teens grow up are left devastated. *It is as if they never really knew this teen or young adult.*

Many are taken by surprise when such teens reject Christianity. How can this possibly happen to young people who once claimed to know God, or may still claim to know Him? This teen may be your child, niece, nephew, grandchild, student, team member, or someone else close to you. As you read this, you may be in the middle of, or may have experienced, a similar heartbreak. There is confusion. There may be guilt and gossip. You wonder, *What happened?* You grieve. You grasp to understand how a *good* kid going down the *right* road could have possibly gotten off course.

How can teens and young adults who are aware of the right path get off track like this? Doesn't Proverbs 22:6 say if you train up a child in the right way, he will not depart from it? Did God's promise fail? The answer is no. To claim Proverbs 22:6 as a fail-proof promise that a child who is raised godly will remain that way is misleading. Proverbs is filled with *wisdom principles*, which are not the same as actual promises. This verse makes the point that *the way* (the direction you point a child, whether right or wrong) will become his "rut," and over time, it will be hard for him to get out of his rut. But it *is* possible. There are no guarantees when it comes to raising children.

As a parent, teacher, coach, or youth worker, you are responsible for faithfully presenting God's Word to children, but ultimately each child will choose to accept or reject direction. God will hold you responsible for faithfully presenting His Word. You are not responsible for the child's choices.

For parents and others who despair of a teen's wrong choices, hope is found in prayer and dedicated Bible study. There are reasons young people choose different routes. Wisdom is needed to help prevent children from taking unexpected detours—the wisdom of presenting them with the true faith.

Hope: Recognize Detours and Roadblocks

The Bible provides God's road map of directions and answers. "All Scripture is breathed out by God and profitable for teaching, for reproof, for correction, and for training in righteousness, that the man of God may be competent, equipped for every good work" (2 Timothy 3:16-17). Failing to carefully teach and apply biblical principles is like giving a child a map with the wrong directions. If you mishandle Scripture, you may have good intentions and unknowingly point children in the wrong direction.

Have you ever had difficulty reading a map that someone has marked and scribbled on? The details of routes and exits become hard to read. That is why we need to make sure God's Word is clearly presented to our young people. When man's opinions and ideas are mixed with biblical truth, it's like messy scribbles that cover up important details on a map. The result is difficulty in determining the correct directions. This makes the destination of Christlikeness more confusing and can lead young people in the wrong direction, leading to detours and roadblocks.

A church whose youth ministry minimizes biblical teaching and is more focused on activities and conforming outward behavior is making the map more confusing. Parents' expectations may drive church and youth leaders to be most concerned with making sure youth look and act like Christians.[1] There is a need for caution; this is the wrong direction. Youth programs that focus on changing behavior in order to meet expected standards may end up de-emphasizing biblical truth. In the end, teens will learn how to *act* like a Christian yet will fail to be in a relationship with Christ.

In his book *What the Bible Says About Parenting*, John MacArthur explains, "Even some of the better Christian parenting programs focus on relatively petty extrabiblical matters and not on the essential biblical principles."[2] God's road map must be carefully applied when training and directing a child down the righteous path. "There is a difference between devotion to principles and devotion to a person. Jesus never proclaimed a cause. He proclaimed a personal devotion to Himself."[3]

Promoting and protecting a child's "self-esteem" is also a dangerous detour from Christlikeness. According to a Web article, self-esteem is defined as "a widely used concept both in popular language and in psychology. It refers to an individual's sense of his or her value or worth, or the extent to which a person values, approves of, appreciates, prizes, or likes him or herself."[4] Self-esteem thus becomes a reason to accuse or blame others. It leads to clever manipulation and a sense of privilege.

This direction is rooted in psychological interpretations rather than Bible principles. Scripture warns, "Cursed is the man who trusts in man and makes flesh his strength, whose heart turns away from the LORD" (Jeremiah 17:5). You fail youth when the goal of Christlikeness is mingled with the worldly message of self-esteem. God intends that we put off the old way of self-love and pride and be remade into the image of Christ (Colossians 3:1-10).

When it comes to raising children, care should be given to handling disappointments, suffering, and persecution in a biblical manner. Raising expectations of praise, privilege, and a life without suffering do not mirror Christlikeness. Tedd Tripp states in his book *Shepherding a Child's Heart*, "For a man to live peacefully, he *must* find the only identity in this life that has worth; that of the *child of God*."[5] God has a good purpose in a child's emotional or physical loss. Romans 8:28-29 is an encouragement to believers who suffer. All things—both good and bad—are meant by God to mold His children into Christlike identity, to help them grow to reflect His image. "He was despised and rejected by men; a man of sorrows, and acquainted with grief; and as one from whom men hide their faces he was despised, and we esteemed him not" (Isaiah 53:3). We should encourage youth to view suffering as a road toward building godly character (James 1:2-4).

Finally, another detour affecting young people is misdirected zeal for them to come to saving faith. After years of teaching in Christian schools, I have come to the conclusion that we have an identity crisis among the children who go to them. Many Christian school students cannot biblically explain salvation. Take your average preteen. Ask him or her to describe how a person gets into heaven. The typical response is, "You have to ask Jesus into your heart." But what does *that* mean? Answers vary: "You have to be saved; you have to pray a prayer and tell Jesus you are a sinner, and you have to *mean it* when you pray." When asked to explain what "saved" means or what kind of prayer to pray, many young people hit a wall. They don't know what to say. The answers they do share are "facts" they were told when they were young. They cannot give a response that is biblically sound. They repeat what they have been taught, but without fully understanding what Scripture teaches. They think becoming identified with Christ (or becoming a Christian) is going forward in a service, praying a prayer, and being assured with a decision card.

Paul Washer is a pastor who has spoken to thousands of teens. He warns of a gospel presentation that may be popular but is unbiblical, weak, and misleading. After emotionally charged altar calls, young people are asked if they want to go to heaven. If they say yes, they are given a model prayer to recite. Then these converts might be asked, "Are you saved?" If the new converts are not sure, they are given a Scripture verse for assurance. Washer refers to such methods as psychological manipulation. Too often these altar calls fail to produce genuine Christians. Salvation should not be pressured, or take on a "game plan" in order to have a good count of salvation decisions. Salvation is a matter of individual reconciliation between a person and God. Salvation requires a solid understanding of sin, repentance, and the resultant life of denying self.[6]

At times teens question their salvation and identity with Christ. That is not a bad thing. What's unfortunate is when young people are reassured of their salvation in an unbiblical way. For example, they are reminded or told of a time they asked Christ into their heart. They are shown a decision card with a date on it. Can you see the problem with giving such reassurance? A mere outward action doesn't necessarily mean true salvation took place. Instead of experiencing a spiritual birth into God's kingdom and being changed by God's amazing grace, these young people are trying to please their parents or teachers by living morally in the strength of their own flesh. They got off at the wrong exit on the map, short of the correct destination.

Many such teens may walk away from a Christianity they could not identify with. Perhaps more dangerous are those who continue onward with false assurance. They think they are on the right path, but aren't. Matthew 7:21-23 warns that *many* are deceived and don't realize they are hopelessly lost and not in a relationship with Christ. They will testify of the works they did for Jesus, but He will reply, "I never knew you; depart from me, you workers of lawlessness" (Matthew 7:23). They may look and behave as Christians, but in their heart is a false identity. They know about Christ, study the Bible, pray, and do the "right things." But their Christian identity is based on knowledge rather than a personal relationship with Christ as a new, born-again child of God. For this reason, it is crucial to encourage youth to examine their hearts. Are they truly related to Christ, identifying with Him?

How clear is the road map you present to your kids or other young people? Are you committed to knowing the way and clearly present-ing biblical truth? Is Christlike identity your focused destination? Do young people see you as a role model living a Christian life for God's glory rather than for personal goals?

Identity Crisis: Know Your Destination

If a person is not sure where he is going, he probably will not get to his destination. And even if he did, how would he know? Teens need a clear understanding of what it means to be a Christian. A Christian is a new creation in Christ. Inviting Christ into one's life isn't simply adding a feature that will make this life better (2 Corinthians 5:17). A Christian is a *child of God*. A child takes on the image of his father, whether earthly or heavenly. In a Christian's case, the child reflects God's character. When teens lack a clear view of the godly destination of Christlikeness (their identity), they will go off track.

Could it be that today's churches and homes are too identified with the vanity of fleeting years lived on this earth? Genuine Christians are not citizens of this world. They are heirs to an eternal kingdom. So don't fail to direct teens to see the awesome glory of a life beyond this one. All too often teens are more in touch with their self-esteem rather than the joy of esteeming God. They aren't taught the God-designed identity and purpose of life: to worship and glorify God. They don't realize that a biblical view of God, others, and self results in *selflessness*. In contrast, selfishness results when there is a wrong view of God, oth-ers, and self.[7]

You want to help youth to see the eternal destination of this life. Bring into focus the value of eternity over this temporary life. If life is represented by a grain of sand, and eternity is represented by all the grains of sand in all the beaches, oceans, and deserts and even by the specks of dust in the universe, then why are we so concerned about this life and what we can get out of it? It seems a bit foolish to be so con-sumed with something as insignificant as a tiny grain of sand; here is the crisis of identity. Sadly, youth see many of their role models place more value on a "grain of sand."

The privileged of this life are Hollywood stars, legendary musicians, the rich and famous. Some youth identify with them, whereas others identify with social and political reforms. And all are vain and empty compared to living as a rich, privileged child of the eternal King. If you are training youth, you are responsible to model a life that affirms the eternal values of kingdom citizens. In essence, teens who walk away from the faith do not fully understand the value of identification with Christ. God's redeemed are destined to God's kingdom, and there is no better end of the road.

We who are Christians fail to reflect Christ when happiness and success in this life are valued above the privilege of growing in Christ-likeness. Youth who leave the faith are usually responding to a message of Christianity that fails to clearly demonstrate what it means to be a kingdom citizen. Christ provides a new life and identity. Heaven is the glorious destination. Christ did not come in order to make life on this earth a heavenly experience. This life is not about self-esteem. It is about esteeming and finding joy in worshiping God. When we keep our focus on the eternal destination, we will provide valuable guidance to youth and teens who are tempted to leave the path of godliness.

The Heart: Identifying Direction

A child's heart and thought life are home to his identity. It is crucial that youth and teens be challenged to biblically examine their identity. Do they understand they were born totally infected with sin (Psalm 51:5; Romans 5:12)? Do they know they sin because they are sinful (Matthew 15:19)? Do they understand that repentance (biblical repentance, not just feeling sorry) is required in order to obtain salvation (Luke 13:3)? Do they understand God's gift of grace (nothing they do) enables them to turn from their sin and be brought into the kingdom of God (Ephesians 1:7; Titus 3:5)? Scripture commands. "Examine yourselves, to see whether you are in the faith. Test yourselves. Or do you not realize this about yourselves, that Jesus Christ is in you?—unless indeed you fail to meet the test!" (2 Corinthians 13:5).

Take care to avoid evaluating the righteousness of a heart by good

deeds and/or compliant behavior. Individuals who appear to be producing good fruit (works) may be living in the flesh. But eventually
such a life will prove to be counterfeit. The Word of God is the evaluation tool. Each person is responsible before God to put their heart to
the test. Are you a real, biblical Christian?

If a young person is truly identified with Christ, Scripture teaches
there *will* be growth and genuine spiritual fruit:

> I am the vine [Christ]; you are the branches [true believers].
> Whoever abides in me and I in him, he it is that bears much
> fruit, for apart from me [relying on self, not grace] you can
> do nothing. If anyone [counterfeit believers] does not abide
> in me he is thrown away like a branch and withers; and the
> branches are gathered, thrown into the fire, and burned (John
> 15:5-6).

Note the last part of John 15:6. The illustration is one of pruning.
Though on the vine, not all branches are producing fruit. When the
vinedresser comes and discovers no fruit he cuts off the branch and
puts it in a brush pile to burn. This pictures how individuals are exam-
ined by God. He sees the heart and knows the fruit. If a person's salvation or spiritual growth is based on self-effort and works instead of the
grace and deliverance of Christ, then God will separate the worthless
branch from the vine. Only Jesus Christ can save a sinner.

Scripture commands each individual, before God, to examine his
own heart. Lovingly challenge youth to an honest evaluation of their
hearts to determine whether there is evidence of biblical salvation. One
of the best examples of the kind of fruit a genuine believer shows is
found in the Beatitudes (Matthew 5:3-12), which appear at the beginning of the Sermon on the Mount (Matthew 5–7). This sermon of
Christ, by God's grace, reveals sin and the need for repentance and salvation, and provides biblical assurance of true faith.

Biblical Direction: The Sermon on the Mount

When directed with love and passion, youth respond well to a challenge. There is no higher goal to put before their lives than grasping
kingdom citizenship. There is nothing more fulfilling than to join in

kingdom living. Direct youth to study the Sermon on the Mount. John MacArthur commented,

> I think we ought to study it because it's the best means I know of evangelism, You say, "What do you mean, evangelism?" I'll tell you this: if we ever live the Sermon on the Mount, it will knock the world over. It's the greatest tool of evangelism there is—to live this kind of life.[8]

The principles in the Beatitudes and sermon are the *gospel* road map for young souls who require and seek direction, hope, and redirection. Matthew 5 opens with the Beatitudes. Here is the highest-quality mirror one can use to check the heart. Here you can verify your profession of salvation and move forward in Christlike identification. Here is one of the clearest pictures of a kingdom citizen. Here a redeemed heart is put on display. Here, by God's grace and Spirit, you discover if heart motives and attitudes reflect the ones described by Christ. A life that displays Sermon on the Mount principles is based on the internal condition of the heart, not on external circumstances or knowledge. Happiness is sourced in a heart right with to God, apart from circumstances.

The Beatitudes show the heart and character of Christ. Genuine kingdom citizens will reflect His image in their character. Each genuine believer, by God's transforming power (grace), will reflect purity, meekness, humility, and steadfastness in the face of struggles and trials. A genuine believer can be distinguished from a hypocrite: A genuine believer develops and exhibits habits of Christlikeness, whereas a hypocrite is one who promotes himself with his religious thoughts and activities. Biblical humility and purity do not reside in his heart.

The first Beatitude is foundational to all that follow: "Blessed are the poor in spirit" (Matthew 5:3). This is contrary to self-esteem. You cannot enter into the kingdom without realizing your spiritual poverty. Unless you face the stark reality that your heart is bankrupt because of sin, you will not mourn over your sin (Matthew 5:4) or begin to hunger and thirst after righteousness (Matthew 5:6).[9] This describes a heart affected by the gospel. It describes a humble heart no longer defending itself, accusing others, or making excuses. Those poor in spirit gain rich grace and citizenship in the kingdom of God.

"Blessed are those who mourn" (Matthew 5:4). Biblical mourning over sin is genuine repentance. It is not just feeling sorry or guilty. The sorrow is not based on a loss of things, expectations, or relationships. The Puritan Thomas Watson explained repentance in his book *The Beatitudes* and said, "The measure of grief over sin should exceed any other loss, the loss of possessions, relationships and even loved ones."[10] Help youth to examine their heart to see if their remorse or sorrow is based on an intense grief over sin. This grief over sin is proof of salvation. The reassurance found in biblical mourning over offending God is the comfort found in forgiveness.

"Blessed are the meek" (Matthew 5:5). Meekness is the result of biblical mourning. Meekness is on display when you choose to suffer wrongs without complaining. You aren't out to defend yourself. You are aware of the undeserved mercy God has given you. A heart of meekness seeks to please without the reward of praise. Because a meek heart understands the great offense of sin, it feels no need to get even or react in self-pity. You do not demand or expect special treatment or privileges.[11] When you are meek, you free yourself from the control of peer pressure because you desire to please God and not others. You don't fret about what you have or don't have or your social position. The meek understand they are going to share the inheritance of the Lord when He reigns on the earth. You'll want to bring youth to this evidence of Christlike identification.

"Hunger and thirst for righteousness" (Matthew 5:6) is the action that results from a heart that is affected by the previous Beatitudes. This hunger is a character trait of a kingdom child. It is a hunger that is never satisfied. It is a continual hunger and desire to be filled with God (Psalm 42:1-2).[12] Ask yourself: "Is hunger for God what drives my young adult?" If so, this is evidence that he or she is identifying with Christ. The contrast is hungering after what is best for self, personal comfort, success in life. Kingdom citizens understand that Jesus alone is the satisfying Bread of Life (John 6:35, 48). Christlikeness is the end, the destination that satisfies.

The merciful, pure in heart, and peacemakers (Matthew 5:7-9) possess character traits that flow from a changed heart, a new identity. Each trait is affirmation of genuine salvation. When our hearts realize the poverty of our souls, we respond with *mercy to others*. When sin produces deep grief we no longer live for self, but live to glorify God. That is, we are *pure in heart* and we look forward to seeing Him. "For now we see in a mirror dimly, but then face to face. Now I know in part; then I shall know fully, even as I have been fully known" (1 Corinthians 13:12). There is coming a day when we will enjoy complete fellowship with the Lord. And finally, we who are meek are not self-focused. We are *peacemakers* who love God. We don't live to promote themselves.[13] The gospel of peace is evident in our witness. Scripture identifies peacemakers as sons of God who clearly reflect His identity.

According to Martyn Lloyd-Jones, "A Christian is something before he does anything; and we have to be a Christian before we can act as a Christian. Now that is the fundamental point. Being is more important than doing, attitude is more significant than action."[14] The Beatitudes are a service center for a sick heart. And the "mile markers" within the Beatitudes serve as a mirror for youth to examine their heart, to make sure they are truly saved. If they fail to identify with kingdom character, then perhaps they will become aware of their spiritual poverty. As they recognize their spiritual bankruptcy, repentance and kingdom citizenship become a possibility.

Encouragement for the Journey

Don't be fearful of telling youth the journey down this path is not easy. Matthew 7:13-14 says, "Enter by the narrow gate. For the gate is wide and the way is easy that leads to destruction, and those who enter by it are many. For the gate is narrow and the way is hard that leads to life, and those who find it are few." Denying self to live for God is the narrow path. It is a hard path; it is costly. Those who walk it should expect trials, opposition, and persecution because their life reflects the character of Christ (Matthew 5:11). It is a life given solely to God (Matthew 6:9-10). Worldliness has to be rejected as needless baggage (Matthew 6:19-24).

But this journey is well worthwhile! For then, life takes on eternal values and purposes. Your identity with Christ gives hope to a world that is lost. You are a welcomed beam of light in darkness and salt that creates a thirst for God (Matthew 5:14-16). Faithfulness brings rewards in the heavenly kingdom (Matthew 5:12; 6:4,6,18); so encourage teens to endure when the way is hard.

Christlike behavior and joy encourages uncommitted teens to join you in this journey. Begging, arguing, preaching at, isolating, or punishing youth who have left the narrow path is not effective when it comes to reaching their hearts. Such responses are rooted in sinful fear and lack of trust. Live in the power of grace (2 Corinthians 12:9; Ephesians 2:5). God uses merciful compassion to draw teens who have left the faith. His love is not harsh or cruel; it is gentle and patient.

Love makes this journey and destination more desirable. Unconditional love, a life committed to biblical truth, and esteeming God attracts teens to the right path. Pray for their hearts to respond to the Spirit of God and His Word. Your joy and zeal for kingdom identification are powerful testimonies; how you live before young people speaks louder than words.

What should you do if teens leave the true faith? *Pray* for them; *love* them; *speak truth* to them; and *display* the right direction through your own submissive obedience to biblical principles. Carefully *represent* the gospel through your attitudes and responses. *Encourage* them with humility. *Teach* biblical repentance. *Help* them to understand God uses the broken and humble heart. *Share* hope with them. *Be wise* and avoid the detours and roadblocks that prevent teens from enjoying the rewards of kingdom identity. And when they have questions, be ready to give biblical answers.

A teen's heart is both the source of his problem and his hope. Use the Sermon on the Mount as a mirror by which a person can examine his heart. Rather than condemning the teen, lovingly challenge him to look within himself, to examine his own heart before God. In his book *Shepherding a Child's Heart*, Tedd Tripp gives encouragement to those who work with youth. Rather than focusing on changing outward behaviors, appearances, and responses, we should get to the deeper issues. Rely on the Holy Spirit and graciously use the Word of God to strike into the heart and conscience of a child. Ask questions that will cause the youth to pronounce himself guilty before God.[15] As Jesus said, "Blessed are the poor in spirit" (Matthew 5:3).

Even when teens stray from the true faith, we can have hope. In order to help them, we need to watch our for possible detours and wrong directions and set kingdom identity as the ultimate goal. Use the mile markers in Christ's Sermon on the Mount to check for evidence of genuine faith, and then rely wholeheartedly on God's Spirit as you seek to live for Christ with zeal and joy.

Recommended Resources

Doriani, Daniel. *The Sermon on the Mount*. Phillipsburg, NJ: Presbyterian & Reformed, 2006.

Fitzpatrick, Elyse and Jim Newheiser. *When Good Kids Make Bad Choices*. Eugene, OR: Harvest House Publishers, 2004.

MacArthur, John. *What the Bible Says About Parenting*. Nashville: W. Publishing Group, 2000.

———. "Hungering and Thirsting After Righteousness." Panorama City, CA: Grace to You, accessed at http://www.gty.org/Resources/Transcripts/2201.

Tripp, Paul. *Age of Opportunity*. Phillipsburg, NJ: Presbyterian & Reformed, 2003.

Tripp, Tedd. *Shepherding a Child's Heart*. Wapwallopen, PA: Shepherd Press, 2005.

Chapter 19

HOPE FOR CAREGIVERS
OF THE ELDERLY

Holly Drew

It looks like those are storm clouds on the horizon. You are getting older. Your parents are already there. As much as we enjoy watching sunsets, they mark the passing of another day. Day after day our lives are passing away; we're like a "mist that appears for a little time and then vanishes" (James 4:14). The difficulties of aging affect every person who lives a long life, and we will *all* ultimately die. The lives of those we love are passing us by, too. So whether your concern is primarily for a loved one (perhaps a parent) or for yourself, the truth is that no matter how much you fight against it, old age is coming.

Perhaps you're feeling concern now because you know that soon you'll need to care for your parents. Or perhaps you're watching a friend struggle with eldercare responsibilities right now. The burden of caring for the aging affected me some years ago and made me aware that I was woefully unprepared for this difficult time of life.

My Story

My parents died several years ago. My mother died when I was a new Christian and my father followed her four years later. During the last few years of my dad's life, I was responsible for much of his care. He suffered from senile dementia, a condition marked by severe deterioration of mental functions. This was more difficult than I had ever imagined. I struggled with my new and demanding responsibilities.

He struggled with the losses that he was experiencing. I loved him very much and wanted to help, but I didn't know how best to care for him. I am sad that I didn't do better and sometimes think how much more effective I would have been had I been more prepared with sound, biblical wisdom and instruction. It's from the perspective of having already walked through many difficulties that I am writing this chapter to you.

So that I can offer the best help possible, I'm going to share honestly about my struggles. Sometimes the simple knowledge that your response to your predicament is "normal" will help more than anything else. What upset me most during the long months of caring for my dad was how angry and impatient I would get with him. Although I knew that he couldn't help what was happening to him, I found myself scolding him or insisting on doing things for him that he wanted to do himself. I became angry when he needed attention while I was busy doing something else. I was also worried about the money—it was expensive to care for him and his life savings were dwindling away. I was tortured by questions about what I would do if his money ran out. Would I have to use my own money? What would become of him? What was I going to do? How long was this going to continue? Would I be able to endure all the way to the end with him? Not knowing the answers made me fearful.

My hope is that neither of my parents suffered because of my ignorance. I know now that the Lord orchestrated our circumstances. He has used these difficulties in my life to help others who are going through what I faced. And He taught me the importance of a biblical approach to caregiving.

As I said earlier, Dad passed away after four years of debilitating deterioration. Years have since passed, and by God's grace, I have grown in the Lord. I now know that the way I responded during those years was not simply on account of the difficult circumstances surrounding my father's decline. My fear, anger, and impatience were the fruit of sin that already resided in my heart. Though I misunderstood my responsibilities and how to perform them, I also possessed pride and unbelief in the midst of the situation, which produced all kinds of evil responses. Most of all, I was unaware of the help that God had already supplied in the Bible. I misunderstood the love of the Lord and His perfect, sovereign plan for His children. I didn't know how His truth could lift up a heart burdened with trouble. In the Old Testament, God spoke through the prophet Jeremiah and said, "'I know the plans I have for you...plans for welfare and not for calamity to give you a future and a hope'" (Jeremiah 29:11 NASB). I have grown to learn that help comes from Jesus Christ by the Holy Spirit through the Word of God and the fellowship of believers.

I assume you are looking into this chapter because the clouds of old age are somehow darkening your day. Perhaps even now you need guidance on your eldercare journey. This stage of life is a great blessing when viewed in the way God wants you to see it. Eldercare is a very important calling, and even a privilege. In caring for aging loved ones, you become, in effect, an integral part of the process of ushering these dear ones into heaven and trusting the Lord to complete what He has begun. "I am sure of this, that he who began a good work in you will bring it to completion at the day of Jesus Christ" (Philippians 1:6). In addition, the circumstances you face will become a blessing to you as they propel you closer to Christ. His abundant, sacrificial love and care will serve as your refuge from whatever guilt or strain you experience in caregiving. So, let's look at aging and eldercare as the Bible speaks of it: the *honor* of it, the *hope* in it, and the *humility* required for it.

The Honor of Aging

Worldly thinking is very self-focused and obsessed with youth and vigor. This obsession actually flows out of the fear of illness and death. But God doesn't view old age negatively, and we must see it as God does. The Bible teaches, "Do not be conformed to this world, but be *transformed by the renewal of your mind*, that by testing you may discern what is the will of God, what is good and acceptable and perfect" (Romans 12:2, emphasis added). Let's focus on transforming our mind about this important issue.

Many of us dread old age. But the Bible tells us that growing older is a blessed gift. It is not a tragic condition, but rather, it is a blessing full of promise. For instance, Proverbs 16:31 says, "Gray hair is a crown of glory; it is gained in a righteous life." Scripture praises the old age of the faithful woman and man. It is considered a crown, a tribute to kings and queens and those who have accomplished honor.

In the Ten Commandments, long life is promised to those who honor their father and mother (Exodus 20:12). In Psalm 92:14 the aged are given this beautiful promise: "They still bear fruit in old age; they are ever full of sap and green." Even with aging bodies and minds, the person who loves the Lord will continue to live fruitfully, accomplishing all that the Lord has for her—even if that means a simple prayer for others or helping others to grow more Christlike through their service to them. "So we do not lose heart. Though our outer self is wasting away," Paul wrote, "our inner self is being renewed day by day" (2 Corinthians 4:16). The body may be deteriorating, but the elderly need not lose heart. The inner spirit is being renewed every day as they walk closely with the Lord; they're actually growing stronger because of the power of Jesus Christ in them.

Hope When Storm Clouds Loom

God honors the elderly, and He has made it very clear who is to care for them. Again, all children (no matter what their age) are to honor their father and mother. We honor them by being willing to care for them when their authority over us is waning. When Paul gave Timothy instructions about his oversight of the church, he wrote,

> If a widow has children or grandchildren, let them first learn to show godliness to their own household and to make some return to their parents, for this is pleasing in the sight of God (1 Timothy 5:4).

That passage emphasizes that it is a *first* priority to care for the needs of one's own family. Jesus affirmed this when He accused the Jewish leaders of disobeying God's command to care for their parents by designating their money for other "more religious" purposes (Matthew 15:3-9). Our hope in caring for our parents is that God will help us and give us grace to do what He has commanded us to do. He promises He will give you the strength you need for eldercare: "Fear not, for I am with you; be not dismayed, for I am your God; I will strengthen you, I will help you, I will uphold you with my righteous right hand" (Isaiah 41:10-11).

Honor toward parents is commanded in Scripture. But what does such honor look like? Honor is shown to a deserving person through special treatment, attention, and cooperation. It is to treat someone with deep respect and a sense of worth or excellence. Honor in the form of caregiving is more than just a kind gesture. It is a debt owed to those who have sacrificed for, nurtured, and taught us. Many of them have spent a lifetime working and caring for our well-being. So honor is not only an expression of godliness, but one of obedience, an obedience that is pleasing to the Lord. It is also an obedience that the Lord Jesus fulfilled flawlessly on the cross as He cared for His mother, Mary, by giving her into the custody of His beloved friend, John. Our hope in caring for our parents or other elderly people is that we can learn from our Lord's perfect example.

Yes, care for the elderly is God's expectation. But remember that it is also a great privilege. Because the Lord declares old age to be a good thing, we should consider it an honor to be considered worthy to do eldercare. As Paul wrote, "I thank Christ Jesus our Lord, who has strengthened me, because He considered me faithful, putting me into service" (1 Timothy 1:12 NASB). Perhaps our service isn't traveling the Mediterranean world preaching the gospel, as Paul did. Perhaps it's simply caring for an aging loved one. But our hope should be that our wonderful Jesus Christ considers us able to do this service for Him and will fortify us for whatever task is at hand. He is "able to do far more abundantly than all that we ask or think, according to the power at work within us" (Ephesians 3:20).

The Humility Required of the Caregiver

You may find it challenging to live out the responsibility of caring for an aging parent. Things will likely become very difficult at times. You may say, "I've cared for my children; *certainly* I can do this for my parent!" But over time, even the most willing participant may become perplexed or exhausted. Remember, babies are cute, cuddly little creatures given by God to parents early in marriage—at a time when parents have more energy and vigor. But when the time comes to care for the elderly, things are different. The elderly are wrinkled and spotted, and perhaps even smelly. And we're faced with caring for them in the afternoon of life, when we ourselves are tired. Changing an infant's diaper elicits a markedly different response than changing that of a parent. And yet the call to eldercare is every bit as noble and God-honoring as the call to childcare—maybe even more so. God is glorified when we accomplish His will in the difficult tasks we face and we demonstrate that the humble nature of Christ is dwelling within us.

Caring for the elderly may cause you to struggle with unexpected problems:

- Crippling diseases will demand extra time for doctor visits, hospital stays, and attention to medications and their side effects.

- Chronic pain can cause the elderly to experience hopelessness and despair, which often lead to anxiety and depression.

- Loss of hearing, decreased vision, low stamina, and other effects of old age will require closer attention, more help, and greater patience from you.

- Elderly people who are chronically helpless may respond by exhibiting combative behaviors such as abusive speech, hitting or throwing things, refusal to cooperate, and the withdrawal of affection.

- The aged person's diminishing brain function causes confusion for both the elderly and the caregiver.[1]

- The care of an aging parent may drain limited resources—theirs or yours.

It is important to remember that ultimately, all the struggles we face are spiritual struggles. Scripture says, "We do not wrestle against flesh and blood, but against the rulers, against the authorities, against the cosmic powers over this present darkness, against the spiritual forces of evil in the heavenly places" (Ephesians 6:12).

The battle may be in *this* world, but ultimately it is spiritual in nature. The difficulties you face are the result of living in a sin-cursed world that is influenced by the evil one, Satan. But the Lord is still in charge of this world, and your circumstances are placed there by Him. You may find comfort in knowing that "he who is in you is greater than he who is in the world" (1 John 4:4).

A Right Response to the Battle

What responses flow from your heart when you're facing the stress of eldercare responsibilities? Are they kind and helpful? Does the soil of your heart produce ripe and good fruit? Or is the response that comes forth like rotten fruit, spoiled and hurtful? How do you think, talk, or act under the pressure you face? Do you say or think things like...

- "They make me angry! Why don't they do it my way?"

- "I get tired of waiting! They are so slow!"

- "There is so much pressure; I am anxious and worried a lot."

- "I never have time to see anyone but Dad or Mom these days."

- "I am just so depressed."

These hurtful, sinful responses are outward displays of unbiblical thinking. They reveal the kinds of thoughts that are going through your mind. These thoughts are what produce ungodly fruit in your life. You may be thinking things like...

- "I don't want this responsibility—it's too much to handle."

- "I want to serve someone who will appreciate me."

- "I want to have some money left for my own future security."

- "I just want life to be normal again."

Do you see how many times the phrase, "I want" appears in that list? If these responses describe you, perhaps you should ask God to help you look deeply into your heart as you ask, "Who or what is controlling my heart and thereby ruling my behavior? The Lord Jesus

Christ or someone or something else? What is motivating me to act in ways that are unloving, in ways that are not pleasing to the Lord?"

The answers will likely reveal the desire or demand that has become your heart's controlling desire. Perhaps you believe that your life is your own and that you ought to be able to live it as you please. Or you might think that you deserve to be treated with appreciation and gratitude, considering all the sacrifices you have made. Maybe fear-filled thoughts of loss and inability to cope are eclipsing your faith in God's ability to sustain you.

Whatever it is that is prompting your sinful responses is a selfish thought or desire that has replaced the desire to help your loved one or please the Lord. Such sinful, selfish thoughts and desires must be put off and replaced with God-honoring thoughts and desires. Ephesians 4:22-24 instructs believers "to put off your old self, which belongs to your former manner of life and is corrupt through deceitful desires, and to be renewed in the spirit of your minds, and to put on the new self, created after the likeness of God in true righteousness and holiness."

You Are Not Alone

When it comes to your eldercare responsibilities, it is important for you to realize you cannot accomplish this task alone. Because of the effects of sin, everyone who is apart from Christ lacks the ability to change and show the love needed to care for others in a sacrificial way. Without Christ, all efforts are fruitless and will not please God or truly help your loved ones. The good news is that Christ loved us so much that He came to earth as a man, sacrificed Himself, and suffered and died on the cross so that you can be forgiven of your sin before God.[2] If you have come to believe this and are now in Christ, the love and forgiveness poured on you from above can now be poured on others: "In the cross lies the power to instill hope that change can actually happen in us, in our relationships, and in those whom we love fiercely and resent intensely at the same time."[3]

As you respond to God's love demonstrated on the cross, you'll find a love for Him that will generate obedience to His commandments and enable you to rely completely on Him. In John 15:5 the Lord teaches, "I am the vine; you are the branches. Whoever abides in me and I in him, he it is that bears much fruit, for apart from me you can do nothing."

You must look to Christ and learn from Him. He is the best example of someone who continually served, healed, and helped others because He felt compassion on those who needed Him. Jesus said of Himself, "The Son of Man came not to be served but to serve, and to give his life as a ransom for many" (Matthew 20:28). He will provide what you need so you can care for those who need you. Scripture says, "We love because He first loved us" (1 John 4:19). We can love those we care for because the Lord first loved us. So, with the help of the Lord and a renewed desire to please Him, your thinking can change by calling to mind what Scripture teaches.

It's also helpful to keep in mind how highly God regards the elderly. Thus it is a privilege to care for them, given they are so honored in the sight of God. You'll want to pray that God grants you the grace to humbly desire to serve as Christ served:

> Do nothing from rivalry or conceit, but *in humility count others more significant than yourselves.* Let each of you look not only to his own interests, but also to the interests of others. Have this mind among yourselves, which is yours in Christ Jesus, who, though he was in the form of God, did not count equality with God a thing to be grasped, but made himself nothing, *taking the form of a servant* (Philippians 2:3-7, emphasis added).

On those days when you feel utterly overwhelmed, remember that God is faithful and has promised that He will not give you more than you can handle. "No temptation has overtaken you that is not common to man. God is faithful, and *he will not let you be tempted beyond your ability,* but with the temptation he will also provide the way of escape, *that you may be able to endure it*" (1 Corinthians 10:13, emphasis added).

If financial strain causes you to worry about future comforts, remember that the Lord will supply for you because you are His child. "Turn away from evil and do good; so shall you dwell forever. For the LORD loves justice; *he will not forsake his saints. They are preserved forever,* but the children of the wicked shall be cut off" (Psalm 37:27-28, emphasis added). More than financial security, the ultimate security—eternal life through faith in Jesus Christ—is priceless and is guaranteed all of His children because of His great steadfast love.

The Lord promises you will have all you need for every good thing. "God is able to make all grace abound to you, so that *having all sufficiency in all things at all times*, you may abound in every good work" (2 Corinthians 9:8, emphasis added). This means that if you need strength to change another diaper, you'll have it. If you need grace to speak kindly even though you've already answered that question five times over the last twenty minutes, if you ask for help, God will supply it for you. And even in the times when you fail to do what is required, God's forgiveness and perfect love will be there for you as well.

You can rest in the knowledge that God's plan for your life is perfect and everything will ultimately work together for your good and for His glory. He knows what is best for you, and He will help you learn to want what He wants. "We know that *for those who love God all things work together for good*, for those who are called according to his purpose" (Romans 8:28, emphasis added).

Having transformed your mind—having put off the sinful, hurtful thoughts and filling your mind with what Christ would have you think and do—you can look at ways to help your frail, aging parent or friend who has been entrusted into your care by the Lord.

Seeing the Elderly with New Eyes

It helps to see the elderly through new eyes, or from a different perspective. When children act their age, they are usually treated with patience and understanding, even enjoyment. The elderly also act in ways that reflect their age. They stumble, drop things, need assistance getting dressed, and say curious things. The same kinds of care and security provided and modeled for children are effective with the elderly as well. You must employ patience when your aging parents now act out their true age with its forgetfulness and frailty. Allow aging parents the privilege of being themselves and give them the honor and respect they deserve.

As you endeavor to extend meaningful care to the aged, the following suggestions may prove helpful:

- *Show compassion.* Ask the Lord to help you show compassion. We are givers of care, not just custodians of bodies. Complaints and worries should not be casually dismissed or challenged. Pain is pain, whatever the age of the person who feels it. Gently direct the elderly person to the God of comfort and understanding (see 2 Corinthians 1:3-5).

- *Listen.* The elderly have a contribution to make. Despite their failures, each person has a history with ethics, ideas, and ways of doing things. Their historical perspective is valuable. Attention given to their past experience and continuing contribution is a way to show respect and give them dignity. You can demonstrate care by listening to their feelings, thoughts and experiences. Let them talk without interruption, even if they ramble and you understand very little of what is said. Sometimes the elderly just need someone to listen.

- *Share.* Include the elderly in your world; share about personal activities, family news, and events in the community. Seek their advice. Let them help with problems and decisions as much as they can. Family participation can lift the spirits of the elderly. They usually love children and their presence (in small doses) is refreshment.

- *Laugh and be joyful.* An atmosphere of joy makes life much more pleasant. Sing and play with the elderly. Do not take things too seriously and do not take the elderly too seriously. Remember, no one really knows how it feels to grow old and become senile. When asked, most elderly people will reply with amusement that they feel just as they did at 25 years of age.

- *Touch.* This expression of affection can extend beyond words and may in extreme circumstances become the only way of communicating. Sometimes simply sitting and holding a hand creates the most memorable visit. Gently massage their back. Old bones and muscles often ache. Give a hug and kiss before leaving.

- *Speak gently.* "A soft answer turns away wrath, but a harsh word stirs up anger" (Proverbs 15:1). Speak to the elderly in a gentle, conversational tone, not a demanding or controlling one. Respect for the elderly is particularly evident in speech. You may find it necessary to explain a situation repeatedly. Exercise patience. Talk *with* them, not *at* them. Pick something truly admirable about them and develop a conversation about it.[4] Appreciate them and express it. Show confidence by telling them something they can do rather than repeating what they cannot do. And never say, "I told you so."

- *Choose battles wisely.* In spite of whatever frustrating circumstances you may encounter, strive to avoid unnecessary conflict. Consider that giving in (as long as it isn't sinful to do so) may keep peace and joy. Be "eager to maintain the unity of the Spirit in the bond of peace" (See Ephesians 4:3). Let them live in the past…why not?

- *Read to them.* Give them the comfort of the Psalms. Almost everyone can recite Psalm 23 and find comfort there. Psalm 91 speaks of the secret place of security for the elderly. Psalm 92 encourages fruitfulness in old age. Psalm 131 reveals the secret for attaining a life of composure and peace in the hope of the Lord. You might also read books about heaven to them.[5]

- *Pray for them and with them.* If they're able, teach them to keep a prayer journal. To the elderly who are frail and nearing death, their constant activity should be directed toward imploring the Lord for His strength and mercy. In addition, the elderly—especially those who are housebound—could be fruitful in the ministry of prayer for friends, family, church members, and missionaries. Help them to "pray without ceasing" (1 Thessalonians 5:17).

Ministering to the *True* Needs

In your caregiving, seek to assist, encourage, comfort, and give hope. Work with the elderly in seeing God's purposes in suffering, helping them to keep a heavenly perspective and to make every attempt to fulfill God's purposes for their lives—even into old age. The daily details and challenges of eldercare ultimately fade away, and the spiritual issues of life and death are what matter most.

As you guide and help the elderly, point out that growing old and becoming frail is challenging but has a spiritual purpose. As people age and approach the time when they must abandon this life and leave all behind, it is appropriate that frailty and feebleness would overtake them, turning their attention to God's strength and comfort and their need for salvation. God has made His children frail "to show that the surpassing power belongs to God and not to us" (2 Corinthians 4:7). God is preparing His own to meet Him. This is great reason to "rejoice always" (1 Thessalonians 5:16).

Everyone needs to keep a heavenly perspective. Heaven is not merely an imaginary place or a state of mind where everlasting truth and beauty reside. The Bible says that heaven is a real place, a beautiful home for those who love God, prepared just for us by Jesus Christ. To be bound to earthly pursuits and cares is fruitless because "the world is passing away along with its desires, but whoever does the will of God abides forever" (1 John 2:17). Life is eternal and people, especially the elderly, must live accordingly. The apostle Paul showed us that in this life we are to live for Jesus, yet there is something much better ahead. He said, "For to me to live is Christ, and to die is gain" (Philippians 1:21).

The Lord desires His own to have their minds set on heaven. Scripture instructs believers to "set [their] minds on things that are above, not on things that are on earth" because their lives are "hidden with Christ," who is above (Colossians 3:2-3). To give hope to those nearing death, we must place emphasis on the promise of a future with the Savior who loves us. Christ promised to prepare a place, to come again, and to receive His own so that where He is we may be also. He comforts and assures believers that their hearts need not be troubled (John 14:1-3). He can be trusted!

Trusting God's Sovereignty

At the time I was caring for my parents, I wish I had known that time alone with the Lord in His Word and in prayer is *vital* to one's well-being, especially during trials. Only the Lord is powerful enough to calm troubled hearts and smooth the stumbling places on the paths that we walk. My prayer today is, "Teach me your way, O LORD, and lead me on a level path" (Psalm 27:11).

I wish I had known and embraced in my heart the magnitude of God's sovereignty. He oversees every detail of life so carefully with wisdom beyond human understanding. He has overseen the details of this frail person's life for many years, and He will not stop now. It is not *all* up to *me*. Everything is proceeding just as it should, according to His perfect plan for His glory and for my good. Scripture promises that "all things work together for good" for those who love God (Romans 8:28).

Most of all, I wish I had understood the depth and height and breadth of the love of Jesus Christ. It has nothing to do with any worthiness on my part or anything I can do to deserve His love. "He doesn't love us because of any prior goodness on our part. He loves us because he chooses to love us, and the depth of our defection from him should produce in us great humility, gratitude, and patience with others' failures."[6]

Focusing more on God's love for me than on my circumstances is the key to fulfilling all He would have me do. Standing firm in His love is the only answer for all fear, anger, frustration, and worry.

Find God in His Word. He's waiting there to comfort, to love, and to walk with you on this sometimes uncertain and lonely path. He will light the way as truly as the sun at daybreak, and even when the sky seems beclouded with storms.

Recommended Resources

Adams, Jay E. *Wrinkled but Not Ruined: Counsel for the Elderly.* Woodruff, SC: Timeless Texts, 1999.

Cornish, Carol W. and Elyse Fitzpatrick. "Counseling Women Facing Dying and Death," in *Women Helping Women.* Eugene, OR: Harvest House, 1997.

Eyrich, Howard and Judy Dabler. *The Art of Aging.* Bemidji, MN: Focus Publishing, 2006.

Fitzpatrick, Elyse. "Counseling Women in the Afternoon of Life," in *Women Helping Women*. Eugene, OR: Harvest House, 1997; *The Afternoon of Life*, Phillipsburg, NJ: Presbyterian & Reformed, 2004.

Rossi, Melody. *May I Walk You Home? Sharing Christ's Love with the Dying.* Bloomington, MN: Bethany House, 2007.

Part 4

A Woman and
Specific Problems

Chapter 20

HELP FOR HABITUAL OVEREATERS

Shannon McCoy

Christina would describe her eating behavior as having a love affair with food. It began early in her teen years. Food was her companion, her friend, and her lover. It seemed as though she thought about food every minute of the day. At first, her relationship with food was blissful. Whenever she was tired, stressed, angry, sad, or even happy, food always came to her rescue. Then she began to set up special times to be alone with her companion. She routinely met with her at favorite fast-food restaurants. At the grocery store, she knew exactly where to find her chosen friends.

Sadly, Christina did not realize that her companion, friend, and lover would soon betray her. Her eating was getting out of control. She became aware of new, shameful behaviors. She started hiding chocolate candy bars and other treats in her T-shirt drawer so that her husband's disapproving eyes wouldn't see. She would secretly eat her co-workers' lunches. Then she would stop by her favorite hamburger joint on the way home from work and consume every morsel before she reached her home and began to prepare her evening meal.

Christina hated to look at herself in the mirror because she had gained more than 100 pounds since her wedding day. She had maxed out her credit cards buying junk food, diet food, exercise equipment, gym memberships, and clothes of every size. She felt guilty because her 11-year-old daughter, who is 25 pounds overweight, was following in her footsteps. She had stopped going to social events and church functions because she was embarrassed to be seen by her friends. She had become so miserable and ashamed that she felt she couldn't even cry out to God one more time. And although she would not say it aloud, Christina had become angry at God for not stopping her from overeating. Her dear friend, food, had become a demanding taskmaster.

Can you identify with Christina? Many of us can. We know what it's like to try to seek comfort in our favorite food. Most of us have rewarded ourselves with a special treat because we think we've had a hard day. How many times have you said that just one more bite won't hurt anything? And then do you continue to tell yourself that you can stop eating any time you want? It may sound strange to those who don't struggle with overeating, but sometimes some of us feel like we're "in love" with a chocolate chip cookie. We even act like we're having an affair: We sneak around, hide, and eat alone. We lie and deceive ourselves and others. But, like all illicit affairs, this one we have with food will end in heartbreak and destruction. In the end, comfort food doesn't really comfort, does it? In the end, it becomes a hated slave master.

A Fleeting Perspective of Life

A habitual overeater is a person who regularly eats more than is necessary or profitable for her body and health. She does so out of sheer pleasure, joyless habit, or both. She does so because her eating is intertwined with her emotions and her desire for distraction from trouble. Although most of us would agree that there's something more to life than living from cookie to cookie, at heart our overeating says something different. Rather than living with an eternal perspective, we live for the moment, for that special taste sensation and the short-lived feelings of well-being, safety, and the pleasure "one more bite" brings.

Rather than living each day faithfully in light of all that the Lord has done for us, we take our eyes off the true purpose of our lives and get tangled up in the difficulties of our daily activities and routines. We forget that even these things, the day-to-day mundane activities we find both boring and challenging, have eternal purpose when accomplished with an eternal perspective. Getting up, getting our family dressed and out the door to school, working at home or the office for eight hours, and picking the kids up and getting something on the table for dinner all have an eternal perspective when they are done for God and His glory. We are working for the Lord, not others or even ourselves (Colossians 3:23).

When we lose this eternal perspective, then life becomes about our pleasure and every little event potentially provides a reason to eat. Are we stressed about being late to work? A donut might help. Are we stuck in traffic? Where's that bag of chips we bought the other day? When eating becomes about something other than hunger and caring for our bodies, we've lost the eternal perspective.

When our life is only about achieving short-term goals like simply making it through another day, it becomes easier to justify overeating. We need something more than making it through our to-do list. We need a higher calling, and when we fail to grasp it, food easily becomes the answer to bringing temporary pleasure and meaning to our lives. Yet the momentary anesthesia produced by our favorite meal or sugary treat fades quickly. Yes, for a moment the boss's demands, our child's bad attitude and disobedience, our loneliness, the argument with our husband, or our financial crises all disappear in the heavenly bliss of a spoonful of chocolate chip ice cream or in the taste of the slow-melting Ghirardelli Milk Chocolate with Caramel Squares. But all too soon the taste fades and we realize that we are slaves shackled to our bad eating habits.

While it's true that like all slaves we desire freedom, sometimes we may not really want the kind of inner change that the Lord desires for us. We might want to change our bad eating habits because they are embarrassing, frustrating, unhealthy, expensive, or make us feel guilty. However, going on a diet to lose those unwanted pounds because the class reunion is coming up, there's a wedding to attend, or just to get attention doesn't have the power to transform slaves into free men and women. Outward, temporary reasons will not motivate us to stop overeating for long. Our problem with overeating is not simply a problem with food. It's a life-orientation problem and when we live with the wrong orientation—a short-term, fleeting orientation—we will never know the satisfaction, fulfillment and peace we are seeking.

The Long-term View of Life

To stop our habitual overeating, we must grasp a long-term view of life. This does not mean we should neglect our daily, seemingly mundane responsibilities, but that we should view them in light of God's overall purpose for us. God created us for His glory. First Corinthians 10:31 says, "So, whether you eat or drink, or whatever you do, do all to the glory of God." Glorifying God with our lives means that we live every moment of every day with His perspective in view.

In her book *Love to Eat, Hate to Eat*, Elyse Fitzpatrick describes it this way:

> What that means is that everything we do—whether we're eating, drinking, reading a newspaper, driving our car, *whatever* we're doing—is to be done with the attitude and in such a way as to cause others around us to say, "Isn't God great! Isn't He wonderful! Isn't it great to know Him through His Son?"[1]

Glorifying God means that we show others how worthy He is of all our love, trust, and belief. It means that we strive to please Him in every aspect of our lives, including our eating habits. One of the primary problems with habitual overeating is that it isn't focused on God's glory. It is self-focused. When we run to food instead of the Lord for our rescue, we show that we do not love Him, trust Him, believe Him, nor please Him as fully as we could. Now, is it okay for us to receive gratification when we eat food? Absolutely—it is right and good to enjoy the pleasure of eating as long as our motive is to glorify God and not to selfishly satiate our desire to live for and please ourselves.

The Right Heart Motive

So how can we change our habits and live in a way that pleases God? Because our habits flow out of our motives, our habits will never change until the motives of our hearts are changed. Our motives are the reasons that we do what we do, and they emanate from the core of our inner person. When we overeat, we do so because we've got wrong motives. We're motivated to please ourselves, numb our hearts, or ignore the trouble around us by concentrating on a temporary pleasure before us. In *Curing the Heart*, the authors write, "For the sort of change to take place that is pleasing to God and has the power to truly change a person there must be a change of heart."[2]

But our problem is that we can't do this on our own. We cannot directly attack wrong motives because they're hidden in our hearts. There is only one Person who can change our heart's motives. The direction we need to go is up. This vertical dimension is often missed by people when they try to lose weight. Yes, we might offer up a prayer or two out of frustration and desperation. But have we really considered God's way of overcoming our overeating?

Women love relationships. We are mothers, sisters, nieces, girlfriends, and co-workers. But the most important relationship we have is the one with Jesus Christ. This relationship is unique; it is like no other. And this is where our hearts can really change and bring honor to God. Jesus alone has the power to change a self-serving, rebellious slave's heart into a generous, God-honoring free daughter.

Only Jesus Christ knows the real inner you, and He's the only One who is powerful enough to transform your motives so they are God-centered rather than self-centered. He can enable you to bring glory to God. A real, powerful, and ongoing relationship with Jesus Christ is the only sure foundation for breaking the cycle of overeating. As He transforms our motives so that now we long to please, honor, and glorify God in our eating habits, we will not run so quickly to a candy bar because our boss, spouse, or child just made us mad. He will teach us how to handle every situation God's way. If you're not sure whether you have such a relationship with Jesus Christ, please turn to Appendix Two. When it comes to real change, you don't need a life coach. You need a heart-transforming Savior. Jesus Christ is the Savior you need.

Three Spiritual Virtues

In the Bible, God has shown us how to live lives that are marked by the desire to please Him. In order to continue pursuing the God-pleasing change we long for, we need to cultivate three specific virtues. These virtues are highlighted in 1 Corinthians 13:13; they are faith, hope, and love.

Faith

The first virtue we need is faith. The Bible defines faith as "the assurance of things hoped for, the conviction of things not seen" (Hebrews

11:1). This assurance or conviction is the mark of a believer and is described in Scripture as being sure of a future reality. The object of our faith is Jesus Christ, not ourselves or our ability to change. Only when we say the same thing about our need for a Savior—that we are utterly incapable of changing our motives or changing our behavior in any deep or lasting way—can we come to know Jesus Christ. We must put our faith in Jesus Christ alone because He alone has the power to change our hearts. When we habitually overeat, we are not living by faith. Rather, we are forgetting God's promises to care for us and supply all we need. Habitual overeating is unbelief; it is seeking to care for ourselves in ways outside of God's good plan for us.

In 1 Corinthians 10:13, God tells us that He has provided a way for His people to escape from any temptation. His faithfulness will not allow us to be tempted to the point that we cannot endure it. But, instead of believing and trusting in God's faithfulness to us, we believe the lie that food is the answer to alleviating our feelings of stress, worry, anger, boredom, or loneliness. We substitute the temporal pleasures of a gallon of ice cream in the place of the eternal pleasure found in our loving and wonderful God. Faith helps us conquer the lie that food is more satisfying than God's presence. God declares that "in [His] presence there is fullness of joy; at [His] right hand are pleasures forevermore" (Psalm 16:11). When we feel "hungry" for pleasure, we can turn to Him and find fullness of joy. It is in faith that we believe that God is this good, this satisfying.

Of course there are times when we do bring God into our situation without a heart of faith. We might scream out to God, "Please stop me from doing what I'm about to do." But when we find that God has not thwarted our plan to eat an entire pizza, we think that He failed us or did not hear our prayer. Living by faith, however, means that we do not plan to sin. Instead, we plan to be obedient and then ask God for help to obey. A better way to pray is this: "Father, I'm going to find myself in a situation in which I'll be tempted to overeat tonight. Please enable me to obey You and find pleasure in You instead of a pizza."

It doesn't help that society constantly pushes the lie that life is supposed to be easy, without stress or suffering. Talk shows, movies, and so-called experts frequently lead us to the conclusion that any situation that causes us pain is wrong. Author Nancy Leigh DeMoss says in her book *Lies Women Believe: And the Truth that Sets Them Free,*

> Unfortunately, most people mindlessly accept whatever they hear and see. We listen to music, read books and magazines, watch movies, listen to advice, and respond to advertisements without asking ourselves important questions: "What is the message here?" "Is it really true?" "Am I being deceived by a way of thinking that is contrary to the Truth?"[3]

The Bible shows us that life is indeed full of suffering. Yet we can successfully persevere through life's difficulties by placing our faith in God, who loves us and has promised never to leave (Hebrews 13:5). Yes, life is difficult, but we're not alone. God's presence in our lives makes even the most trying circumstances meaningful and joyful. Running to food in response to suffering will never change our hearts or bring true satisfaction. Only Jesus Christ can do that. He's an expert on suffering, and He knows how to sustain us in the midst of it (Hebrews 4:15-16).

Faith in Jesus Christ and His beauty will expose the lie that food is ultimately satisfying. Faith in Him will help us see how our overeating hinders true pleasures and continues to enslave us. Putting all of our trust in Him, instead of what we want to taste, enables us to become more and more aware of the truth that sets slaves free. It will also build more faith within us to believe that God really will help us overcome our bad eating habits and that food is not the answer to our problems. God has promised that by faith we can please Him and that He "rewards those who seek Him" (Hebrews 11:6).

Hope

The second virtue is hope. The object of our hope is the same as the object of our faith. The Bible tells us that we are to have a "steadfastness of hope in our Lord Jesus Christ in the presence of our God and Father" (1 Thessalonians 1:3 NASB). Biblical hope is a confident expectation in God's goodness rather an implication of uncertainty as in "I hope so." Biblical hope is not wishful thinking, but a confident assurance that God will do what He has promised. We can have an outrageous hope in Him because He is the "God of hope" (Romans 15:13) and we know that He holds our future in His hands. We put our hope in the fact that we will attain all that God has for us because our achievements are not based on our abilities but rather on His. When we're concerned about the future—about whether our hearts or circumstances will ever change—hope assures us that God will comfort and sustain us in ways that food never could.

The opposite of hope is despair. Living through the daily activities of life can sometimes lead us to despair. We wonder how we'll make it through whatever crisis may be threatening us, and so we turn to food. Then the realization that we've overeaten again will breed even more despair. Hope in God's character and in His love for us as demonstrated at the cross will help us conquer the despair that fills our hearts in such times. While it's true that we may not have all the answers and that we may have struggled with our eating habits for years, we can continue to hope in God's goodness and His power to change us. Putting our hope in God empowers us to live without despair as we persevere through the struggles and sufferings of the present day.

God's purpose for us is to make us like Jesus Christ. Although Jesus enjoyed food, He was never mastered by it. Our hope is that God is transforming us to become more and more like Him—someone who loved His Father and others more than He loved the pleasures of this life.

When we turn to God and put our faith and hope in His faithfulness, He will enable us to put our bad eating habits to death. Hope placed in the personal promises of God is secure, for God acts and intervenes in our daily lives and can be trusted to fulfill His promise to transform us. We can put our hope in the fact that as we focus on pleasing God, food will no longer have the power to enslave us.

Hope anchors the soul and settles the mind. It leads us to persevere in spite of our failures and ongoing struggles. It assures us that even though we sometimes fail, victory has already been accomplished by our risen Savior. We can have the assurance that the things we hope for are real (Hebrews 11:1) and that we will never be disappointed by the Lord (Romans 5:5).

Love

The third virtue we need to cultivate as we pursue God-pleasing change is love. Love is a determination to act sacrificially for the good of others. In Matthew 22:37, Jesus commanded, "You shall love the Lord your God with all your heart and with all your soul and with all your mind." That means we are to love God with everything that we are and with every aspect of our lives. Love for God is the only power strong enough to break the power of habitual overeating.

When we are practicing overeating as a way of life, we are actually expressing hatred instead of love toward God and ourselves. We are not caring for His creation, our bodies, and in fact are causing harm to ourselves. There are many diseases and health-related illnesses that are directly related to bad eating habits. Some of those are heart disease, diabetes, high blood pressure, gallstones, aching joints, and even some cancers.

The Bible tells us that we love God because He first loved us (1 John 4:19). He showed love for us when He gave us His Son, Jesus Christ, who died on the cross to save us from our sin. As we meditate on God's love for us in Christ, we'll find that our hearts are being transformed from people who love food and self-indulgence to people who love God and disciplined living. Love for God *because* of His love for us will enable us to conquer this enslaving habit and rest in His work for us.

Moving in the opposite direction of God's will for our lives brings on devastating consequences. Faithlessness, hopelessness, and lovelessness are root problems for habitual overeaters. Putting our faith and hope and love by using the comforts and pleasures of food is futile and will end in more despair in the long run.

Loving the Lover of Your Soul

Like Christina, you need to see that your life is "more than food" (Luke 12:23). Your life—everything on your to-do list today—has eternal significance because everything belongs in Jesus Christ and should be accomplished for His glory. Even if you have to face real difficulties today or your day is filled only with the mundane, everything you do and everything you eat must be viewed in the eternal perspective of God's fame and pleasure.

Living a life of faith, hope, and love may sound impossible to you right now. If it does, it's because you're looking only at yourself and your ability. Instead of thinking about the strength you'll need to some-how pull yourself up by your own bootstraps, focus on the work that Jesus Christ has already accomplished for you. He is the source of this triad of virtues. He is the source of your faith—because of what He's done, you can believe that true change is possible. He is the source of your hope—because He is ruling right now as the ascended King of heaven, you can remain assured He will transform your heart and life in His time and by His power. And He is the source of your love—because He first loved you, you can love Him and choose to find your pleasure in Him rather than in food. He's done everything for you and given you everything you need. Because of His work, you can find the grace you need to overcome this sin in your life and break free.

Recommended Resources

DeMoss, Nancy Leigh. *Lies Women Believe: And the Truth that Sets Them Free*. Chicago: Moody, 2001.

Eyrich, Howard and W. Hines, *Curing the Heart: A Model for Biblical Counseling*. Ross-shire, UK: Christian Focus, 2002.

Fitzpatrick, Elyse. *Love to Eat, Hate to Eat*. Eugene, OR: Harvest House, 1999.

Chapter 21

Breaking the Chain
of Generational Sin

⸶ Nanci McMannis ⸶

Years ago, my daughter was caught cheating on a first-grade spelling test. She imagined the worst—getting kicked out of school, confessing to mom and dad, going back to kindergarten, or hearing "You're stupid" from her brother and sisters. But that's not what happened. She had a wise and loving teacher who simply asked her why she had cheated. "I didn't want to make a mistake," she confessed as a big tear rolled down her cheek. Getting down on her knees, the teacher spoke kindly and said, "My job is to teach you. But I can't help you if you cheat or hide behind someone else's work. By making mistakes, we learn what we need to work on."

While that story may be simple, the lesson is profound: *The Lord wants us to learn from our mistakes by taking individual responsibility for our sin.*

Since the first sin committed in the Garden of Eden, all of us have turned excuse-making, blame-shifting, and covering up into an art form. Adam blamed Eve (and by implication, God). Eve blamed the serpent. We're all excuse-makers and because it's so much a part of our life, most of us don't think it's a big deal. But owning up to and taking individual responsibility for our actions *is* a big deal—especially to God. The clear biblical truth is that if we fail to learn from the sins of the past, if we cover them up or blame someone else, we'll probably repeat them—whether it's our own sin or the sin of our parents or grandparents. *We* are responsible—not our parents or anyone else—for what we choose to do. And like my daughter in the aforementioned story, we can choose to hide or try to cover up, or we can choose to fight our sin honestly and openly with God's help.

What Is Generational Sin?

Generational sin is a willful, unbiblical pattern of disobedience learned from one generation by the next. Every family passes their patterns of sin on to the descendants because every family is comprised of sinners. Everyone has sinned and fallen short of the glory of God (Romans 3:23)—in this we're all alike. But every family is also unique in their particular sin patterns. For example, one family might respond to difficulties through overeating. Another family might resort to alcohol. Whatever the case, every family faces the challenges of life in their own sinful way. No family is immune from sin.

In this chapter, when I speak of "generational sin," I am not saying there is a particular pattern of sin that is passed on through our genes or that there are curses that *force* families to sin in a certain way. As fallen people, as part of the human race, we all are guilty of both original sin (the sin nature) and personal sin (the particular way our nature manifests itself every day).

There are some Christians who are concerned and confused about what are called "generational sins." Some people teach that there are "family curses" or "sins of the father" that predetermine how we respond to life. In this chapter, I will address these misconceptions and also give you hope that you do not have to sin in the same way that your parents (or grandparents) did. The biblical term "sins of the fathers" has to do with God warning His special people that He was a jealous God and that there are consequences for violating His laws (Exodus 20:3-6). But Jesus Christ fulfilled all the law and offers hope for change to individuals who repent and place their faith in Him.

Hide-and-Seek

Hiding behind someone else's strengths or weaknesses, or claiming that we sin because of "generational curses," gets in the way of our learning. In addition, making excuses or blaming others for our own decisions complicates our lives. Each of us needs to take personal responsibility for what we do in life. Recently I ran into a 26-year-old former Sunday school student who told me about how her life was all messed up. "I feel like I've lost my faith. There's lots of baggage, you know—sins of the father." She blamed her struggles on her family and on hypocrisy in the church. She took no responsibility for her choices. The reality is families, friends, and even churchgoers will let you down because everyone sins.

When we take responsibility for and learn from our decisions, we move forward. We make change possible. The Bible calls this repentance, and it is one of the greatest gifts God has given man. "For human beings the whole possibility of redemption lies in their ability to change. To move across from one sort of person to another is the essence of repentance: the liar becomes truthful, the thief honest, the lewd pure, the proud humble."[1]

None of us chose the family we were born into, but by faith we can believe that God chose our particular family for us. Many of us today feel hopeless, trapped, and chained to the consequences of our family's sin. Perhaps you have pledged or promised yourself never to repeat the past. But the pattern you once hated is now the reality of your life. We can search for answers, but "nothing that the world has to offer can change the human heart," says Elyse Fitzpatrick in her book *Counsel from the Cross.* "We need to set our eyes on something beyond ourselves or our failures. We need to glimpse something that is more powerful. We need to see Jesus Christ and the transforming glory of God."[2]

When we turn to the pages of Scripture, we can gain clarity and learn from our mistakes. Too often the things we learn or believe are based on preconceived notions or the influence of friends, relatives, or supposed media experts. "The Scriptures' self-testimony is that it was written so that we might have hope (Romans 15:4), know truth (John 17:17), and have life (John 6:63, 68)."[3]

In the same way that my daughter's teacher's job was to guide her toward what was required, right, and honorable, God gives us guidance through the Scriptures so that we can have a solid foundation for understanding exactly what God wants us to do. By looking to God, we avoid falling into generational sin patterns, behaviors, or responses that are habitual, familiar, and destructive. According to Scripture, only God's truth can set us free (John 8:32).

Many people who struggle with generational sin believe their problem stems from growing up in an ungodly home. Mary Somerville writes, "If my child's salvation depends entirely on my ability to start them off right, then he or she is certainly doomed!"[4] She goes on to say that through the work of the Holy Spirit, God's grace helps us in spite of our sin. "No matter what we once were, whether through your own rebellion or through our parents' sin, we do not have to remain that way (1 Corinthians 6:9-11)."[5] How exciting to think that God can transform us no matter what our family history! We're talking here about the kind of transformation that changes the very nature of a person. God begins this change when we honestly recognize our sin and admit how short we fall from His perfect and holy standard.

Spiritual Blindness

Sometimes we are blind to our own problems yet aware of the faults in others (Matthew 7:1-5). Doubting God's ability or His willingness to forgive us can also cause us to stumble and lose hope. The Bible teaches that God has given us everything we need for life and godliness (2 Peter 1:3). He is the creator of man and knows us better than we know ourselves. The kind of life we live is a choice *we* make every day. And God, by His grace, has given us the answers to our problems and the Spirit to help us overcome them.

When it comes to breaking away from the past, we have to come to a point at which we decide that enough is enough. In the midst of our sorrow and deep reflection, we have to take responsibility for what our lives have become. And when we cry out for help, God will listen. He will grant His children the grace to take responsibility for their sins. God desires real transformation in our mind and heart—not just our outward behavior. He knows our thoughts and intentions (Hebrews 4:12); there is nothing we can hide from Him.

God's View

Growing up in a messed-up home is not a legitimate excuse for making sinful choices in life. "For while we were still weak, at the right time Christ died for the ungodly" (Romans 5:6). The fact that we have all sinned and fallen short of God's perfect standard was dealt with by Jesus Christ on the cross of Calvary (Romans 3:23). Jesus paid the ransom for our sin with His blood (Romans 5:8-10). If we are His, we are no longer His enemy. But we need to agree with what God says about our sin. As Christians, we are in a war against the enemy, Satan. We're also fighting against our flesh and the world. Our family's unbiblical patterns play into these battles, and learning to say what God says about our sin is a first step toward overcoming the problem.

Ownership

God wants us to take responsibility for our own actions. Only when we do so can we know happiness in the life to come. Remember, Jesus said that in this world we will experience trouble. The good news of Jesus Christ is that He fulfilled the requirements of God's law so our trouble with God has been handled by His Son in our place. "For God did not send his Son into the world to condemn the world, but in order that the world might be saved through him" (John 3:17). Even though our problem with God has been handled, we continue to have problems with our own sin. According to Scripture, our problem is that we love the world and pleasing ourselves more than we love Jesus. "This is the judgment: the light has come into the world, and people loved the darkness rather than the light because their works were evil" (John 3:19). Jesus is the light of the world. He understands our sinfulness and our natural unwillingness to change. "We do not have a high priest who is unable to sympathize with our weaknesses, but one who in every respect has been tempted as we are, yet without sin" (Hebrews 4:15). We don't have to suffer on our own. When we become a child of God, we can approach the throne of grace with confidence. Instead of shame and sorrow, we can receive mercy and grace to help us in our time of need (Hebrews 4:16).

Motives

God is not ignorant of our motives. We think we can hide or blame others for our sinful practices, but we can't. We want what we want, and we don't want anyone—including God—to rule us. Illustrator

Mary Englebreit has it right when she quips, "It's good to be queen." We love to sit on the throne and have the world revolve around us. Our bent is to selfishly put our wants above others' needs.

There is an expression in biblical counseling: "Just two choices on the shelf: serving God or serving self."[6] Denying ourselves is not easy. Everyone—those from good homes and those from very broken ones—must learn to obey the Lord. "Because God is man's creator, man owes him his allegiance, obedience, and worship."[7] It is a believer's job to make God look good and bring Him glory no matter what their circumstance, trial, or stumbling block.

In Christ Alone

There are many people who say they believe in Jesus' name, but they do not confess Him as their personal Savior and Lord. If we refuse to say that we sin or that those we love sin, we refuse the help of the One who was born to "save his people from their sins" (Matthew 1:21).[8] Jesus redeems sinners who then, by faith, follow and trust Him, acknowledging that He is Lord over their whole life. The Christian is one who has been made a new creation. Her old sin nature has been replaced with a new nature (2 Corinthians 5:17); she is no longer what she once was.

Contentment in Him

God made us to live in fellowship with Him, and He knows us better than we know ourselves. We will never know satisfaction or contentment in this life until we give our whole life to Him. Confusion about generational sin is a significant roadblock that can get in the way of our finding satisfaction in our relationship with Him. We can become so trapped in the circumstances of surviving each day that we fail to look up and see that our lives can be different. God sent His son Jesus to die for needy, brokenhearted, messed-up people who recognize they are sinners. Instead of hiding in the dark or behind someone else, we need to focus on Christ's sacrifice for us, acknowledge our faults, repent, and turn to God. We need to "identify and take responsibility for the specific lies, false beliefs, desires, expectations, and fears that poison [our] relationship with God"[9] and then rest in what He has accomplished for us.

No Place to Hide

What God perfectly created out of nothing was cursed because of man's rebellion (Genesis 3:6). This was not a "magical" curse spoken by a distant god, but a judgment from our loving heavenly Father, who cannot turn a blind eye to sin and disobedience. Because He is perfectly pure and righteous, He could not excuse our first parents' sin. But like a loving Father, He provided a way for man to get back to Him. In the garden "He came not in fury, but in the same condescending way He had walked with Adam and Eve before."[10] God pursued Adam and pressed him to confess, but Adam refused to take responsibility for what he had done. Instead, he blamed God, and in turn, Eve blamed the serpent (Genesis 3:12-14). "The basic reluctance of sinful people to admit their iniquity is here established. Repentance is still the issue. When sinners refuse to repent, they suffer judgment; when they do repent, they receive forgiveness."[11]

Taking Responsibility

True godly repentance requires us to acknowledge our personal guilt (Jeremiah 3:13). Mere tears are not a true indication of heart change: "Godly grief produces a repentance that leads to salvation without regret, whereas worldly grief produces death" (2 Corinthians 7:10). The Corinthian believers who took responsibility for their sins became hungry for righteousness and indignant against sin. They longed to see their relationship with God restored and justice served. God promises us that when "we confess our sins, he is faithful and just to forgive us our sins and to cleanse us from all unrighteousness" (1 John 1:9). He also says, "If we say we have not sinned, we make him a liar, and his word is not in us" (verse 10).

Forgiveness

Because God cannot turn a blind eye to sin, He cannot simply ignore it or sweep it under the rug. Sin has to be punished. Following Adam and Eve's sin in the garden, God made a temporary atonement for sin by killing an animal (a blood sacrifice) to cover man's shame (Genesis 3:21). The fig leaves the couple had tried to hide behind only served to draw more attention to their sin. God clothed Adam and Eve with animal skins, and in doing so, He pointed out that forgiveness for sin always comes at the price of blood.

John the Baptist said of Jesus Christ, "Behold, the Lamb of God, who takes away the sins of the world!" (John 1:29). What the animal sacrifice could only do temporarily and symbolically was replaced at the cross of Calvary with the permanent and perfect sacrifice of Jesus Christ. "God presented him as a sacrifice of atonement, through faith in his blood" (Romans 3:25 NIV). The redeemed of God have been saved by grace alone through faith alone in Christ alone (Ephesians 2:8). Jesus Christ was and is the perfect sacrifice for sin. Believers in Christ have been bought with a price—the blood of the Lamb.

Zero Debt

When Jesus cried, "It is finished" on the cross of Calvary (John 19:30), He accomplished what the Father had sent Him to do—save His people from God's wrath. According to Jerry Bridges, "Jesus exhausted the wrath of God. It was not merely deflected and prevented from reaching us; it was exhausted." He goes on to say, "Jesus bore the full, unmitigated brunt of it. God's wrath against sin was unleashed in all its fury on His beloved Son. He held nothing back."[12] Making excuses for our sin hinders our ability to receive the most incredible gift ever given. The cross is our only hope for change.

Learning from the Past

Families today are no different than those of previous generations, who quickly forgot what God requires: obedience to His Word and sacrificial love for others. Although growing up in a home where the parents seek to honor God is a blessing, the truth is that our sin condition is not predetermined by whether we have a wicked or wise father. Not until we come to saving faith in Jesus Christ and our spiritual eyes are opened do we become transformed. And not until then can we lovingly serve others by helping undo the past one relationship at a time. The hopelessness of the past can now have a purpose—to bring glory to God today and bring hope to others. God's name is proclaimed when tragedy is turned into triumph.

Fear Factor

Some families feel trapped in generational sin because of fear. They believe that something or someone has cursed them, and thus there is no hope for change. In the book *And the Word Came with Power*, missionary and Wycliffe Bible translator Joanne Shetler challenged this kind of fear and thinking, which she witnessed among the Balangao people (formerly headhunters) of the northern Philippines. For generations this tribe had lived in fear of what spirits could do to them. During her translation of the Gospel of Mark (chapter 5), Joanne spoke of Jesus casting out demons from a man. Her Balangao assistant interrupted her, "You translated that part wrong...people can't cast out demons. They come when they want, and they leave when they want. The demons are in control, not people."

The assistant's eyes opened wide when Joanne said with authority that "Jesus wasn't an ordinary man. He was God and He was stronger than the spirits."[13] Joanne's prayer was that God's supernatural power might change these people forever. Change did come—and has continued to this day.

Scripture says "The fear of the LORD is the beginning of knowledge" (Proverbs 1:7). "The fear of the Lord is a state of mind in which one's own attitudes, will, feelings, deeds, and goals are exchanged for God's."[14] When we put our trust in Jesus Christ, we allow Him to be our Master, and we become His servant. And if God is for us, nothing can touch us (Romans 8:38-39). "God has charged Himself with full responsibility for our eternal happiness and stands ready to take over the management of our lives the moment we turn in faith to Him."[15]

When we give our life to Christ, His righteousness is deposited into our account. "What kind of sinner you were before doesn't exist anymore."[16] Your past is past. "He made Him who knew no sin to be sin on our behalf, so that we might become the righteousness of God in Him" (2 Corinthians 5:21). Once we become believers, we are given provision for doing battle against the flesh, Satan, and the world through the indwelling of the Holy Spirit. No matter what our present circumstance, God alone is able to save us from the stumbling block of past sins and a fallen world.

"People change when they see that they are responsible for what they believe about God," says David Powlison. "Life experience is no excuse for believing lies; the world and devil don't excuse the flesh."[17] What patterns and habits a parent displays in the home does not change the truth that an individual makes his own choices. "People change when biblical truth becomes more loud and vivid than previous life experience. People change when they have ears to hear and eyes to see what God tells us about Himself."[18] And the truth about God from Scripture is this:

> He does not deal with us according to our sins, nor repay us according to our iniquities. For as high as the heavens are above the earth, so great is his steadfast love toward those who fear him; as far as the east is from the west, so far does he remove our transgressions from us. As a father shows compassion to his children, so the LORD shows compassion to those who fear him. For he knows our frame; he remembers that we are dust (Psalm 103:10-14).

Taking Responsibility Leads to Freedom

The Lord wants us to learn from our past by taking responsibility for our sins and not making excuses for them. Using Scripture as our standard, we have hope for change and instructions to live by. "At one time you were darkness, but now you are light in the Lord. Walk as children of light (for the fruit of light is found in all that is good and right and true), and try to discern what is pleasing to the Lord" (Ephesians 5:8-9). When we come to Christ honestly and without excuse for our sins or the sins of our families, He willingly adopts us as His beloved children. Change occurs when our heart is pliable to the Spirit of God. Overcoming the stumbling block of generational sin is possible when we admit our need, repent, and allow Christ to be Lord over our past, our present, and our future.

Reducing the whole matter to individual terms, we arrive at some vital and highly personal conclusions. In the moral conflict now raging around us, whoever is on God's side is on the winning side and cannot lose; whoever is on the other side is on the losing side and cannot win.

Here there is no chance, no gamble. There is freedom to choose the side we will join, but no freedom to negotiate the results of the choice once it is made. By the mercy of God we may repent of a wrong choice and alter the consequences by making a new and right choice.[19]

What will you choose? Are you willing to leave excuses behind and learn from what Scripture says about the past? *The Lord wants us to learn from our mistakes by taking responsibility for our sin and by not making excuses anymore.* Surrendering our past to God assures us of strength for today and hope for tomorrow. In the power of God's grace we can choose today to put aside all of our past and live our life for Him, asking Him to use the mistakes of our past for His glory. He's good enough, powerful enough, and wise enough to turn your life around and free you from the sins you never thought you'd find freedom from. Trust Him today...and believe that He loves you more than you can imagine and that you'll always find Him very nearby.

Recommended Resources

Fitzpatrick, Elyse and Carol Cornish. *Women Helping Women.* Eugene, OR: Harvest House, 1997.

Fitzpatrick, Elyse and Dennis Johnson. *Counsel from the Cross.* Wheaton, IL: Crossway, 2009.

Lane, Timothy and Paul Tripp. *How People Change.* Greensboro, NC: New Growth, 2006.

————. *Relationships: A Mess Worth Making.* Greensboro, NC: New Growth, 2006.

Mack, Wayne. *Your Family God's Way.* Phillipsburg, NJ: Presbyterian & Reformed, 1991.

Powlison, David. *Seeing with New Eyes.* Phillipsburg, NJ: Presbyterian & Reformed, 2003.

Tozer, A.W. *Knowledge of the Holy.* New York: HarperCollins, 1978.

Chapter 22

The Taboo Topic: Pornography and Women

§ *Rachel Coyle* §

The forbidden scene was on instant replay. For some reason it enticed the young woman. Over and over the images appeared, alluring her to a point of no return. She was captivated, overcome by a desire to linger on even though she knew the scene was not pleasing to God. How was it possible for her to hate it and indulge in it at the same time? She knew she should turn it off immediately and run from this temptation. But there was just one problem: It was all in her mind. How could she escape what she envisioned over and over inside her head? Her thoughts were getting out of hand…whether she was at work with colleagues, alone in her car, having lunch with a friend, or whatever else she was doing, the images kept surfacing in her mind. Embarrassed and ashamed, she was a captive to her thoughts.

The scene above illustrates the powerfully pervasive influence of pornography. It becomes quickly and easily ingrained in the mind, and becomes a disturbing presence that can rear its ugly head unexpectedly at any time, in any place. So it is with good reason that Scripture admonishes Christians in no uncertain terms when it comes to matters of sexual purity.

From Captivated to Captive

The matter of women using pornography is a sensitive topic. Many of us are uncomfortable talking about it. When pornography is discussed, it is usually addressed as a man's problem. Rarely do we ever hear a preacher or Christian speaker warn women about the dangers of pornography. It seems taboo—forbidden—to suggest that *women* use pornography. The fact is that there are many women among us who not only use pornography, but are in bondage or addicted to it.[1]

Because pornography can be so alluring, repeated use of it seemingly has the ability to "take over" our mind. We find ourselves thinking about it so much that it feels uncontrollable; we secretly plan ways to indulge in it without others knowing about it; we may even eventually pursue other forms of sexual immorality in order to achieve the same sense of pleasure or high that we initially obtained from pornography. This is what it means to be addicted to pornography. The Bible describes addictions in terms of slavery:[2] "For whatever overcomes a person, to that he is enslaved" (2 Peter 2:19). Pornography appeals to our hearts on so many levels and the pleasure from it can be so powerful that we may quickly find ourselves overcome and enslaved by a desire for it.

Pornography is a growing problem among women. Rather than pretend that this problem doesn't exist, it is time we admit that it does and try to help each other. Perhaps you're reading this chapter today because you've struggled with it yourself. Many women are fascinated by pornographic videos, pictures, books, and magazines that tantalize the imagination. It is not uncommon to feel embarrassed, isolated, or unsure of where to turn for help. After all, isn't pornography something only men use? Again the answer is no! If this is your struggle, you are not alone.

Maybe you can relate to one of these women:[3] Denise was exposed to pornography before her teenage years. She became intrigued by it and secretly sought it out, but eventually it seemed to seek her out. Like the woman at the opening of this chapter, Denise's thoughts felt out of control. Michelle began experimenting with pornography during college and, over a period of ten-plus years, was involved with it off and on. Even when she stopped using it, impure memories flooded back into her mind when triggered by books and innocent movies. Heather's involvement began out of curiosity, but over time she became deeply enslaved to it. Over time, her addiction digressed to more perverted sexual behavior.

Denise, Michelle, and Heather are all real women who eventually experienced freedom from pornography—the complete freedom that only the Lord Jesus Christ can give. Yes, freedom is possible through Jesus Christ and the power of His Word. Read on!

It's More Than Meets the Eye

Pornography is available in many forms. Most of us associate pornography with what we can see with our eyes: pictures, movies, television, Web sites, etc. Some women do look at such images, which tend to comprise the form of pornography that men use. However, there is another more subtle, more socially acceptable, yet dangerous form of pornography that women are drawn to: reading material. *Erotic literature, even if it doesn't have any actual pictures, is pornography.* Scenes and stories that entertain the imagination have the greatest tendency to attract women.[4] Romance novels, magazine articles, and Internet chat rooms may contain contents that conjure up impure images in our minds. They can warp our expectations and beliefs about relationships and sex.

As I have helped women who struggle with pornography, I have learned that pornographic images and the imagination often go hand-in-hand. That is, once we intentionally look at pornography, we will likely want to read it and secretly imagine it as well. Reading certain romance novels and looking at actual pornography go hand-in-hand. Perhaps you not only understand this thought conceptually, perhaps you've experienced it, too.

The Power of the Mind's Eye

The fact is, our *mind's* eye (what we think about or imagine) is just as powerful and dangerous as our *physical* eye (what we look at). In Matthew 5:27-28, Jesus says, "You have heard that it was said, 'You shall not commit adultery.' But I say to you that everyone who looks at a woman with lustful intent has already committed adultery with her in his heart." Jesus teaches that both our physical eye and our mind's eye can cause us to sin. Sin is not just what we *do*; we can have sinful thoughts as well (Matthew 15:19; Mark 7:21). Although Jesus makes reference to men in this passage, the lesson is the same for women: We can commit adultery in our hearts by having lustful, impure *thoughts* about any man.[5]

Applying this principle to pornography, from God's perspective there is no difference between watching a pornographic video and reading a graphic romance novel that conjures up an impure fantasy. Both are sinful, both are dangerous, both embed images deeply into our memories, and both can lead to addiction or—in biblical terms— *slavery to sin* (see Romans 6:12-16; 2 Peter 2:19).

Please understand that I am not saying that every romance novel is pornographic, or that everyone who reads romance novels is enslaved to pornography. Rather, I'm referring to steamy or graphic literature. We need to stop and consider what we are allowing into our mind, and how this may influence our expectations, beliefs, and behavior. Most importantly, we should consider whether or not the books or magazines we read please Almighty God or make us love Him more.

What Is the Problem? Why Is It Sin?

Although there is much more to say on this subject, here are three reasons we ought to consider pornography in any form as sin:

Pornography Is Sexually Immoral

Although the word *pornography* is not found in the Bible, the original Greek text of the New Testament uses several variations of its root word, *porneia*.[6] Most modern Bible versions translate this word (and its variations) into words such as "fornication" and "sexual immorality." Therefore, if you want to learn God's opinion of pornography, you can study the Bible's uses of these terms. (See the "Living What You Learn" section near the end of this chapter to get started.)

Pornography Misrepresents God's Purposes for Sex

Pornography distorts God's purposes for the sexual relationship. Sex is reserved for a marriage relationship between a man and a woman. It is pure and honorable within this covenant (Genesis 2:24; Hebrews 13:4). God did not design sex for our own selfish purposes. It is a gift that spouses give to one another (see Proverbs 5:18-19; 1 Corinthians 7:3-5). God never intended sex as a form of entertainment for "onlookers." It is private and intimate between husband and wife alone.

Pornography Promotes Impure Thinking

I mentioned earlier that all forms of pornography cause impure sexual images to become embedded in our memories. As the opening story illustrated, these images can creep into our minds at any time and any place. Pornographic literature actually *encourages* us to dwell on impure scenarios. This blatantly violates what the Lord teaches through the apostle Paul in Philippians 4:8. We are to think upon whatever is true, honorable, right, pure, lovely, and commendable. Pornography does not meet these criteria.

Jesus Christ: God's Gift of Grace

If we want to break free from the chains of pornography, then we need to live in the grace of God. Jesus Christ is God's gift of grace for all people (2 Timothy 1:9; Titus 2:11). The most important question we can consider has eternal ramifications: Have we given our life to Jesus Christ as Savior and Lord? Jesus' work on our behalf is the only way to have a relationship with God (John 14:6), and God is the only One powerful enough to give us genuine, lasting freedom from the sin of pornography.

The Bad News

The bad news is that we are all sinners (Isaiah 53:6; Romans 3:10-12). Sin is any deviation from God's standards of right and wrong, which are revealed to us in the Bible. We *all* sin with our actions (what we do), our minds (what we think), and with our mouths (what we say). No one can claim to be without sin except Jesus Christ alone (2 Corinthians 5:21; Hebrews 4:15). Indulging in pornography is just one of the thousands of sins we can commit, but it is especially dangerous because of the way it enslaves us and harms others. But God has an answer to the problem of sin and the habitual use of pornography.

The Good News

This brings me to the good news. The living God is a God of grace.

He always has been and always will be. He gives us something we do not deserve and could never earn: forgiveness from our sin. God has always required a blood sacrifice in order to forgive sins (Hebrews 9:22). In Old Testament times animal sacrifices, which the people had to do repeatedly, served as a type or pointed to a greater, perfect sacrifice that would make forgiveness possible. And then Jesus came. Jesus is called "the *Lamb of God*, who *takes away* the sin of the world" (John 1:29, emphasis added). He is the perfect sacrifice, the final sacrifice; He died once, for all people (Hebrews 7:27; 1 Peter 3:18). But the story does not end there—Jesus not only died for our sin, He's alive! God raised Him from the dead, proving to the world that He has the power to defeat sin (Acts 2:24; 13:37-39). Unlike animal sacrifices of old that merely covered sin for a time, Jesus completely takes our sin away. He *forgives once and for all* when we admit that we are sinners, believe that Jesus died and rose again, trust His forgiveness, and follow Him. This is what salvation is all about. Jesus Christ came into the world to save sinners and to set us free from sin (1 Timothy 1:15; see also Romans 6:5-11,17-23). (If you're not sure whether you're a Christian, please turn *now* to Appendix Two at the back of the book.) Your eternal salvation is more important than your overcoming pornography, and you'll never find true and lasting freedom from it without God's help.

God's help is available to all His children, including those who struggle with enslaving sins such as pornography. With the help of God's power, we can fight against our sin. Perhaps you're already a Christian and yet you continue to battle with pornography. Because sin thrives in dark and secret places, you need to throw open the doors of your heart and bring everything out into the light! Flooding your heart with God's light begins when you confess your sin to God and receive and rest in His complete forgiveness (1 John 1:8-9).

Then you need to learn how to live in God's grace, walking daily in His Spirit so that you do not carry out the desires of the flesh. And although you may know that what you're doing is wrong and that you should change your behavior you may wonder just how to get from here to there. God does not leave you in the dark about this issue. He addresses it very clearly in the Bible!

Replace and Renew

At the moment of salvation, we are instantly released from the punishment of sin (hell), but we still need to learn how to live victoriously over sin. We will all continue to wrestle with sin until the Lord takes us to be with Him in heaven. And while we're still here on this earth, God's goal is that we become more like the Lord Jesus Christ, doing all for His glory (Romans 8:29; 1 Corinthians 10:31). This ought to become our goal as well! In theological terms, this process is called "progressive sanctification." [7]

Growing More Godly

The instant-gratification culture we live in today has made us accustomed to getting what we want as soon as we want it. Microwaves, cell phones, credit cards…you want it now? You got it. I confess that I, too, tend to want instant results. But this mind-set presents us with a problem: We want God to change us quickly and painlessly, too. We ask, "Couldn't God just say the word and set me free from the grip of pornography?" Certainly He *could*, and maybe for some of us He will. But in His wisdom, God designed spiritual growth, or sanctification, as a gradual process that calls for our ongoing obedience to Him. Ephesians 4:22-24 is a key passage that describes God's pattern for progressive sanctification: [8]

> Put off your old self, which belongs to your former manner of life and is corrupt through deceitful desires, and…be renewed in the spirit of your minds, and…put on the new self, created after the likeness of God in true righteousness and holiness.

Progressive sanctification, that slow process of change into Christlikeness, advances through three steps: The first is to put off the old self, the second is to be renewed in the spirit of your mind, and, the third is to put on the new self.

According to that passage, we are not merely to *break* old sinful habits; we must *replace* them with righteousness (thoughts, words, and deeds that please God). Each of these steps are integral to true change. Perhaps you have tried to break your habit of pornography to no avail. Could it be that you did not apply the principle of replacement?

Although it is imperative that we take all measures to *stop* using pornography—turn off the Internet, throw away the DVDs, destroy books and magazines, and so on—simply stopping is not enough. We must also literally *replace* our behavior with actions that please God and glorify Him. This may include walking away from the computer, turning off the TV, listening to Christian music, writing a letter, praying for others, and so on. The idea is to focus our mind and body on doing things that please the Lord. We are to "put off" sin and "put on" righteousness.

Now, make sure you don't overlook the instruction sandwiched in between the put-off/put-on steps. Ephesians 4:23 exhorts us to "be renewed in the spirit of [our] minds." This renewal is crucial to experiencing victory over sin. For lasting change to occur, your thoughts, beliefs, motives, attitudes, and desires need to undergo a radical transformation. This transformation begins when you compare your standards with those of God's Word. And when you become aware of areas in which your thoughts and desires are out of line with His, you can pray that the Lord will help you bring them in line. Of course, such renewal will require that you study the Bible (preferably on a daily basis) and learn to apply it to your life. I cannot overemphasize the importance of renewing your mind, especially through daily study of the Scriptures. That's why I will address this more thoroughly and practically in the section titled "Know the Heart of the Matter."

Living What You Learn

Here are a few exercises designed to help you on your way to freedom from pornography. As you begin to work through these exercises, you'll want to keep a notebook or journal in which you can record your answers and progress. *Be as specific as possible* with your answers. For the application portion of each project, you may find it helpful to seek guidance from a pastor, biblical counselor, or mentor.

GAIN A BIBLICAL UNDERSTANDING OF PORNOGRAPHY

1. Using an English dictionary and a Bible dictionary, look up the words *fornication* and *immorality*. Record the definitions in your notebook or journal.

2. Read the following passages and write down everything God says about fornication and sexual immorality (where it comes from, what to do about it, how it is defined, etc.): Mark 7:21; Acts 15:20; Romans 1:28-32; 1 Corinthians 6:13,18; 2 Corinthians 12:21; Galatians 5:19-21; Ephesians 5:3-5; Colossians 3:5-7; and 1 Thessalonians 4:3-7.

3. Look up the word *pornography* in an English dictionary and write down the meaning(s).

4. What is your conclusion regarding God's perspective of pornography? What do you think of it? What opinion *should* you have?

KNOW THE HEART OF THE MATTER

In the same way that a nasty weed will continue to sprout in a beautiful garden unless you pull out the roots below ground level, sin will continue to sprout up in your life until you attack its origin: your heart. The heart is the "inner you."[9] The Bible tells us that all of life's issues flow from the heart (Proverbs 4:23). Your heart encompasses your thoughts, beliefs, feelings, desires, and choices.[10] Ultimately, your heart is what causes you to sin (see Mark 7:21-23). For this reason, you need to examine your thoughts, beliefs, feelings, desires, and choices. Then you need to identify those that are unbiblical and bring them in line with God's Word. You also need to know what drives you to use pornography. The best way to examine your heart is with questions like these:

• What motivated you to use pornography in the first place?

• What keeps you going back for more?

• What draws you to pornography?

• What do you want from it? (Personal pleasure? Escape from painful feelings? To avoid responsibilities?)

Take some time right now to write your answers to all these questions. Try to come up with additional questions that will help you understand your thoughts, beliefs, feelings, desires, and choices regarding pornography. Ask God to show you what is in your heart that is not pleasing to Him so that you can apply the put-off/put-on principle and, by His grace, cultivate a heart that is fully His.

Keep a Journal of Tempting Times[11]

To start a "Journal of Tempting Times," on each page of your journal or notebook create four columns. Then do the following:

1. Record *when* you are tempted to use any form of pornography and *what* you are tempted to do.

2. Describe the *circumstances* surrounding the temptation. (For example, "It was right after I had an argument with my husband." "I had a bad day at work." "I was bored.")

3. Write down what you were *thinking* during the time of the temptation. ("I am so stressed out about my family." "I just wanted a high." "I have so much do to and not enough time.")

4. Record what you *actually did* following the temptation. (Remember, temptation itself is not sinful, but this is the point at which you make the choice either to please God or to sin against Him.)

As you are faithful to keep track of your temptations, pay attention to patterns that emerge. Use a highlighter to note similarities or patterns you see as you review your list and add to it daily. Take note of the following:

- What form(s) of pornography you are most drawn to

- What circumstances tend to trigger temptation

- What you want when you are tempted (for example, distraction from challenges or certain people, a high, control, etc.)

- If or how your thoughts send you on a downward spiral into sin

Recognizing specific patterns will help you prepare for the battle ahead of time. Consider what these patterns reveal about your heart—your thoughts, feelings, attitudes, desires, and so on—and what they tell you in terms of changes you need to make with God's help. Ask the Lord to help you remain diligent about studying the Bible and learning godly ways of handling situations that would usually tempt you to use pornography (Psalm 119:9-11).

PUT ON NEW HABITS[12]

The steps below are designed to help you live out Romans 6:12-14. By learning to put on new habits, you will live in the grace of God and no longer as a slave to pornography. On a page in your journal, make three columns and do the following:

1. *Put Off*—Make a list of actions, thoughts, and words that you need to put away in regard to your struggle with pornography. *Be specific*. Include particular situations that have occurred.

2. *Renew Your Mind*—List Bible references that apply to your situation. Focus on verses that emphasize what you *should* do, think, and say rather than what you should not do. Use a concordance or ask a pastor, biblical counselor, or mentor to help you find applicable Bible verses.

3. *Put On*—List specific actions that you can do to replace the sinful behaviors. Remember, it is not enough to *stop* doing something; record what you will *start* doing instead. For every item in the "Put Off" column you should have a solution in this column. And make sure the solution is realistic.

Review this list daily and add to it as you can. Refer to the book of Proverbs in the Old Testament and Galatians, Ephesians, Philippians, and Colossians in the New Testament. These are all treasure troves that provide lists of what we ought to put off and put on.

Compelled by Love

Love for the Lord Jesus is the only motivation for change that really works. When you love the Lord, you want to do what pleases Him. In fact, your obedience to Him is a reflection of your love for Him (1 John 5:3). Why do you want to change? Is it because you genuinely love the Lord? Or is it because you are afraid of consequences that might occur if you continue on in pornography?[13] Are you concerned about what others might think of you?

Prayerfully consider why you want to stop using pornography, then journal your thoughts. This is important because the only motive that will enable you to persevere when change becomes a challenge is a love for Christ that makes you want to please Him more than anything else (see 2 Corinthians 5:14-15). Be assured you are not in this alone; God will help you. God *wants* you to depend on Him, and you need His strength to succeed.

Finally, remember that change is a gradual *process*. At times you may find it somewhat painful to break free from the bondage of pornography. But the Lord will comfort you as you seek to honor and obey Him in this area of your life (see Psalm 103:10-14). He is a good and gracious God. Where your sin is great, His grace is greater (Romans 5:20). Keep pressing on, and ask the Lord for His grace and help.

Recommended Resources

Fitzpatrick, Elyse. *Idols of the Heart.* Phillipsburg, NJ: Presbyterian & Reformed, 2001.

Welch, Edward T. *Addictions: A Banquet in the Grave.* Phillipsburg, NJ: Presbyterian & Reformed, 2001.

Chapter 23

Women Struggling with Same-sex Attraction

❧ Karrie Hahn ❧

What made you turn to this chapter? Perhaps you are curious about the topic of homosexual desires and Christianity. Maybe you are trying to come alongside a friend experiencing homosexual desires, and you want to know how to help her. Or maybe you have turned to this chapter because you are desperately seeking answers for your own struggles—you are looking for help and hope as a Christian woman experiencing homosexual desires. Whatever the case, I hope you find helpful guidance and encouragement in the gospel of Jesus Christ as the only true source of the help and hope you or others long for.

Listen to the news, watch a talk show, or read a magazine article, and you'll quickly discover that homosexuality is a hot topic these days. Even entire church denominations are caught up in contentious debates over whether or not homosexuality is a sin. Thankfully God is not silent on this issue, and His Word gives us clear instruction that cuts through the cultural confusion of our day. While homosexual advocates have tried to reinterpret Bible passages and make them appear to not condemn homosexuality, God's Word plainly tells us that homosexuality is a sin. Embracing this truth is the first step toward freedom. The good news that Jesus Christ came to save sinners means that there is a *provision* for our sin and *power* to change. But first a person has to agree with God that homosexuality is sin before that person can experience the freedom that Jesus died to obtain.

When talking about homosexuality, it's important for us to define some terms. When the Bible mentions homosexuality, it always refers to homosexual desires that find full expression through homosexual behavior. Biblically speaking, a homosexual is a person who engages in homosexual behavior despite God's instructions about and design for male-female sexuality. However, there are also Christian women who experience homosexual desires yet choose not to engage in a homosexual lifestyle out of obedient love to the Lord. Their battle has to do with handling the presence of homosexual desires as well as abstaining from engaging in the various expressions of sin that these desires can produce. If that describes you, your identity is not that of a homosexual. Rather, you are a believer in Jesus Christ who battles homosexual desires. This is a key distinction—1 Corinthians 6:9-11 says,

> Do you not know that the unrighteous will not inherit the kingdom of God? Do not be deceived: neither the sexually immoral, nor idolaters, nor adulterers, nor men who practice homosexuality, nor thieves, nor the greedy, nor drunkards, nor revilers, nor swindlers will inherit the kingdom of God. And such *were* some of you. But you were *washed*, you were *sanctified*, you were *justified* in the name of the Lord Jesus Christ and by the Spirit of our God (emphasis added).

Some members of the Corinthian church *were* homosexuals, but their new life in Christ changed their identity so radically that they were no longer homosexuals. If a woman embraces Christ as Savior and Lord, agrees that homosexuality is sinful, yet fights against sinful expressions of homosexual desire in her life, she is not a homosexual.

Homosexual desires can be defined as experiencing a longing to relate to other women, either emotionally or physically, in a manner that contradicts God's design for woman-to-woman relationships, male-female relationships, and a pure relationship with Him. While these desires are a manifestation of the sin nature, they do not necessarily constitute a conscious and deliberate choice for a woman. These desires, however, can easily become willful sin when acted upon. As mentioned, homosexual desires may be physical, emotional, or a combination of both. Physical desires might include a longing to be physically close to or sexually intimate with another woman. These desires can lead to sins such as sexual thoughts, fantasies, masturbation, or pornography. Emotional desire, on the other hand, can show itself through infatuations with another woman or an overly dependent relationship in which you think you cannot live without the other woman. These desires can lead to sins such as manipulation and control, jealousy and envy, and various other distortions of biblical love for others.

If that is true for you, your struggle may have been shaped in part by the suffering that results when others sin against you (that is, sexual abuse or abandonment). But it's also possible that you have no concrete explanation for factors that may have shaped the presence of homosexual desires in your life. Regardless of your experience, the common denominator for every woman with homosexual desires is the pursuit of seeking satisfaction in another person (the creation) more than in God (the Creator). The real problem lies in the failure to love the Lord with all your heart, soul, mind, and strength, as well as your failure to love others as you love yourself. Instead, you place love for other people above a love for God, and that leads you to use other people for your own satisfaction rather than love them in purity according to God's Word. Though seeing and acknowledging your sin is difficult, the good news is that there is hope for you.

If you are experiencing homosexual desires, you must understand that Christ and His gospel have everything to do with your situation. Let me suggest three ways that the gospel makes provision for you and relates to your struggle: The first truth is that the gospel is the only source of true *hope*. The second truth is that the gospel is the only source of true *power*. And the third truth is that the gospel is the only source of true *motivation*. Let's unpack each one of these truths so that you can more fully understand how the gospel makes provision for your every need in the midst of your struggle.

Hope, Power, and the Motivation to Change

Hope

Life is miserable for those who lack hope. Proverbs 13:12 says, "Hope deferred makes the heart sick, but a desire fulfilled is a tree of life." If you have been trying to gain victory and freedom over your homosexual desires with little success, you may be feeling hopeless. Despite your attempts and efforts, the change you long for may seem to elude you. Hope, which can be defined as the confident expectation that God will do all that He has promised to do, may be in short supply in your soul.

Only the gospel contains the reservoir of hope that can replenish your drought of hopelessness. Because we who are believers are in Christ, God's Word says that we are "born again to a *living hope* through the resurrection of Jesus Christ from the dead" (1 Peter 1:3). How do you gain access to living hope when your hope is dying? The answer, according to this passage, is by realizing how the resurrection of Jesus Christ intersects with your life as a believer. All your sins and failures in this life can never change the fact that Jesus has been raised in glory, and you will be raised with Him! In fact, God already sees you as though you've been raised with Christ because you belong to Him (Colossians 3:1). Not only can you have hope that God fully loves and accepts you despite your sin; you can also have hope that the resurrected Christ can help you in your struggles against sin no matter how much you seem to fail. Hebrews 4:14-16 says,

> Since then we have a great high priest who has passed through the heavens, Jesus, the Son of God, let us hold fast our confession. For we do not have a high priest who is unable to sympathize with our weaknesses, but one who in every respect has been tempted as we are, yet without sin. Let us then with confidence draw near to the throne of grace, that we may receive mercy and find grace to help in time of need.

If you are a Christian, you are united to Christ and raised with Christ, and you are never without hope in Him.

Power

Not only does the gospel give the hope you need to persevere, it also gives you the power to change. Change that you attempt in your own power is always short-lived and is a sure pathway to discouragement. The apostle Paul, in his prayer for the Ephesians, prayed that the believers in Ephesus would know

what is the immeasurable greatness of his power toward us
who believe, according to the working of his great might that
he worked in Christ when he raised him from the dead and
seated him at his right hand in the heavenly places, far above
all rule and authority and power and dominion, and above
every name that is named, not only in this age but also in the
one to come (Ephesians 1:19-21).

In other words, Paul prayed that God would enable the Ephesian
Christians to understand the kind of power that was at work within
them. What kind of power is that? According to this passage, it's the
power God displayed when He took Jesus' dead body and raised it to
life incorruptible. That's the same power that is at work in us as believers. Sin is powerful, but Christ is more powerful. And because we are
united to Him, that source of power will never be exhausted or extinguished. His power will always continue to work in us until the day we
see Him face to face. Yes, His power is greater than our greatest sin.

Motivation

Most importantly, the gospel is the only source of true motivation
for change. What motivates you to try to change your homosexual
desires? Do you fear that God will punish you? Are you trying to earn
His love? Do you want to get rid of the guilt you feel? There are countless
reasons why you might seek change, but only one of them is right. Every
attempt at battling homosexual desires will fall short if your motive is
wrong. And what is the only motive that provides the ability to truly
pursue holiness? What is the only thing that can bring true hope and
power to your struggle against homosexual desires? The answer is *love*.

Now, I'm not talking so much about the love that you have for God.
Rather, I'm talking about knowing and believing God's love for you.
We often think about Christian growth primarily in terms of what we
do (our pursuit of holiness), yet Scripture talks about pursuing other
types of growth in addition to growth in godly character. We must continually seek growth in our understanding of what *Christ has done for us*
and *who we are in Him* before we can rightly pursue holiness. Second
Peter 3:18 urges us to "grow in the grace and knowledge of our Lord

and Savior Jesus Christ." What this means is that as you seek to grow in your understanding of God's character and the gospel, you will grow in your desire to pursue holiness in response to God's incomprehensible love. First John 3:1-3 makes the connection between comprehending God's love and growing in practical righteousness in this way:

> *See what kind of love the Father has given to us,* that we should be called children of God; and so we are…Beloved, we are God's children now, and what we will be has not yet appeared; but we know that when he appears we will be like him, because we shall see him as he is. *And everyone who thus hopes in him purifies himself as he is pure* (emphases added).

We often wrongly try to "purify" ourselves apart from being controlled by God's love. Yet God tells us that it is only when we see His prior love for us that we have the hope and power to seek purity!

Answering Your Questions

The gospel of Jesus Christ is what gives you hope, power, and motivation to fight against your homosexual desires and pursue purity. Now, as you pursue this path of holiness, you may find yourself asking some of the questions that women with homosexual desires commonly ask.

Question 1: I never consciously chose to be attracted to other women. How did this happen?

Romans 1 helps us understand who we are as human beings before God and sheds light on the question of how all sin, including homosexual desires, happens. Because we are all born as sinners, all of us have rejected God and chosen to worship things other than Him. The word *worship* simply refers to that which we love, serve, prioritize, need, and live for. This is the true root of every sin that we commit—worship of God is exchanged for the worship of someone or something else (ultimately driven by worship of ourselves). Because of this truth, the notion of an inborn and morally neutral "homosexual orientation" falls short of biblical reality. The larger fact is that we are all born with a sin orientation that may express itself in a variety of ways—including an orientation toward homosexual desire.

While sinful expressions of homosexual desire is a conscious choice for the person who engages in them in the same way that lying, disobedience to parents, and gossip are conscious choices, the heart desire for each of these sinful behaviors, including homosexual desires, is not necessarily a conscious choice that a person makes. Counselor and author Ed Welch makes helpful observations on this point:

> Like many other sins, homosexuality does not have to be learned. Like the child who never witnessed a temper tantrum but can be proficient at throwing one, it can be an instinctive ability of the human heart. Homosexuality is natural in the same way that anger or selfishness is natural. They are embedded in our humanness. Indeed, homosexuality is "natural," but only in the sense that it is a natural expression of the sinful nature rather than some sort of morally neutral, God-given constitution. The fact that many homosexuals cannot remember choosing homosexuality can also be explained by Scripture. Most sin works on a level where we do not feel that we self-consciously choose it.[1]

Author Albert Mohler offers additional insight on this:

> We must stop confusing the issues of moral responsibility and moral choice. We are all *responsible* for our sexual orientation, but that does not mean that we freely and consciously *choose* that orientation. We sin against homosexuals by insisting that sexual temptation and attraction are predominantly chosen. We do not always (or even generally) choose our temptations. Nevertheless, we are absolutely responsible for what we *do* with sinful temptations, whatever our so-called sexual orientation.[2]

A full understanding of the sin orientation we are all born with leaves the option of a morally neutral, inborn homosexual orientation a biblical impossibility. Rather, it is accurate to say that (1) we are all born with sinful hearts that exchange the worship of God for the worship of something that is not God; (2) everyone is born with tendencies toward certain types of sinful desires and behaviors; (3) some people experience homosexual desires that may have never been consciously chosen; and (4) all sinful behavior and desires, including homosexual desires and the sins that result from them, are dealt with in the same way—the sinless life, substitutionary death, and triumphant resurrection of Jesus Christ.

Question 2: How can I gain victory over my homosexual desires? How much change should I expect?

Ultimate and complete victory against sin will not take place until we die or when Christ returns. We are guaranteed to win the battle because Christ is the victor (1 Corinthians 15:56-57). But in the here and now, we struggle in the fight.

Some seasons of the battle may seem more victorious than others. At times you might feel great strength and power; at other times you may feel weakness and a sense of defeat. Therefore, part of being victorious means *enduring to the end,* regardless of how victorious you feel. While the fight against sinful expressions of homosexual desires may never come to a complete end in this life, learning every day to choose Christ over sin will weaken fleshly desires, strengthen your resolve to put sin to death, and bring increasing holiness over time.

If you define victory in terms of a complete cessation of all temptation for the rest of your life, your expectations need to be challenged in the light of God's Word. You must be willing to fight because you love and trust Jesus, no matter what form victory takes in this life. The truth is that you can experience tremendous growth and change as you pursue the Lord with a purely motivated heart. Even if the temptations never fully cease in this life, you can know the great victory of being an overcomer. David Powlison notes:

> We love gazelles. Graceful leaps make for a great testimony to God's wonder-working power. And we like steady and predictable. It seems to vindicate our efforts at making the Christian life work in a businesslike manner. But, in fact, there's no formula, no secret, no technique, no program, and no truth that guarantees the speed, distance, or time frame. On the day you die, you'll still be somewhere in the middle, but hopefully further along. When we lengthen the battle, we realize that our business is the direction...God's people need

to know that, so someone else's story doesn't set the bar in a place that is not how your story of Christ's grace is working out in real life.[3]

Don't define victory as the absence of homosexual desires. True victory occurs each time you choose to fight temptation and sin and love God instead. While miraculous victory and freedom from homosexual desires may occur for some women, there is no guarantee this will be true for everyone. You must decide what truly matters most to you: not "feeling" certain desires, or enduring by fighting them until the battle is done. By remembering what God has in store for those who love Him and setting your mind on things above, you can remain encouraged in the hope of what lies ahead in eternity.

Question 3: How can I break free?

The thought you might battle homosexual desires for the rest of your life may discourage you. It is difficult to have hope when there is no guarantee that you will win the battle in this life. Experiencing freedom is often defined in terms of freedom from homosexual desires. However, the Lord gives us a *different* definition of freedom that can bring hope and strength to those who ask, "How long, O Lord?" Romans 6:17-18 says,

> Thanks be to God, that you who were once slaves of sin have become obedient from the heart to the standard of teaching to which you were committed, and, having been set free from sin, have become slaves of righteousness.

For believers, freedom is not defined as the *absence* of temptation and sinful desires; rather, freedom in Christ means it is now possible for us to *fight against, deny,* and *put to death* those sinful desires. Author David White notes,

> Freedom is not the absence of temptation; it is the increasing ability to choose holiness out of love for Christ, despite the relentlessness of temptation. To live in freedom from sexual sin usually means ongoing temptations and the suffering they bring, but be encouraged: your struggle against sexual sin

matters to God! The daily decision to die to yourself and to lay your sexual desires on his altar is a precious sacrifice of obedience that is a delight to the Lover of your soul.[4]

We are often tempted to be shortsighted and fail to see the significance of small moments of obedience when no one else is around to see us. And we often don't live as though God sees all things. Yet He is intimately acquainted with all our ways (Psalm 139:1-3), and He sees what we do in secret when no one else is watching (Matthew 6:3-6). What a difference having this eternal perspective would make in our battles against sin! We need to live with an awareness that no act of obedience done out of love for Christ will go unnoticed or unrewarded in the final day.

So, true freedom is not equivalent to heterosexuality and marriage. True freedom is living every day fighting sin, believing that God's promises are better, and knowing He does and will reward those who seek Him.

One woman reflects on this issue in her article "What Does Healing Look Like?"

> There is probably not a one of us that would not give nearly anything for a normal life—some sort of heterosexual fantasy involving a nice house complete with a spouse and children. But what if healing is not about heterosexuality? What if we frustrate ourselves out of true healing because we have the wrong goal?
>
> Daniel 3 tells the familiar story of three Hebrew men who refused to bow down and worship an idol, even when the consequence of their choice was certain death. In verse 17, the men acknowledge that God is able to deliver them from their fate. However, it is verse 18 that catches my attention. They concede that their decision to be obedient will stand even if God does not deliver them. What a commitment! They had absolutely no assurance of deliverance! They placed their faith in God Himself rather than an outcome they hoped for.
>
> This challenges me to a similar commitment. I know that God is able to completely deliver me from homosexual desires… but if He does not, let it be known that I will not serve other

gods (my own lust, fantasies, sinful desire, etc.)…I think that
is what healing looks like. I believe it is having integrity when I
have no idea what the outcome will be…I am closer to healed
than I have ever been with the simple freedom I have found in
pursuing Christ rather than a change in sexual orientation.[5]

Question 4: Why does God allow me to struggle this way? I never consciously chose these attractions.

Human beings have the innate drive and capacity for evaluating
and interpreting life. This is one of the characteristics that sets us apart
from anything else in God's creation, and we most often ask the question "Why?" when we face trials, difficulties, and disappointments in
our lives.

There are both right and wrong ways for us to ask the why questions of life. The wrong way includes anger and bitterness against God,
fueled by a sinful pride that demands for God to explain Himself and
denies that we should have to face difficulties in life. By contrast, the
right way asks why without sinning against the Lord. It's okay to ask
why in genuine confusion and bewilderment as you pray for God to
shine His light onto a dark path, or you ask Him to reveal what He
wants you to learn through the trials you face. Some questions might
receive answers now, some questions might get answers later, and some
might never get answers in this life. Whatever the case, make sure that
your desire for answers doesn't get in the way of pursuing the Lord and
cause you to get stuck in a pit of bitterness and despair.

Psalm 131 offers wisdom in regard to humbling ourselves and being
content with not knowing all of the answers. In verse 1, David acknowledged that he refused to be filled with pride before the Lord, and proclaimed that he did not seek to understand things that were beyond
him. Like David, you must recognize that having all the answers to
your questions is not what will set you free. By realizing God's fatherly
care for you, you can break free of the need to know all the answers.
The result of this trust, according to verse 2, is a heart that is calm and
quiet like a child resting in his mother's arms. When the why questions threaten to derail your trust in the Lord and humility before Him,
turning to this psalm can help renew your thinking.

A unique opportunity to honor God is presented in the midst of unanswered questions. Though you may not know the answer to why the Lord would allow certain struggles in your life, you have a choice to make. If you choose to, you can view your struggle as giving you a context to show God, Satan, angels, demons, and mankind that God is worthy of all your praise, love, trust, and obedience—even if He never answers your questions. In the book of Job, one of Satan's comments to God is, "Does Job fear God for no reason?" (1:9). From a human standpoint, it makes logical sense for us to worship God if He makes life relatively prosperous and enjoyable. On the other hand, worshiping God goes against the grain of human nature in times of great trial and pain. One of the sweetest offerings that you can give to the Lord is a heart and life that chooses to live for Him even if He never answers the why questions in this life.

The Road to Real Change

The hope, power, and motivation that comes from God's love for you in Jesus Christ can bring real change to your life, no matter how great your weaknesses and failures. Embrace His love for you that is shown so powerfully in the gospel. Embrace your true identity in Christ. And to take the next step, embrace biblical community in a solid local church. When you become a believer, God gives you a spiritual family of brothers and sisters, and you are all members of the body of Christ. By committing yourself to the kind of relationships with other believers that God's Word describes, you will be able to receive biblical instruction, wise counsel, encouragement, and exhortation from others who are also sinners saved by God's grace. Whatever your unique situation, struggles, circumstances, and life experiences, there is hope and help in Jesus Christ and His people.

Recommended Resources

Fitzpatrick, Elyse and Dennis Johnson. *Counsel from the Cross.* Wheaton, IL: Crossway, 2009.

Mohler, Albert. "Is Your Baby Gay? What If You Could Know? What If You Could Do Something About It?" at www.albertmohler.com.

Powlison, David. "Making All Things New: Restoring Joy to the Sexually Broken," in *Sex and the Supremacy of Christ*. Eds. John Piper and Justin Taylor. Wheaton, IL: Crossway, 2005.

Schaife, Heather. "What Does Healing Look Like?" in *Pure Intimacy*, www. pureintimacy.org.

Welch, Edward T. *Addictions: A Banquet in the Grave*. Phillipsburg, NJ: Presbyterian & Reformed, 2001.

———. *Homosexuality: Speaking the Truth in Love*. Phillipsburg, NJ: Presbyterian & Reformed, 2000.

White, David. "Suffering with Temptation: Understanding the Battle." Philadelphia: Harvest USA, Fall/Winter 2008.

APPENDICES

Resources for More Help

Recommended Resources by Chapter

Chapter 1—Biblical Counseling: Real Help for Real Women

Fitzpatrick, Elyse and Dennis Johnson. *Counsel From the Cross.* Wheaton, IL: Crossway, 2009.

Chapter 2—Do God's Promises Apply to You?

Lawson, Steven. *Absolutely Sure.* Sisters, OR: Multnomah, 1999.

MacArthur, John. *The Gospel According to Jesus.* Grand Rapids: Zondervan, 1988.

Parsons, Burk. *Assured by God.* Phillipsburg, NJ: Presbyterian & Reformed, 2007.

Peace, Martha. *Attitudes of a Transformed Heart.* Bemidji, MN: Focus Publishing, 2002.

Piper, John. *Finally Alive.* Fern, Scotland: Christian Focus, 2009.

———. *God Is the Gospel.* Wheaton, IL: Crossway, 2005.

Chapter 3—Interpreting God's Word Accurately

ESV Study Bible. Wheaton, IL: Crossway, 2008.

Pearch, Dora Leigh. *Back to the Source: 10 Steps for Personal Bible Study.* Mesa, AZ: Pearch Publishing, 2007.

Zuck, Roy B. *Basic Bible Interpretation.* Colorado Springs: Victor, 1991.

Chapter 4—Spiritual Discernment: How Can I Know What Is True?

Adams, Jay E. *A Call to Discernment*. Woodruff, SC: Timeless Texts, 1998.

Bridges, Jerry. *The Gospel for Real Life*. Colorado Springs: NavPress, 2002.

Challies, Tim. *The Discipline of Discernment*. Wheaton, IL: Crossway, 2007.

Lutzer, Erwin W. *Who Are You to Judge?* Chicago: Moody, 2002.

MacArthur, John. *Fool's Gold*. Wheaton, IL: Crossway, 2005.

Chapter 5—Establishing a Biblical Ministry to Women

Buckley, Ed. *Why Christians Can't Trust Psychology*. Eugene, OR: Harvest House, 1993.

Duncan, J. Ligon and Susan Hunt. *Women's Ministry in the Local Church*. Wheaton, IL: Crossway, 2006.

ESV Study Bible. Wheaton, IL: Crossway, 2008.

Grudem, Wayne. *Systematic Theology*. Grand Rapids: Zondervan, 1994.

House, Wayne. *Charts of Christian Theology & Doctrine*. Grand Rapids: Zondervan, 1992.

Ryken, Leland. *The Word of God in English*. Wheaton, IL: Crossway, 2002.

Tripp, Paul. *Instruments in the Redeemer's Hands*. Phillipsburg, NJ: Presbyterian & Reformed, 2002.

Chapter 6—Dealing with Your Emotions God's Way

Borgman, Brian. *Feelings and Faith: Cultivating Godly Emotions in the Christian Life*. Wheaton, IL: Crossway, 2009.

Bridges, Jerry. *Trusting God: Even When Life Hurts*. Colorado Springs. NavPress, 1988.

Fitzpatrick, Elyse. *Idols of the Heart*. Phillipsburg, NJ: Presbyterian & Reformed, 2001.

Lane, Timothy S. and Paul David Tripp. *How People Change*. Winston-Salem, NC: Punch Press, 2006.

Williams, Sam. "Toward a Theology of Emotion." *Southern Baptist Journal of Theology, Volume 7*. Southern Baptist Theological Seminary, 2003; 2006, 58.

Chapter 7—Christ, God's Answer to Your Fear

Fitzpatrick, Elyse. *Overcoming Fear, Worry, and Anxiety.* Eugene, OR: Harvest House, 2001.

Mack, Wayne. *Fear Factor.* Tulsa, OK: Hensley Publishing, 2002.

Welch, Edward T. *When People Are Big and God Is Small.* Phillipsburg, NJ: Presbyterian & Reformed, 1997.

Chapter 8—Help for Overcoming Anger

Bridges, Jerry. *Respectable Sins.* Colorado Springs: NavPress, 2007.

Jones, Robert D. *Uprooting Anger.* Phillipsburg, NJ: Presbyterian & Reformed, 2005.

Mack, Wayne. *Anger and Stress Management God's Way.* Merrick, NY: Calvary Press, 2005.

Chapter 9—The Difficult Road Through Depression

Bridges, Jerry. *Trusting God: Even When Life Hurts.* Colorado Springs: NavPress, 1988.

Fitzpatrick, Elyse M. *Because He Loves Me.* Wheaton, IL: Crossway, 2008.

———. *Comforts from the Cross.* Wheaton, IL: Crossway, 2009.

———. *A Steadfast Heart.* Phillipsburg, NJ: Presbyterian & Reformed, 2006.

Fitzpatrick, Elyse and Dennis Johnson. *Counsel from the Cross.* Wheaton, IL: Crossway, 2009.

Piper, John. *When the Darkness Will Not Lift.* Wheaton, IL: Crossway, 2006.

Tada, Joni Eareckson and Steven Estes. *When God Weeps.* Grand Rapids: Zondervan, 1997.

Welch, Edward T. *Depression: A Stubborn Darkness.* Greensboro, NC: New Growth, 2004.

Chapter 10—About Medicines: Finding a Balance

Fitzpatrick, Elyse. *Because He Loves Me.* Wheaton, IL: Crossway, 2008.

———. *Idols of the Heart: Learning to Long for God Alone.* Phillipsburg, NJ: Presbyterian & Reformed, 2001.

Fitzpatrick, Elyse and Laura Hendrickson, M.D. *Will Medicine Stop the Pain?* Chicago: Moody, 2006.

Welch, Edward T. *Blame It on the Brain? Distinguishing Chemical Imbalances, Brain Disorders, and Disobedience.* Phillipsburg, NJ: Presbyterian & Reformed, 1998.

Chapter 11—*Single Women and the Test of Loneliness*

Brownback, Lydia. *Fine China Is for Single Women Too.* Phillipsburg, NJ: Presbyterian & Reformed, 2003.

Elliot, Elisabeth. *Passion and Purity.* Grand Rapids: Revell, 2002.

———. *The Path of Loneliness.* Grand Rapids: Revell, 2001.

Farmer, Andrew. *The Rich Single Life: Abundance, Opportunity & Purpose in God.* Gaithersburg, MD: Sovereign Grace, 1998.

Harris, Joshua. *Boy Meets Girl: Say Hello to Courtship.* Sisters, OR: Multnomah, 2005.

———. *Not Even a Hint: Guarding Your Heart Against Lust.* Sisters, OR: Multnomah, 2003.

Mahaney, C.J. *Sex, Romance, and the Glory of God.* Wheaton, IL: Crossway, 2004.

McCulley, Carolyn. *Did I Kiss Marriage Goodbye?* Wheaton, IL: Crossway, 2004.

Piper, John and Justin Taylor, eds. *Sex and the Supremacy of Christ.* Wheaton, IL: Crossway, 2005.

Chapter 12—*Way Beyond the Man of Your Dreams: Help for Single Moms*

Bridges, Jerry. *Trusting God: Even When Life Hurts.* Colorado Springs: NavPress, 1988.

George, Elizabeth. *Loving God with All Your Mind.* 2d ed. Eugene, OR: Harvest House, 2005.

MacArthur, John. *Our Awesome God.* Wheaton, IL: Crossway, 1993.

Pink, Arthur W. *The Attributes of God.* Grand Rapids: Baker, 2004.

Tozer, A.W. *The Knowledge of the Holy.* New York: HarperCollins, 1978.

Chapter 13—Does Anyone Hear Me? Facing Loneliness in Marriage

Burroughs, Jerry. *The Rare Jewel of Christian Contentment*. Gaithersburg, MD: Sovereign Grace, 2001.

DeMoss, Nancy Leigh. *Lies Women Believe: A Life-Changing Study for Individuals and Groups*. Chicago: Moody, 2002.

Ellen, Nicolas. *Happy Even After: Biblical Guidelines for a Successful Marriage*. Mustang, OK: Dare 2 Dream, 2007.

————. *With All Your Heart: Identifying and Dealing with Idolatrous Lusts*. Mustang, OK: Dare 2 Dream, 2008.

Fitzpatrick, Elyse. *Helper by Design: God's Perfect Plan for Women in Marriage*. Chicago: Moody, 2003.

Hunt, June. "Loneliness: How to Be Alone But Not Lonely." *Biblical Counseling Keys*, 2005, 1-13.

Mahaney, C.J. *How Can I Change? Victory in the Struggle Against Sin*. Gaithersburg, MD: People of Destiny International, 1993.

Wiersbe, Warren W. *Lonely People*. Grand Rapids: Baker, 2002

Chapter 14—Healing for Hidden Wounds from Verbal Abuse

Adams, Jay. *How to Overcome Evil*. Phillipsburg, NJ: Presbyterian & Reformed, 1977.

Bridges, Jerry. *Trusting God: Even When Life Hurts*. Colorado Springs: NavPress, 1988.

Peace, Martha. *Damsels in Distress*. Phillipsburg, NJ: Presbyterian & Reformed, 2006.

Vernick, Leslie. *The Emotionally Destructive Relationship*. Eugene, OR: Harvest House, 2007.

Chapter 15—Faithful Parenting: Reaching Your Child's Heart

Elliff, Jim. *How Children Come to Faith in Christ* [sound recording]. Little Rock, AR: Family Life Today, 2006.

Plowman, Ginger. *Don't Make Me Count to Three!* Wapwallopen, PA: Shepherd Press, 2003.

Priolo, Lou. *Teach Them Diligently.* Woodruff, SC: Timeless Texts, 2000.

Tripp, Tedd. *Shepherding a Child's Heart.* Wapwallopen, PA: Shepherd Press, 1995.

Chapter 16—The Perfect Mom Syndrome

Bridges, Jerry. *Trusting God: Even When Life Hurts.* Colorado Springs: NavPress, 1988.

Fitzpatrick, Elyse. *Idols of the Heart: Learning to Long for God Alone.* Phillipsburg, NJ: Presbyterian & Reformed, 2001.

———. *Overcoming Fear, Worry, and Anxiety.* Eugene, OR: Harvest House, 2001.

Mack, Wayne. *Anger and Stress Management God's Way.* Merrick, NY: Calvary Press, 2004.

Priolo, Lou. *Pleasing People.* Phillipsburg, NJ: Presbyterian & Reformed, 2007.

———. *Teach Them Diligently.* Woodruff, SC: Timeless Texts, 2000.

Younts, John A. *Everyday Talk.* Wapwallopen, PA: Shepherd Press, 2004.

Chapter 17—Raising Children Who Are Challenged

Fitzpatrick, Elyse and John Newheiser, with Dr. Laura Hendrickson. *When Good Kids Make Bad Choices.* Eugene, OR: Harvest House, 2003.

Hendrickson, Dr. Laura. *Finding Your Way on the Autism Spectrum.* Chicago: Moody, 2009.

Hubach, Stephanie. *Same Lake, Different Boat: Coming Alongside People Touched by Disability.* Phillipsburg, NJ: Presbyterian & Reformed, 2006.

Langston, Kelly. *Autism's Hidden Blessings.* Grand Rapids: Kregel, 2009.

Chapter 18—Training Teens in the True Faith

Doriani, Daniel. *The Sermon on the Mount.* Phillipsburg, NJ: Presbyterian & Reformed, 2006.

Fitzpatrick, Elyse and Jim Newheiser. *When Good Kids Make Bad Choices.* Eugene: OR: Harvest House, 2004.

MacArthur, John. *What the Bible Says About Parenting.* Nashville: W. Publishing Group, 2000.

————. "Hungering and Thirsting After Righteousness." Panorama City, CA: Grace to You, accessed at http://www.gty.org/Resources/Transcripts/2201.

Tripp, Paul. *Age of Opportunity.* Phillipsburg, NJ: Presbyterian & Reformed, 2003.

Tripp, Tedd. *Shepherding a Child's Heart.* Wapwallopen, PA: Shepherd Press, 2005.

Chapter 19—Hope for Caregivers of the Elderly

Adams, Jay E. *Wrinkled but Not Ruined: Counsel for the Elderly.* Woodruff, SC: Timeless Texts, 1999.

Cornish, Carol and Elyse Fitzpatrick. "Counseling Women Facing Dying and Death," in *Women Helping Women,* eds. Elyse Fitzpatrick and Carol Cornish. Eugene, OR: Harvest House, 1997.

Eyrich, Howard and Judy Dabler. *The Art of Aging.* Bemidji, MN: Focus Publishing, 2006.

Fitzpatrick, Elyse. "Counseling Women in the Afternoon of Life," in *Women Helping Women.* Eugene, OR: Harvest House, 1997. *The Afternoon of Life.* Phillipsburg, NJ: Presbyterian & Reformed, 2004.

Rossi, Melody. *May I Walk You Home? Sharing Christ's Love with the Dying.* Bloomington, MN: Bethany House, 2007.

Chapter 20—Help for Habitual Overeaters

DeMoss, Nancy Leigh. *Lies Women Believe: And the Truth that Sets Them Free.* Chicago: Moody, 2001.

Eyrich, Howard and W. Hines. *Curing the Heart: A Model for Biblical Counseling.* Ross-shire, UK: Christian Focus Publications, 2002.

Fitzpatrick, Elyse. *Love to Eat, Hate to Eat.* Eugene, OR: Harvest House, 1999.

Chapter 21—Breaking the Chain of Generational Sin

Fitzpatrick, Elyse and Dennis Johnson. *Counsel from the Cross.* Wheaton, IL: Crossway, 2009.

Fitzpatrick, Elyse and Carol Cornish. *Women Helping Women.* Eugene, OR: Harvest House, 1997.

Lane, Timothy and Paul Tripp. *How People Change.* Greensboro, NC: New Growth, 2006.

———. *Relationships: A Mess Worth Making.* Greensboro, NC: New Growth, 2006.

Mack, Wayne. *Your Family God's Way.* Phillipsburg, NJ: Presbyterian & Reformed, 1991.

Powlison, David. *Seeing with New Eyes.* Phillipsburg, NJ: Presbyterian & Reformed, 2003.

Tozer, A.W. *Knowledge of the Holy.* New York: HarperCollins, 1978.

Chapter 22—The Taboo Topic: Pornography and Women

Fitzpatrick, Elyse. *Idols of the Heart.* Phillipsburg, NJ: Presbyterian & Reformed, 2001.

Welch, Edward T. *Addictions: A Banquet in the Grave.* Phillipsburg, NJ: Presbyterian & Reformed, 2001.

Chapter 23—Women Struggling with Same-sex Attraction

Fitzpatrick, Elyse and Dennis Johnson. *Counsel from the Cross.* Wheaton, IL: Crossway, 2009.

Mohler, Albert. "Is Your Baby Gay? What If You Could Know? What If You Could Do Something About It?" at www.albertmohler.com.

Powlison, David. "Making All Things New: Restoring Joy to the Sexually Broken," in *Sex and the Supremacy of Christ.* Eds. John Piper and Justin Taylor. Wheaton, IL: Crossway, 2005.

Schaife, Heather. "What Does Healing Look Like?" in *Pure Intimacy,* www.pureintimacy.org.

Welch, Edward T. *Addictions: A Banquet in the Grave.* Phillipsburg, NJ: Presbyterian & Reformed, 2001.

———. *Homosexuality: Speaking the Truth in Love.* Phillipsburg, NJ: Presbyterian & Reformed, 2000.

White, David. "Suffering with Temptation: Understanding the Battle." Philadelphia: Harvest USA, Fall/Winter 2008.

Biblical Counseling Training Centers

Following is a list of training centers where you can receive formal or informal training in the practice of consistently biblical counseling:

- The Master's College, www.masters.edu
- The Institute for Biblical Counseling and Discipleship, www.ibcd.org
- The National Association of Nouthetic Counselors, www.nanc.org
- Fairbanks Baptist Bible Institute, www.akhabc.com
- Birmingham Theological Seminary, www.birminghamseminary.org
- Briarwood Presbyterian Church, eadams@briarwood.org
- Eastwood Counseling Ministries, LouisPaul@aol.com
- Biblical Counseling Center of Sonoma County, www.counselfromthebible.org
- Valley Bible Church Biblical Counseling Center, www.livetheword.squarespace.com
- Biblical Counseling and Education Center, www.bcecvisalia.net
- Grace Community Church, www.gracechurch.org/ministries/logos
- HOPE Biblical Counseling and Training Center, www.hopebiblicalcounseling.org
- American University of Biblical Studies, annie.mcfadden@att.net
- Grace Church Counseling Ministries, pastor@gracechurchislands.org
- Clear Horizons Biblical Counseling Ministries, www.redeemer-pca.org

- Faith Biblical Counseling Center,
  www.FaithBibleChurch.us
- Faith Theological Seminary, www.faith.edu
- Biblical Counseling Center, www.biblicalcounselingctr.org
- Rod & Staff Ministries, lorraensign@aol.com
- Crossroads Bible College, www.crossroads.edu
- Faith Biblical Counseling Ministries,
  www.fbcmlafayette.org
- Trinity Theological Seminary, www.trinitysem.edu
- Redeeming Grace Biblical Counseling Center,
  www.redeemer-pca.org
- Southern Baptist Theological Seminary, www.SBTS.edu
- Biblical Family Soulcare, www.soulcare.org
- Grace Counseling Ministries, gcm@gbcnet.org
- Hollis Center Baptist Church, www.hcbaptist.org
- Biblical Counseling Center, www.bccmi.org
- Morning Star Counseling Center, tdymond@prodigy.net
- Biblical Counseling Center of Southeast Michigan,
  www.bcceastmi.com
- Central Baptist Theological Seminary,
  www.centralseminary.edu
- Mt. Carmel Ministries, www.mtcarmelmin.org
- Sonrise Biblical Counseling Ministry, bplatt@gobbc.edu
- Baptist Bible College Counseling Ministry,
  www.boggc.edu
- Southeastern Baptist Theological Seminary,
  www.sebts.edu

- Pastors for Nouthetic Ministry, fbc610@Bellsouth.net
- Victorious Biblical Counseling Ministry, ibcclemons@aol.com
- Biblical Counseling Center of Grand Island, New York, www.biblepres.org
- Faith Fellowship Biblical Counseling Center, www.faithfellowship.us
- Wheelersburg Baptist Church, wbc@wheelersburgbaptist.com
- Beamsville Counseling and Discipleship Center, www.beamsvillechurch.com
- Clearcreek Chapel Counseling Ministries, www.clearcreekchapel.org
- Biblical Counseling Institute, www.bci-ohio.com
- The Fountain Counseling Ministries, www.thefountainofgrace.org
- Christian Counseling and Educational Foundation, www.ccef.org
- The Institute for Nouthetic Studies, www.nouthetic.org
- Redeemer Biblical Counseling Training Institute, RBCTI@redeemerarp.org
- Expository Counseling Center, www.jirehbiblchurch.org
- Western Reformed Seminary, registrar@wrs.edu
- Biblical Counseling Ministries, Inc., www.bcmin.org

Counseling

If you're looking for a counselor in your area, please visit www.nanc
.org, where you'll find a list of certified counselors by state.

Audio Recordings

If you are looking for audio recordings of teachings by well-known biblical counselors, please visit www.soundword.com and peruse their library. Look especially at the conferences sponsored by NANC, IBCD, or The Wayne Mack Library.

Annual Conferences (Open to all)

If you would like to attend a conference on biblical counseling, please visit the following websites:

- The Master's College—MABC Department: In July of each year The Master's College sponsors a biblical counseling conference for women called Women Discipling Women at Grace Community Church in Sun Valley, California. For more information see: www.masters.edu.

- The Institute for Biblical Counseling and Discipleship: Annually in June, IBCD sponsors a biblical counseling conference in the suburbs of San Diego, California. See www.ibcd .org for more information.

- The National Association of Nouthetics Counselors: In the first week of October, NANC sponsors a national biblical counseling conference. This conference moves around the country from year to year. NANC also holds regional training conferences. Information on all these conferences can be accessed at www.nanc.org.

- The Christian Counseling and Educational Foundation: Every year in November, CCEF sponsors a conference in Pennsylvania. For more information, see www.ccef.org.

- Faith Baptist Counseling Ministries: In February, FBCM sponsors a week-long training course in biblical counseling on six different levels. For more details about the conference, held in Lafayette, Indiana, see http://www.faithlafayette.org/ FBCM/Conferences/Biblical_Counseling/Biblical_Coun seling_Training.aspx.

- Grace Fellowship Church of Northern Kentucky: In the fall, GFC sponsors three monthly weekend conferences for training in biblical counseling. See http://www.graceky.org/index .php?c=counseling1 for more information and a schedule of speakers.

HOW TO BECOME A CHRISTIAN: THE BEST NEWS EVER

§ *Elyse Fitzpatrick* §

This book is the product of the labors of 23 different women. Some are personal friends of mine; others I know only through the privilege of editing their chapters. Some live in Southern California like me; others are scattered throughout the country. A few are grandmothers like I am; and others are younger women with young families or no families at all. Aside from collaborating together on this book and loving women enough to spend time and resources to help them, we all have at least one thing in common: We're all Christians.

Now, when I say we're all Christians it's hard for me to know what you might think that means. After all, in the South, just about everybody says that they're "Christian." Here in Southern California, where I live, just about everybody says that they're "spiritual" and smile politely when I say I'm a Christian counselor. "Oh, how nice…I'm spiritual, too," they say.

So, in light of the great gap that exists in our day between what I'll call biblical Christianity and everything else that passes itself off as spirituality, it's wise that we make sure we're understanding specific terms in the same way. We don't want differing definitions to cause confusion regarding what is meant by the terms *Christian* and *spiritual*.

Before I begin, though, let me say this: This discussion of definition of terms isn't some insignificant bypath for people who are superspiritual or really religious. It means everything. As you'll soon see, I believe the Bible teaches there is only one truth—and if we fail to believe it, we'll spend eternity agonizing over having made a mistake from which there is no recovery. Yes, it's that serious.

The Truth You *Have* to Believe

The Truth About Our Sin

In its most basic form, here is the first part of the truth you have to believe: *You are more sinful and flawed than you ever dared believe.* When I say you are sinful, I don't mean that you are and I'm not. No, every woman who contributed to this book—and in fact, every person who ever lived (besides One)—is far more sinful than we know. The Bible says that "all" have sinned (Romans 3:23). That "all" means everybody. It means Mr. Good-guy who walks old ladies across the street, and it means Jeffrey Dahmer, who slaughtered them and hid them in his basement. That "all" means everybody who has ever lived.

When I use the word *sinful*, what I mean is that we have all violated or broken God's law. Now, I know that people generally say things like, "Oh, well. Nobody's perfect. We all make mistakes from time to time." That's not what the Bible is talking about. No, when the Bible says that we are sinful, it basically means that we have all broken God's law and that this lawbreaking is not a little boo-boo. No, it's treasonous and punishable by death.

What is this law? Simply this:

> You shall love the Lord your God with all your heart and with all your soul and with all your mind. This is the great and first commandment. And a second is like it: You shall love your neighbor as yourself (Matthew 22:37-39).

God's law is that we love Him and our neighbor with everything we are, everything we have, all the time. It's that we always put His pleasure above our own and that we always treat others the same way. We worship only Him; we love, serve, and delight in Him above all others. And that we love, serve, and delight in laying down our lives for others. That's what His law tells us, and that's what we (yes, all of us) have completely failed to do.

That's not to say that on occasion we don't get it right. Of course we do. As my husband Phil likes to say, "Even a blind squirrel finds a nut sometimes." Because God created us in His image, we know that we should love like this and sometimes we actually get close to it. But we *never* do it perfectly, without self-reference or self-aggrandizement, and we *never* do it consistently. The Bible calls this "never getting it right" sin. The truth is that we all know we should worship and serve only God and we all know that we should love our neighbor the way we already love ourselves (Romans 1:18-22). How do I know this Law of Love is something you should obey? For this simple reason: You expect others to obey it. You expect others to love you and care for you in the same way that you love yourself, and we all get mad when people fail to treat us the way we think they should. We all get indignant when we hear about wicked people like Jeffrey Dahmer because we know that people should love and care others, not murder and cannibalize them.

Even if you object to this kind of "sin" talk, I'm sure it won't take long for you to remember ways that you loved yourself more than anyone else, and that you've even done so today. Here are a few examples to help jog your memory:

Have you ever wished that a slow driver would just disappear? Have you ever cursed him in your heart? Have you ever purposely ignored someone you thought was beneath you? Have you taken cuts in line or gone to church so people would think you were good? Have you ever looked at the sizes of the pieces of pie and taken the biggest? Have you ever talked disparagingly about a coworker? Have you ever yelled at your children or lusted after a man? Have you ever stolen a paper clip? Have you ever lied on your taxes? Have you ever coveted a coworker's advancement and groused because it wasn't yours?

In all those ways and millions of others like them, we have failed to love our neighbor. We have sinned…and we haven't even talked about the ways that we've all failed to love God as we should or that we don't love our neighbor *because* we don't love God. *We are all more sinful and flawed than we ever dared believe.*

God, on the other hand, is perfectly holy, loving, faithful, good, merciful, and just. That means that He's different than us. It also means that He's greater than us and that because He created us, He has the right, as a great Creator King, to make laws about how we should live and demand that we obey. He also has the right to bless us for compliance and punish us for rebellion. He has the authority and power to make laws and then insist that we obey them. When we fail to do so, that's called sin.

The Truth About His Love

Remember that I said that our sin is the *first* part of the one truth we need to know? Well, here's the second part: Although we are more sinful and flawed than we ever dared believe, we are also *more loved and welcomed than we ever dared hope!* After everything I've just said about our sin, that's a pretty shocking statement, isn't it? You might be thinking, *I thought you just said that we were sinners and that God punishes sin. What's up? Am I really better than you said? Or is God more flexible or...?* No, everything I said about God, His love-law, and our sin is true. But there's a very shocking something else that's also true: It's the good news about the work that God's Son, Jesus Christ, has done. This good news is frequently called the *gospel*, which is just a word that means "good news." And it's because of this good news that we can be assured God loves and welcomes us. But how can He?

God can love us (and still be a just Judge and uphold His holy love-law) because He has taken the punishment for our sin upon Himself. He has poured out all of His just wrath upon Himself and He has perfectly loved the way we should have loved. Then He transferred this perfect record of love to the account of all those who trust in Him. He's done for us everything we could not do. This, by the way, is what makes Christianity different from all other religions. Every religion has laws and a higher power of some sort who must be obeyed. There are always blessings for obedience and cursings for disobedience. The shocking dissimilarity between Christianity and all other religions is that in Christianity, the holy God has taken the cursings for disobedience upon Himself! But still, you may be wondering, *How?*

The Story of Jesus Christ

Christianity isn't primarily a story of how you get the help you need to get your act together and have a happy home life. The truth is that Christianity isn't primarily a story about us at all! While it's true that we have a part to play in the story, we're not the star of the story. Jesus Christ is. Here's His story:

Eons of years ago, before there was even a world or a person living on it, God the Father and God the Son made an agreement. This agreement is called the Covenant of Redemption. In this covenant or agreement, it was decided that God the Father would send God the Son to earth to make a way for His wayward children to return to Him. In order for this reunion to take place, God the Son agreed to take the blame for all our sin and to be punished for it by His Father. He also agreed to perfectly fulfill the love-law and to let the record of His perfect obedience be transferred to us. In order for God the Son to be our perfect representative, He had to become exactly like us, meaning that He would have to live the same kind of life we live but He would have to do it perfectly. This is called the *incarnation,* and it is the story that we celebrate every year at Christmas.

With full agreement on both sides, God the Father sent God the Son into the world to reclaim it. His mother, Mary, who was a virgin, became pregnant through the agency of the Holy Spirit's work, not through the normal way women conceive. He was God's Son and Mary's Son, too. He was the God-Man. For the first time ever, God the Son left His Father's house—and all His majesty—to be clothed in the humble flesh of human beings. The Son who created the light was enclosed in the darkness of Mary's womb and then born in a cattle stall in Bethlehem.

Aside from His unique beginnings, Jesus lived a life very similar to the lives we live. He was an infant, a child, a teenager, a young man. He had brothers and sisters and a mom and dad. He had friends and as He grew older, He worked in His earthly father's home business. He was a carpenter. He lived the same sort of life that we live but with one enormous difference: He *always* loved God and He *always* loved all people. He always shared His toys. He always obeyed His parents. He always let others go first and always chose to worship God and put God's glory above all else. He never sinned. His perfect life is of immeasurable importance to us, as you'll soon learn.

When Jesus was 30 years old, He knew that it was time for Him to enter into a more public phase of His agreement to redeem or rescue us. He began to gather people around Him. These people were not the important religious people of the day. No, many were lowly fishermen. He also gathered all sorts of women around Him—and they weren't necessarily the sort of women that you would expect the Savior of the world to love. But He did anyway. The Bible says that he "went about doing good" (Acts 10:38). He spoke about God's laws and did many miracles that were signposts proclaiming that He really was God. And He continued to love.

About three-and-a-half years after Jesus began His ministry, the religious leaders of Israel decided that His message of love was taking away their place of honor and threatening their message of following the traditions of Moses, so they began a plan to silence Him. They bribed one of His followers, Judas, who betrayed Him and arranged for His arrest. He was arrested at night and brought before the religious leaders, who tried to condemn Him on trumped-up charges. Eventually Jesus proclaimed that He was God, and His fate was sealed. He was condemned by the religious leaders to die. But because they were under the rule of Rome, they did not have the right to execute Him themselves. So they had to get Pontius Pilate, a ruler in Israel, to agree with their plan—and eventually he did. Jesus was sentenced to die on a cruel Roman cross even though all He'd ever done was love His Father and all His people.

About now it would be easy for us to think: *Those rats! Why would they do that? If I had been there, I would have stopped that from happening! Why are people so mean?* Although it's easy to think something like that, we have to take care that we don't miss the point. The point is that it wasn't the religious leaders or the irreligious Romans who were ultimately responsible for the death of the God-Man, Jesus Christ. It was God. Remember, God the Father and God the Son had made an agreement to rescue His people. This was God's plan. You see, God is willing to take His own medicine. If He tells us that we must love our neighbor and lay down our life for him, He's willing to do the same, even if it costs Him His very Son's life. So, Jesus Christ died the death we should have died, taking the responsibility for all our sin upon Himself. God the Father poured out every bit of just wrath He has for our sin on His Son. Jesus cried out, "It is finished," and He let Himself die. But that's not the end of the story.

Jesus' friends and family took His lifeless body down from the cross and laid it in a tomb. They had to set His body in the tomb quickly because all the people in Jerusalem were in the midst of a religious observance and Jesus' friends and family couldn't properly bury Him until afterward. So, on what was the first Easter Sunday, they went back to the tomb (which had been guarded by Roman soldiers) and discovered the most astonishing thing: Jesus Christ wasn't there! The women who arrived first saw an angel, who told them that Jesus had risen from the dead. This is called the *resurrection,* and it is why Christians are so happy on Easter. That Jesus arose again confirms that God the Father accepted Jesus' sacrifice for our sin and that He vindicated His life and message by raising Jesus from the dead. And because of the resurrection, the perfect record of all the good Jesus ever did is able to be transferred to everyone who will trust in Him. This is called our *justification*. This word simply means "just as if I'd never sinned," and also "just as if I'd always obeyed."

That's why Jesus' perfect record of loving in every season of life is so important to us today. If we trust in His life and death and resurrection, we are not only forgiven of all our sin, but we're also granted His perfect record of obedience. You see, when God made a covenant to rescue sinners, He followed it through all the way to the end. Jesus was right when He said He had finished all the work His Father had given Him to do. Then, after teaching His disciples for 40 days, Jesus ascended into heaven to return to His Father's home, having accomplished the plan that had been agreed upon eons and eons ago.

Your Response

That is the good news. Christianity isn't about helping you become a better person. It's about you finally understanding that you can't be better, and Someone has been better in your place. It's news that you can choose to accept or reject. Accepting this news means that you transfer your trust from yourself onto Jesus Christ. It means that you talk to God and tell Him that you want to trust in Jesus Christ to make you acceptable to God.

So that you can grow in your understanding of how trustworthy God is and what your grateful response to such love should be, we encourage you to do two things: First, begin to read the Bible. We recommend that you start with the book of John, which is in the New Testament. Second, we recommend you find a good church. A good church is one that believes this entire message exactly like it's been presented here. If you need help finding a good church, you can contact The Master's College in Santa Clarita, California, and ask them for a referral.

Of course, there's another option: You can choose to reject this story as being false. You can continue to believe in your own ability to make life work and you can try hard to love others in your own power. Ultimately, however, you'll come to the realization that you can't do it. We pray that that realization will not come too late for you.

I know I've given you a lot to think about in this appendix. Here are a few summary points for you to remember and think about:

1. You are more sinful and flawed than you ever dared believe (remember the love-law).

2. You are more loved and welcomed than you ever dared hope (God keeps His love-law).

3. God the Father and God the Son made an agreement to rescue all those who would trust in Him.

4. The rescue plan is called the *gospel* or the *good news,* and it's simply the story of the life, death, resurrection, and ascension of Jesus Christ.

5. You can choose to accept this news and transfer your trust from yourself to Jesus Christ. Jesus saves only those who stop trusting in their own goodness and trust only in His.

6. You can choose to reject this news and keep trusting in yourself and hoping that you'll be good enough. If so, you are rejecting the love of the Father and the Son and you will live without it for eternity.

It is our prayer that you would choose to accept this good news. If you have done so, we invite you to let us know of your decision by contacting me through Harvest House Publishers or through my Web site at www.elysefitzpatrick.com.

ABOUT THE CONTRIBUTORS

Karen Avinelis lives in Porterville, California, with her husband, Tom. She is the mother of two children and grandmother of one. She holds an MA in biblical counseling from The Master's College in Santa Clarita, California and has been practicing biblical counseling in her church for ten years. She and her husband helped found and are currently involved in operating the Porterville Biblical Counseling Center. Combining years of experience in the home, church body, and local community with her formal education, Karen desires to share the importance of finding one's foundation for all of life and faith in God's wisdom and the person of Jesus Christ.

Maureen Bonner lives in Victoria, Minnesota, with her husband, Bill, their "adopted" Hungarian daughter, two cats, and a dog. They have three children and four grandchildren. Maureen worked in the medical field for over 25 years before returning to school to study for Christian ministry. She also holds an MA in biblical counseling from The Master's College. Ten years ago Bill and Maureen planted a new church in their community. At Waterbrooke Fellowship she enjoys serving in counseling and prayer, women's ministries, and congregational care.

Rachel Coyle lives in Germany with her husband, Philip, and their two young daughters. She is an Army wife and full-time homemaker. She holds an MA in biblical counseling from The Master's College and is a NANC-certified counselor. She has had the privilege of counseling, teaching, and discipling women for more than ten years.

Lynn Denby lives in Simi Valley, California, with her husband, Dennis, with whom she enjoys traveling and hiking. After homeschooling their three children through high school, she had the privilege of completing her MA in biblical counseling at The Master's College. She has a passion for counseling women one-on-one and leading small-group Bible studies. Presently, as part of her church's women's ministry board, she is helping to oversee spiritual growth and prayer among the women at her church.

Holly Drew is married, has two grown children, and helps her husband, Geoff, at home, in his medical office, and on the mission field, recently serving twice with a medical mission team in Malawi, Africa. She received her MA in biblical counseling at The Master's College in Santa Clarita, California. She enjoys serving in her church in hospitality and through teaching, counseling, and discipling women.

Venessa Ellen is a native of Beaumont, Texas. She surrendered her life to Christ and to His call to serve His kingdom in 1990. Venessa holds an MA in biblical counseling from The Master's College and an MA in Christian education from Southwestern Baptist Theological Seminary. Currently she is pursuing a PhD in women's ministries from Southwestern Baptist Theological Seminary, located in Fort Worth, Texas. She is an adjunct professor at the College of Biblical Studies, where she teaches, counsels, trains, and mentors women. For more than 18 years Venessa has communicated her burden for the women of God in conferences, seminars, Bible studies, and retreats. Venessa and her husband, Nicolas, reside in Houston, Texas, and are the proud parents of two lovely daughters, and they have two handsome grandsons named Jeremiah and Cameron.

Barbara Enter lives in Georgia with her husband, Jack. She is the mother of three and the grandmother of five. Barbara received her BS degree from Georgia Southern University and her MA degree in biblical counseling from The Master's College. She teaches Precept Bible studies, is an occasional conference speaker, and counsels at Providence Church Counseling and Discipleship Center in Duluth, Georgia, of which her husband is the director.

Elyse Fitzpatrick lives with Phil, her husband of nearly 40 years, in Southern California. She is the mother of three adult children and has six grandchildren with whom she loves to body board and bike ride in the beautiful Southern California sunshine. Elyse is deeply involved in the counseling, home group, and women's ministries of her local church, Valley Center Community Church. She holds an MA in biblical counseling from Trinity Theological Seminary and is a NANC-certified counselor. She is the author of 15 books as well as numerous teaching CDs and DVDs. She is a frequent conference speaker who has spent decades training and encouraging women to love Christ, His Word, and one another.

Debra Gentry is married to Ray and the mother of two daughters in their twenties, April and Allison. She lives in Georgia, where she ministers and counsels alongside her husband, a pastor. She regularly teaches and counsels women in her church and community. She has an MA in biblical counseling from The Master's College in Santa Clarita, California.

Karrie Hahn lives in Southern California and holds an MA in biblical counseling. She serves as the associate dean of women at The Master's College in Santa Clarita, California, where she disciples, counsels, and teaches young women. She enjoys traveling, running, hiking, and exploring Los Angeles for the best ethnic food restaurants.

Dr. Laura Hendrickson is trained as a medical doctor and board-certified psychiatrist, and counsels women at the Institute for Biblical Counseling and Discipleship in San Diego. The mother of an adult son who has recovered from autism, Laura is the author of *Finding Your Child's Way on the Autism Spectrum: Discovering Unique Strengths, Mastering Behavior Challenges*, and coauthor of *Will Medicine Stop the Pain? Finding God's Healing for Anxiety, Depression, and Other Challenging Emotions* and *When Good Kids Make Bad Choices: Help and Hope for Hurting Parents*. Laura is a frequent conference speaker and a visiting guest lecturer at The Master's College in Santa Clarita, California.

Joan Kulper and her husband, Ray, have lived in White Salmon, Washington, since 1977. She has two daughters and five grandchildren. She received a BA and MA in biblical counseling from The Master's College in Santa Clarita, California. She is a NANC-certified counselor and has had a counseling ministry at First Baptist Church in Hood River, Oregon, for the past ten years.

Connie Larson, a pastor's wife for 34 years, graduated from The Master's College with her MA in biblical counseling in 2007. She and her husband, Steve, live in Southern California, where she currently assists in directing the counseling ministry at her church. As the mother of three married children and grandmother of six, she still finds time to teach, speak, mentor, and counsel women. Her passion is to help women of all ages learn how to live godly in the real-life challenges of daily living.

Shannon McCoy lives in Southern California with her daughter, Raven. She has an MA in biblical counseling from The Master's College in Santa Clarita, California. She is a cytotechnologist (reads pap smears under a microscope) by profession, loves counseling women, and has a passionate concern for women's physical health and spiritual growth. She is currently working toward NANC certification as a counselor.

Nanci McMannis lives in Southern California with her husband, Bob. She is the mother of four children, with one grandchild on the way. She holds an MA in biblical counseling from The Master's College. She enjoys counseling women at her local church and is a NANC-certified counselor.

Martha Peace is a women's Bible teacher and nouthetic counselor to women at Faith Bible Church, Sharpsburg, Georgia. She conducts seminars for women on topics such as "The Excellent Wife," "Becoming a Titus 2 Woman," "Personal Purity," "Having a High View of God," and "Raising Kids Without Raising Cain." She is the author of *The Excellent Wife* and six other books. Martha worked for eight years as a counselor to women at the Atlanta Biblical Counseling Center. Her previous work experience also includes six years as an instructor of women's classes at Carver Bible College and Institute in Atlanta, Georgia, and 13 years as a registered nurse. She is currently on the adjunct faculty of The Master's College. She and her husband, Sanford, have two grown children and twelve grandchildren.

Janet Rickett has been married to Brian, pastor and professor, for over 16 years. She has been involved in various ministries and has served as the director of development of a Los Angeles-area pregnancy clinic, where she counseled women in crisis pregnancies. They recently moved to central Arkansas to plant a church. She holds an MA degree in biblical counseling from The Master's College and a BA in elementary education from the University of Central Arkansas.

Barbara Scroggins lives in Southern California with her husband, Nathan, and their two children. She is a homemaker and homeschool teacher. She holds an MA in biblical counseling from The Master's College, has been involved in discipleship and counseling in the local church for ten years, and occasionally teaches a biblical counseling course for women at The Master's College.

Mary L. Somerville and her husband, Bob, live in Valencia, California, where they teach at The Master's College. She was formerly a pastor's wife for many years and was on part-time staff with Young Life for 14 years spearheading a ministry to teen mothers. She has authored the book *One with a Shepherd: The Tears and Triumphs of a Ministry Marriage,* which has been translated into Russian. Mary and Bob have two children and six grandchildren. Mary likes to travel and explore new places with her husband, including visiting their children in South Africa. She holds an MA from Trinity Evangelical Divinity School.

Jan Steenback lives in the upstate area of South Carolina with her husband, Rick. She is a mother of two and grandmother of two. She has been a teacher at a Christian school for more than 25 years and has an MA in biblical counseling from The Masters College in California. She finds joy in teaching youth from a biblical perspective and opportunities to counsel women and youth.

Janie Street is a wife, homemaker, and piano teacher. She is the mother of four and grandmother of three. She lives in Southern California with her husband, John, and her twin college-age sons. She enjoys counseling young women and teaching an occasional biblical counseling course at The Master's College in Santa Clarita, California.

Mary Wilkin lives in the Minneapolis area. She is a physician who specializes in pediatric critical care medicine and currently works part-time. Her passion has changed from medicine to biblical counseling and she enjoys helping women become true worshipers of God. She is involved in women's ministry at Bethlehem Baptist Church, where she leads Bible studies and counsels. She loves encouraging women to come alongside other women in counseling and discipleship relationships. She is a NANC-certified counselor and is pursuing an MA in biblical counseling from The Master's College. She also enjoys cooking and cross-country skiing.

NOTES

Women Who Teach What Is Good

1. See Elyse Fitzpatrick and Carol Cornish, *Women Helping Women* (Eugene, OR: Harvest House), 1997, especially chapter 4.

Chapter 2—Do God's Promises Apply to You?

1. John Piper, *God Is the Gospel* (Wheaton, IL: Crossway, 2005), p. 12.

2. Ibid., emphasis added.

3. Mark 1:15.

4. John MacArthur writes, "Because ours is such a free and prosperous society, it is easier for Christians to feel secure by presuming on instead of depending on God's grace. Too many believers become satisfied with physical blessings and have little desire for spiritual blessings. Having become so dependent on their physical resources, they feel little need for spiritual resources. When programs, methods, and money produce impressive results, there is an inclination to confuse human success with divine blessing. Christians can actually behave like practical humanists, living as if God were not necessary. When that happens, passionate longing for God and yearning for His help will be missing—along with His empowerment." John MacArthur, *Alone with God* (Colorado Springs, CO: David C. Cook, 2006), p. 16.

5. Those who don't have a personal relationship with Jesus Christ, the Bible says, are spiritually dead. Ephesians 2:1-3 says, "You were dead in the trespasses and sins in which you once walked, following the course of this world, following the prince of the power of the air, the spirit that is now at work in the sons of disobedience—among whom we all once lived in the passions of our flesh, carrying out the desires of the body and the mind, and were by nature children of wrath, like the rest of mankind."

6. Burk Parsons, *Assured by God: Living in the Fullness of God's Grace* (Phillipsburg, NJ: Presbyterian & Reformed, 2007), p. 11.

7. Steven J. Lawson, *Absolutely Sure* (Sisters, OR: Multnomah, 1999), p. 35.

8. John F. MacArthur, *The Gospel According to Jesus* (Grand Rapids: Zondervan, 1988), p. 201.

9. Carolyn McCulley, *Radical Womanhood* (Chicago: Moody, 2008), p. 26.

10. Joshua Harris, *Stop Dating the Church* (Sisters, OR: Multnomah, 2004), p. 84.

11. This verse is not saying Christians cannot possess things. Rather, it is saying they are not to idolize or worship them. God made us to worship Him alone.

12. Dictionary.com, "metaphor," in *Dictionary.com Unabridged (v 1.1)*. Source location: Random House, Inc. at http://dictionary.reference.com/browse/metaphor. Accessed September 8, 2009.

Chapter 3—Interpreting God's Word Accurately

1. Bernard S. Cayne, ed., *The New Lexicon Webster's Encyclopedic Dictionary of the English Language* (New York: Lexicon, 1990), pp. 453-54.

2. Roy B. Zuck, *Basic Bible Interpretation* (Colorado Springs: Victor, 1991), p. 19.

3. Bernard Ramm, *Protestant Biblical Interpretation* (Grand Rapids: Baker, 1970), pp. 2-3.

4. Dr. John D. Street, "BC531s: Hermeneutics," unpublished class syllabus (Santa Clarita, CA: The Master's College and Seminary, 2005), p. 6.

5. Zuck, *Basic Bible Interpretation*, p. 79.

6. Cayne, ed., *Webster's Encyclopedic Dictionary*, p. 397.

7. Dr. John D. Street, "BC518s: Counseling and the Book of Proverbs," unpublished class syllabus, (Santa Clarita, CA: The Master's College and Seminary, Summer 2005) p. 5.

8. Source unknown.

9. J.I. Packer, *Knowing God* (Downers Grove, IL: InterVarsity Press, 1973), pp. 14-15.

Chapter 4—Spiritual Discernment: How Can I Know What Is True?

1. Using the United States Homeland Security System as our guide, we will follow the color scheme as our warning system: Green, low risk of terrorist attack; Blue, guarded risk; Yellow, elevated risk; Orange, high risk; and Red, severe risk.

2. Tim Challies. *The Discipline of Spiritual Discernment* (Wheaton, IL: Crossway, 2007), p. 61.

3. Tim Challies site is at www.discerningreader.com and is designed to help the Christian community use discernment with relation to the books they read.

4. John MacArthur, Jr., *How to Get the Most Out of God's Word* (Dallas, TX: Word, 1997), p. 6.

5. Challies, *Spiritual Discernment*, p. 70.

Chapter 5—Establishing a Biblical Ministry to Women

1. William W. Goode, "Biblical Counseling and the Local Church," in John F. MacArthur Jr. and Wayne A. Mack, *Introduction to Biblical Counseling* (Dallas, TX: Word, 1994), p. 306.

2. *Humanism* is "a doctrine, attitude, or way of life centered on human interests or values; especially a philosophy that asserts the dignity and worth of man and his capacity for self-realization through reason and that often rejects supernaturalism...Psychology is simply the seductive daughter of humanism." Webster's Dictionary, Internet definition.

3. John MacArthur, *The MacArthur Study Bible* (Nashville, TN: Word, 1997), p. 1952.

4. Wayne Grudem, *Systematic Theology* (Grand Rapids: Zondervan, 1994), p. 73.

5. Ibid., p. 116.

6. Elyse Fitzpatrick and Carol Cornish, gen. eds., *Women Helping Women* (Eugene, OR: Harvest House, 1997), p. 63.

Chapter 6—Dealing with Your Emotions God's Way

1. Robert Plutchik, "The Nature of Emotions," *American Scientist* 89, no. 4 (July/August 2001).

2. Sometimes our emotions are the result of physical problems, such as lack of sleep or medications we're taking for some condition or other. Even in these cases, however, our emotions are affected by what we think about the way we feel.

3. William Garden Blaikie and Robert Law, *The Inner Life of Christ* (Minneapolis: Klock & Klock, 1982).

Chapter 7—Christ, God's Answer to Your Fear

1. Elyse Fitzpatrick, *Overcoming Fear, Worry, and Anxiety* (Eugene, OR: Harvest House, 2001), p. 20.

2. Wayne Mack, *Fear Factor* (Tulsa, OK: Hensley Publishing, 2002), pg. 51.

3. Ibid., p. 50.

4. Although God might not physically deliver you from a giant in the same way he delivered David from Goliath, He has promised to deliver you from spiritual giants who threaten to kill your faith. God has a specific plan for your life, just as He did for David's. Those plans are not exactly the same, but His character remains the same. Just as He was faithful to rescue David, He is faithful to you today.

5. Psalm 33:8-9,13,18-20.

6. I John 4:14.

7. 2 Corinthians 5:21.

8. Matthew 3:1-2.

9. Romans 6:17-18.

10. Ephesians 2:4-5,8-10, emphasis added.

11. Ephesians 4:22-24.

12. Isaiah 43:1-3.

Chapter 8—Help for Overcoming Anger

1. Millard J. Erickson, *Christian Theology* (Grand Rapids: Baker, 1985), p. 387.

Chapter 9—The Difficult Road Through Depression

1. John Piper, *When the Darkness Will Not Lift* (Wheaton, IL: Crossway, 2006), p. 25.

2. Be encouraged to pray this heartfelt prayer along with Saint Augustine: "God of our life, there are days when the burdens we carry chafe our shoulders and weigh us down; when the road seems dreary and endless, the skies gray and threatening; when our lives have no music in them, and our hearts are lonely and our souls have lost courage. Flood the path with light, we beseech Thee: turn our eyes to where the skies are full of promise; tune our hearts to brave music; give us the sense of comradeship with heroes and saints of every age; and so quicken our spirits that we may be able to encourage the souls of all who journey with us on the road of life, to Thy honor and glory." Edythe Draper, *Edythe Draper's Book of Quotations for the Christian World* (Wheaton, IL.: Tyndale House, 1992), p. 121.

3. The great reformer Martin Luther often wrote about his struggles with depression. He recognized that Satan had a role in this, being the "accuser of our brothers" (Revelation 12:10) who causes believers to dwell on their past sins. In the hymn "A Mighty Fortress Is Our God," Luther assures us that although our ancient foe, Satan, is crafty, the Man of God's own choosing—Christ Jesus—will win the battle for us.

4. What follows is the story of Francis, a radiant wife and grandmother in my daughter's church. When you see her bright smile and the line of women wanting to be discipled by her, you would never guess that she struggled with severe depression for 21 years. She never hesitates to tell others about it.

Francis was hospitalized and institutionalized for depression and attempted suicide three times. She was treated with strong psychotropic medicines and shock therapy. This led to horrible migraines and more drugs to counteract the side effects. She confesses now that "the shocking reality was that depression had become a 'hiding place' to me. As painful as it was, it numbed me from my painful life at the time. I felt safer in the mental institution because I felt unable to function in my role as a wife or mom. At least here, while I was in this place, I was not a danger to myself."

But God, in His mercy, caused her to run to His Word right out of the middle of a psychotherapy session. She escaped to her hospital room and searched the Scriptures for the help that she needed. She shares, "On this particular day, I remember so clearly, how I clung to these truths, 'For in this HOPE we were saved. But HOPE that is seen is not HOPE. For who HOPES for what he sees? But if we HOPE for what we do not see, we wait for it with patience' (Romans 8:24-25). Then I read on to discover that we are 'more than conquerors through him who loved us' (Romans 8:37). This was the first turning point in the struggle. I became confident in my LIVING HOPE!"

Francis went to a biblical counselor for a period of 18 months. She says, "God enabled me to repent of my sinful anger, resentment, bitterness, and unforgiving spirit, which were the root cause of this terrible bondage. In the past, I used to confess these sins to God but had not learned how to biblically put off these sinful attitudes and how to put on Christ."

She continues, "Studying the character of God, His greatness, His goodness, His sovereignty, and His supremacy over all things helped me to let go of all my anxiety and depression and gradually to get off of all medication. I've gone 13 years without it, and I am so thankful to Him for what He has done. He created in me a desire to know Him more and to grow in grace and the knowledge of Him" (2 Peter 3:18).

"It is because of His truth that I am in my right mind today," Francis testifies. "He is the 'lifter of my head' (Psalm 3:3), the health of my countenance and my LIVING HOPE (Psalm 42–43)! His grace is sufficient for me. His power is made perfect in my weakness. O the power of the cross! Jesus said 'If you abide in My Word, you are truly my disciples, and you will know the truth, and the truth will set you free' (John 8:32). I am truly free!"

Chapter 10—About Medicines: Finding a Balance

1. You can find a counselor who has been certified as being trained and competent in biblical counseling at www.nanc.org.

2. C.H. Spurgeon, *Sermons*, vol. 18 (New York: Funk & Wagnalls, n.d.), pp. 351-52.

Chapter 11—Single Women and the Test of Loneliness

1. John Piper and Wayne Grudem, eds. *Biblical Foundations for Manhood and Womanhood* (Wheaton, IL: Crossway, 2002), p. 93.

2. Amber Anderson, "Surf Here Often?" *Christianity Today,* June 22, 2001, at http://ChristianityToday.com.

3. Jay E. Adams, *The Christian Counselor's New Testament and Proverbs* (Stanley, NC: Timeless Texts, 2000).

Chapter 13—Does Anyone Hear Me? Facing Loneliness in Marriage

1. Nicolas Ellen, *Happy Even After: Biblical Guidelines for a Successful Marriage* (Mustang, OK: Dare 2 Dream, 2007).

2. June Hunt, "Loneliness: How to Be Alone but Not Lonely," *Biblical Counseling Keys* (Dallas: Hope for the Heart, 2005), pp. 1-13.

3. Ibid.

4. Robert B. Hughes and J. Carl Laney, *Tyndale Concise Bible Commentary* (Wheaton, IL: Tyndale House, 2001), p.11.

Chapter 14—Healing for Hidden Wounds from Verbal Abuse

1. Jerry Bridges, *Trusting God: Even When Life Hurts* (Colorado Springs: NavPress, 1988), p. 200.

Chapter 15—Faithful Parenting: Reaching Your Child's Heart

1. Tedd Tripp, *Shepherding a Child's Heart* (Wapwallopen, PA: Shepherd Press, 1995), p. 138.

Chapter 18—Training Teens in the True Faith

1. John MacArthur, *What the Bible Says About Parenting* (Nashville: W. Publishing Group, 2000), p. 12.

2. Ibid., p. 11.

3. Oswald Chambers, *Studies in the Sermon on the Mount* (1960; repr. Grand Rapids: Discovery House, 1995), p. 17.

4. Nancy Adler and Judith Stewart, "Self-Esteem," 1991. MacArthur Network on SES of Health, at http://www.macses.ucsf.edu/Research/Psychosocial/notebook/selfesteem.html. Accessed August 29, 2009.

5. Tedd Tripp, *Shepherding a Child's Heart* (Wapwallopen, PA: Shepherd Press, 2005), p. 41.

6. "Joel Osteen vs. Paul Washer, Part 1 of 3," at http://www.youtube.com/watch?v=h4EjvgNheQk. Accessed August 9, 2008.

7. Dennis and Dawn Wilson, *Parenting in the Information Age* (West Jordon, UT: Tricord, 1996), p. 57.

8. John MacArthur, "Happiness Is…" at http://www.gty.org/Resources/Transcripts/2197. Accessed December 23, 2007.

9. Thomas Watson, *The Beatitudes* (Carlisle, PA: The Banner of Truth Trust, 2000), pp. 42-43.

10. Ibid., p. 32.

11. Daniel Doriani, *The Sermon on the Mount* (Phillipsburg, NJ: Presbyterian & Reformed, 2006), p. 20.

12. John MacArthur, "Hungering and Thirsting After Righteousness," at http://www.gty.org/Resources/Transcripts/2201.

13. Martyn Lloyd-Jones, *Studies in the Sermon on the Mount* (Grand Rapids: Eerdmans, 1967), pp. 63, 65, 72.

14. Ibid., p. 81.

15. Ted Tripp, *Shepherding a Child's Heart*, pp. 173-74.

Chapter 19—Hope for Caregivers of the Elderly

1. For a discussion regarding the depletion of brain function, see the book *Blame it on the Brain?* by Dr. Edward T. Welch (Phillipsburg, NJ: Presbyterian & Reformed, 1998), pp. 38, 68-70.

2. To learn more about forgiveness and salvation through faith in Jesus Christ, see Appendix Two of this book.

3. Elyse Fitzpatrick and Dennis Johnson, *Counsel from the Cross* (Wheaton, IL: Crossway, 2009), p. 12.

4. Practice what is taught in Philippians 4:8: "Finally, brothers, whatever is true, whatever is honorable, whatever is just, whatever is pure, whatever is lovely, whatever is commendable, if there is any excellence, if there is anything worthy of praise, think about these things." Surely there is *something* about which they can be honored.

5. Good books about heaven include *The Glory of Heaven* by John MacArthur, *Heaven, Your Real Home* by Joni Eareckson Tada, and *Heaven* by Randy Alcorn.

6. Elyse Fitzpatrick and Dennis Johnson, *Counsel from the Cross*, p. 153.

Chapter 20—Help for Habitual Overeaters

1. Elyse Fitzpatrick, *Love to Eat, Hate to Eat* (Eugene, OR: Harvest House, 1999), p. 19.

2. Howard Eyrich and W. Hines, *Curing the Heart: A Model For Biblical Counseling* (Ross-shire, UK: Christian Focus Publications, 2002), p. 45.

3. Nancy Leigh DeMoss, *Lies Women Believe: And the Truth that Sets Them Free* (Chicago: Moody, 2001), p. 35.

Chapter 21—Breaking the Chain of Generational Sin

1. A.W. Tozer, *The Knowledge of the Holy* (New York: HarperCollins, 1961) p. 52.

2. Elyse Fitzpatrick and Dennis Johnson, *Counsel from the Cross* (Wheaton, IL: Crossway, 2009), p. 38.

3. Ibid., p. 188.

4. Mary Somerville, "Counseling Mothers of Rebellious Teens," in *Women Helping Women*, eds. Elyse Fitzpatrick and Carol Cornish (Eugene, OR: Harvest House, 1997), p. 290.

5. Mary Somerville, "Counseling Mothers of Rebellious Teens," p. 290.

6. Mark Dutton, *The Goal of Life* (Lafayette, IN: Faith Baptist Counseling Observation Video #4, n.d.).

7. Elyse Fitzpatrick and Dennis Johnson, *Counsel from the Cross*, p. 186.

8. Ibid., p. 188.

9. John MacArthur, *The MacArthur Study Bible* (Nashville, TN: Word, 1997), p. 180.

10. Ibid., p. 20.

11. Ibid.

12. Jerry Bridges, *The Gospel for Real Life* (Colorado Springs: NavPress, 2003), p. 55.

13. Joanne Shetler and Patricia Purvis, *And the Word Came with Power* (Portland, OR: Multnomah, 1992), pp. 74-75.

14. John MacArthur, *The MacArthur Study Bible*, p. 865.

15. A.W. Tozer, *The Knowledge of the Holy*, p. 63.

16. Mike Fabarez, "The Bible and Your Salvation" (Aliso Viejo, CA: Compass Bible Church, taped January 24, 2009).

17. David Powlison, *Seeing with New Eyes* (Phillipsburg, NJ: Presbyterian & Reformed, 2003), p. 177.

18. Ibid.

19. A.W. Tozer, *The Knowledge of the Holy*, p. 112.

Chapter 22—The Taboo Topic: Pornography and Women

1. When I began researching this issue in February 2004, there were 3535 women enrolled in *Way of Purity* by Mike Cleveland (previously titled *Pure Freedom* [Bemidji, MN: Focus, 2002]). This is a Christ-centered course designed to help men and women find freedom from pornography and other sexual sins. In February 2009, 7653 women were enrolled in the same course. For more statistics on women and pornography, check out Family Safe Media at http://familysafe media.com/pornography_statistics.html#anchor7 and American Family Online at http://www .afo.net/statistics.htm.

2. Edward T. Welch, *Addictions: A Banquet in the Grave* (Phillipsburg, NJ: Presbyterian & Reformed, 2001), p. 6.

3. Each of the names used here are pseudonyms for real women and their actual situations.

4. Sara June Davis and Lindy Beam, *Fantasy World: Pure Thinking in a Sea of Unrealistic Images* (Colorado Springs: Focus on the Family, 2000), p. 6; Jimmy Evans, *The Secret Power of Sexual Purity* (Amarillo, TX: Family & Marriage Today, 2000), p. 7.

5. It is not sinful to think about being romantic with your husband, but lustfully impure thoughts are always sinful.

6. The Greek text uses the following variations of this word: *porneia* ("sexual immorality, fornication...a generic term for sexual sin of any kind"); *porneuō* ("to commit sexual immorality of any kind"); *pornē* ("a woman who practices sexual immorality for payment"); and *pornos* (a male or female "who is sexually immoral"). James Strong, John R. Kohlenberger III, and James A. Swanson, *The Strongest Strong's Exhaustive Concordance of the Bible* (Grand Rapids: Zondervan, 2001), p. 4196.

7. There are two types of sanctification: *positional*, occurring the moment of salvation, and *progressive*, which occurs all through a Christian's life and is the process of becoming more like Jesus (see 1 Corinthians 1:2; 6:11; and Romans 6:1-14).

8. An abridged version of this material originally appeared in my article "No More Chains: Part 2," *MTL Magazine*, July/August 2008 [online magazine], at www.mtlmagazine.com.

9. Elyse Fitzpatrick, *Idols of the Heart: Learning to Long for God Alone* (Phillipsburg, NJ: Presbyterian & Reformed, 2001), p. 93.

10. Ibid., pp. 93-95.

11. A portion of this material originally appeared in my article "No More Chains: Part 1," *MTL Magazine*, March/April 2008 [online magazine], at www.mtlmagazine.com.

12. A portion of this material originally appeared in my article "No More Chains: Part 2," *MTL Magazine*, July/August 2008 [online magazine], at www.mtlmagazine.com.

13. Penny Orr, "Counseling Women with Addictions," in *Women Helping Women*, gen. eds. Elyse Fitzpatrick and Carol Cornish (Eugene, OR: Harvest House, 1997), p. 385.

Chapter 23—Women Struggling with Same-sex Attraction

1. Edward T. Welch, *Homosexuality: Speaking the Truth in Love* (Phillipsburg, NJ: Presbyterian & Reformed, 2000), p. 13.

2. Albert Mohler, "Is Your Baby Gay? What If You Could Know? What If You Could Do Something About It?" at www.albertmohler.com.

3. David Powlison, "Making All Things New: Restoring Joy to the Sexually Broken," in *Sex and the Supremacy of Christ*, eds. John Piper and Justin Taylor (Wheaton, IL: Crossway, 2005), p. 82.

4. David White, "Suffering with Temptation: Understanding the Battle," *Harvest News* (Fall/Winter 2008).

5. Heather Scaife, "What Does Healing Look Like?" in *Pure Intimacy*, http://www.pureintimacy.org.

**Another Outstanding Counseling Resource for Women
by Elyse Fitzpatrick and Carol Cornish, general editors**

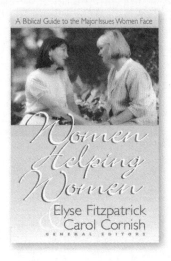

W*omen Helping Women* is a one-of-a-kind resource written for Christian women who desire to share with other women the comfort, hope, and encouragement the Bible has to offer in response to the problems of today—problems related to

- difficult marriages
- infertility
- divorce
- addictions
- singleness
- post-abortion issues
- dietary habits
- rebellious teens
- single parenthood
- marriage to unbelievers
- care of dying parents
- and more

Counsel that is based on God's Word is more powerful than we can ever imagine. God created us and knows us completely, and only He can provide us with true freedom, peace, and joy.

This book offers clear biblical advice along with consistently practical help for bringing about true and lasting change. A powerful resource for every woman who desires to counsel—whether a caring sister in Christ or a trained professional.